D0850944

Ten Steps
to a
Results-Based
Monitoring
and
Evaluation
System

A Handbook for Development Practitioners

Ten Steps to a Results-Based Monitoring and Evaluation System

Jody Zall Kusek
Ray C. Rist

THE WORLD BANK
Washington, D.C.

Library of Congress Cataloging-in-Publication Data

Kusek, Jody Zall, 1952–
   Ten steps to a results-based monitoring and evaluation system : a handbook for development practitioners / Jody Zall Kusek and Ray C. Rist.
      p.   cm.
   Includes bibliographical references and index.
   ISBN 0-8213-5823-5
   1. Government productivity—Developing countries—Evaluation.
2. Performance standards—Developing countries—Evaluation.   3. Total
quality management in government—Developing countries—Evaluation.
4. Public administration—Developing countries—Evaluation.   I. Rist, Ray
C.   II. Title.

JF1525.P67K87 2004
352.3'5—dc22   2004045527

February 9, 2009

Contents

Boxes

Tables

Figures

Preface

An effective state is essential to achieving sustainable socioeconomic development. With the advent of globalization, there are growing pressures on governments and organizations around the world to be more responsive to the demands of internal and external stakeholders for good governance, accountability and transparency, greater development effectiveness, and delivery of tangible results. Governments, parliaments, citizens, the private sector, nongovernmental organizations (NGOs), civil society, international organizations, and donors are among the stakeholders interested in better performance. As demands for greater accountability and real results have increased, there is an attendant need for enhanced results-based monitoring and evaluation of policies, programs, and projects.

Monitoring and evaluation (M&E) is a powerful public management tool that can be used to improve the way governments and organizations achieve results. Just as governments need financial, human resource, and accountability systems, governments also need good performance feedback systems.

There has been an evolution in the field of monitoring and evaluation involving a movement away from traditional implementation-based approaches toward new results-based approaches. The latter help to answer the "so what" question. In other words, governments and organizations may successfully implement programs or policies, but have they produced the actual, intended *results*. Have governments and organizations truly delivered on promises made to their stakeholders? For example, it is not enough to simply implement health programs and assume that successful implementation is equivalent to actual improvements in public health. One must also examine *outcomes* and *impacts*. The introduction of a results-based M&E system takes decisionmakers one step further in assessing whether and how goals are being achieved over time. These systems help to answer the all important "so what" question, and respond to stakeholders' growing demands for results.

This handbook is primarily targeted toward officials who are faced with the challenge of managing for results. Developing countries in particular have multiple obstacles to overcome in building M&E systems. However, as we shall see, results-based M&E systems are a continuous work in progress for both developed and developing countries. As we have learned, when implemented properly these systems provide a continuous flow of information feedback into the system, which can help guide policymakers toward achieving the desired results. Seasoned program managers in developed countries and international organizations—where results-based M&E systems are now in place—are using this approach to gain insight into the performance of their respective organizations.

This handbook can stand alone as a guide on how to design and construct a results-based M&E system in the public sector. It can also be used in conjunction with a workshop developed at the World Bank entitled "Designing and Building a Results-Based Monitoring and Evaluation System: A Tool for Public Sector Management." The goal of the handbook is to help prepare you to plan, design, and implement a results-based M&E system within your organization. In addition, the handbook will also demonstrate how an M&E system can be a valuable tool in supporting good public management.

The focus of the handbook is on a comprehensive ten-step model that will help guide you through the process of designing and building a results-based M&E system. These steps will begin with a "Readiness Assessment" and will take you through the design, management, and, importantly, the *sustainability* of your M&E system. The handbook will describe these steps in detail, the tasks needed to complete them, and the tools available to help you along the way.

Please also note the additional materials available in the annexes that can be used to enhance your understanding of the strategy described here for building your own results-based M&E system.

We owe a special note of gratitude to the Policy and Operations Review Department of the Dutch Ministry of Foreign Affairs, specifically to Rob D. van den Berg and Hans Slot. Through their financial support (via a Dutch Trust Fund at the World Bank) and their intellectual encouragement, they have been prime supporters of this initiative. That this handbook has come to fruition is profoundly due to their consistency and vision.

We also want to acknowledge with special thanks the contribution of Dr. Barbara Balaj to the preparation of this handbook. Her keen analytic insights, her thoughtful critiques, and her sustained support were invaluable. Her involvement significantly strengthened this handbook.

We would also like to acknowledge the comments and critiques from the following colleagues here in the Bank, Osvaldo Feinstein and Laura Rawlings. We also want to thank Jonathan Breaul and Frans Leeuw for their constructive reviews as well. Their efforts are most appreciated.

Building a results-based M&E system takes time. There will be many twists and turns along the road, but the journey and rewards are well worth it.

Jody Zall Kusek
Ray C. Rist
Washington, D.C.

About the Authors

Jody Zall Kusek is the World Bank Africa Region Results Monitoring and Evaluation Coordinator. She advises on strategies to improve the capacity of M&E in both Bank and client organizations. Previously she was a Senior Evaluation Officer at the World Bank, implementing Bankwide improvement initiatives in the area of results-based monitoring and evaluations. Before joining the World Bank, Ms. Kusek was Director of Performance Planning for the U.S. Secretary of the Interior and Principal Management Advisor to the U.S. Secretary of Energy. Previous work also includes leading the Natural Resource Management Performance Review for former U.S. President Clinton. She has worked in Albania, Egypt, the Kyrgyz Republic, Mozambique, Romania, and Zambia to support the development of national monitoring and evaluation systems. She has recently published 10 articles in the area of poverty monitoring system development and management, and serves on the editorial board of a U.S. government knowledge and learning journal.

Ray C. Rist is a Senior Evaluation Officer in the Operations Evaluation Department of the World Bank. His previous position in the Bank was as Evaluation Advisor and Head of the Evaluation and Scholarship Unit of the World Bank Institute. Prior to coming to the World Bank in 1996, his career included 15 years in the United States government with appointments in both the Executive and Legislative Branches. He served as a university professor with positions at Johns Hopkins University, Cornell University, and George Washington University. Dr. Rist was the Senior Fulbright Fellow at the Max Planck Institute in Berlin, Germany, in 1976 and 1977. He has authored or edited 24 books, written more than 125 articles, and lectured in more than 60 countries. Dr. Rist serves on the editorial boards of nine professional journals and also serves as chair of an international working group that collaborates on research related to evaluation and governance.

Introduction

Building a Results-Based Monitoring and Evaluation System

While the role of the state has changed and evolved during recent history, it is now readily apparent that good governance is key to achieving sustainable socioeconomic development. States are being challenged as never before by the demands of the global economy, new information and technology, and calls for greater participation and democracy.

Governments and organizations all over the world are grappling with internal and external demands and pressures for improvements and reforms in public management. These demands come from a variety of sources including multilateral development institutions, donor governments, parliaments, the private sector, NGOs, citizens' groups and civil society, the media, and so forth.

Whether it is calls for greater accountability and transparency, enhanced effectiveness of development programs in exchange for foreign aid, or real results of political promises made, governments and organizations must be increasingly responsive to internal and external stakeholders to demonstrate tangible results. "The clamor for greater government effectiveness has reached crisis proportions in many developing countries where the state has failed to deliver even such fundamental public goods as property rights, roads, and basic health and education" (World Bank 1997, p. 2). In short, government performance has now become a global phenomenon.

Results-based monitoring and evaluation (M&E) is a powerful public management tool that can be used to help policymakers and decisionmakers track progress and demonstrate the impact of a given project, program, or policy. Results-based M&E differs from traditional implementation-focused M&E in that it moves beyond an emphasis on inputs and outputs to a greater focus on outcomes and impacts.

Building and sustaining results-based M&E systems is not easy. It

1

requires continuous commitment, time, effort, and resources—and champions—but it is doable. Once the system is built, the challenge is to sustain it. There are many political, organizational, and technical challenges to overcome in building these systems—both for developed and developing countries. Building and sustaining such systems is primarily a political process, and less so a technical one. There is no one correct way to build such systems, and many countries and organizations will be at different stages of development with respect to good public management practices in general, and M&E in particular. It is important to recognize that results-based M&E systems are continuous works in progress.

Developed countries, particularly those of the Organisation for European Co-operation and Development (OECD), have had as many as 20 or more years of experience in M&E, while many developing countries are just beginning to use this key public management tool. The experiences of the developed countries are instructive, and can provide important lessons for developing countries. Developed countries have chosen a variety of starting points for implementing results-based M&E systems, including whole-of-government, enclave, or mixed approaches—that may also be applicable to developing countries. For their part, developing countries face a variety of unique challenges as they try to answer the "so what" question: What are the results and impacts of government actions?

This introduction is divided into three parts. First, it focuses on the new challenges in public sector management, namely the many internal and external pressures facing governments and organizations to manage for results. Second, it examines the use of M&E as a public management tool that can be utilized to track and demonstrate results. Third, it documents the M&E experience in developed countries, as well as the special challenges facing developing countries.

PART 1

New Challenges in Public Sector Management

There has been a global sea change in public sector management as a variety of internal and external forces have converged to make governments and organizations more accountable to their stakeholders. Governments are increasingly being called upon to demonstrate results. Stakeholders are no longer solely interested in organizational activities and outputs; they are now more than ever interested in actual *outcomes*. Have policies, programs, and projects led to the desired results and outcomes? How do we know we are on the right track? How do we know if there are problems along the way? How can we correct them at any given point in time? How do we measure progress? How can we tell success from failure? These are the kinds of concerns and questions being raised by internal and external stakeholders, and governments everywhere are struggling with ways of addressing and answering them.

One public management lesson drawn from more than 25 years of experience in OECD and developed countries is that building greater accountability within government will improve its overall functioning. The same should also hold true for the developing world.

International and External Initiatives and Forces for Change

There are an increasing number of international initiatives and forces at work pushing and prodding governments in the direction of adopting public management systems geared toward reform and, above all, results. These include:

- Millennium Development Goals (MDGs)
- Highly Indebted Poor Country (HIPC) Initiative
- International Development Association (IDA) funding
- World Trade Organization (WTO) membership
- European Union (EU) enlargement and accession
- European Union Structural Funds
- Transparency International.

The MDGs are among the most ambitious of global initiatives to adopt a results-based approach toward poverty reduction and improvement in living standards. The eight comprehensive MDGs (box i.i) were adopted by 189 U.N. member countries and numerous international organizations in 2000. They consist of a series of goals for the international community—involving both developed and developing nations—to achieve by the year 2015.[1]

This new development agenda emphasizes the need to measure the results of aid financing. Are development initiatives making a difference and having an impact? How will governments know whether they have made progress and achieved these goals? How will they be able to tell success from failure, or progress from setbacks? How will they identify obstacles and barriers? And at the most elementary level, do they even know their starting points and baselines in relation to how far they must go to reach their goals?

The MDGs contain some elements of a results-based M&E approach. For example, the MDG targets have been translated into a set of indicators that can measure progress. Box i.ii contains an ex-

Box i.i
Millennium Development Goals

1. Eradicate extreme poverty and hunger
2. Achieve universal primary education
3. Promote gender equality and empower women
4. Reduce child mortality
5. Improve maternal health
6. Combat HIV/AIDS, malaria, and other diseases
7. Ensure environmental sustainability
8. Develop a global partnership for development.

Source: United Nations

"The MDGs symbolize a focus on results. . . . The new development paradigm emphasizes results, partnership, coordination, and accountability. . . . [It] combines a results-orientation; domestic ownership of improved policies; partnerships between governments, the private sector, and the civil society; and a long-term, holistic approach that recognizes the interaction between development sectors and themes."
(Picciotto 2002, p. 3)

ample of just one of the ways in which the goals have been articulated into a series of targets and indicators.

More generally, the building and sustaining of comprehensive results-based M&E systems at the country and donor levels will be key to measuring and monitoring achievement of the MDGs.

The 2002 Monterrey, Mexico, conference specifically addressed means of achieving the MDGs. A new international consensus was forged whereby developed countries would provide increased levels of aid in conjunction with better governance, reform policies, and a greater focus on development effectiveness and results on the part of developing countries.

The MDGs are also posing special challenges to the international evaluation community. It is becoming increasingly clear that a new evaluation architecture is necessary. A foundation must be laid to build results-based M&E systems beyond the country level by harmonizing and coordinating them internationally with U.N. agencies, multilateral and bilateral donors, civil society, and the like. This will be the future challenge in expanding M&E.

Many countries, particularly the developing countries, must now vie to become a part of international initiatives, organizations, and blocs in order to reap the desired socioeconomic, political, and security benefits. Part of the bargain inevitably involves adhering to a set of specific requirements, conditions, and goals—including monitoring and evaluation. If these governments are going to become a part

Box i.ii

Example of Millennium Development Goal, Targets, and Indicators

Goal: Eradicate extreme poverty and hunger

Target l.   Halve, between 1990 and 2015, the proportion of people whose income is less than US$1 a day

Indicator 1.   Proportion of population below US$1 per day

Indicator 2.   Poverty gap ratio (incidence × depth of poverty)

Indicator 3.   Share of poorest quintile in national consumption

Target 2.   Halve, between 1990 and 2015, the proportion of people who suffer from hunger

Indicator 4.   Prevalence of underweight children (under 5 years of age)

Indicator 5.   Proportion of population below minimum level of dietary energy consumption

Source: United Nations 2003.

of the global community, they must open themselves up to increased scrutiny and be more transparent and accountable to their stakeholders. In this context, they must learn to manage for results. Box i.iii describes the impact one external organization, Transparency International (TI), is having on the move toward accountability.

The following are examples of the kinds of international initiatives and requirements set forth for joining international organizations and blocs—and for reaping the benefits of membership and inclusion. Together they have created a global force for public accountability and proven results:

- **Highly Indebted Poor Country Initiative.** In 1996, the World Bank and the International Monetary Fund (IMF) proposed the Highly Indebted Poor Country (HIPC) Initiative, the first comprehensive approach to reduce the external debt of the world's poorest and most heavily-indebted countries. HIPC also aims at supporting poverty reduction, stimulating private sector–led growth and improvement in a country's social indicators. As a

---

Box i.iii
Transparency International

"Transparency International is the only international organization exclusively devoted to curbing corruption" (TI 1997).

Transparency International's (TI's) annual Corruption Perception Index—which ranks 102 countries by perceived levels of corruption among public officials—is cited by the world's media as the leading index in the field. TI's Bribe Payers Index ranks the leading exporting countries according to their propensity to bribe.

TI is politically nonpartisan, and has chapters in 88 countries that carry out the anticorruption mission at the national level, helping to spread public awareness of corruption issues and the attendant detrimental development impact. "Corruption undermines good government, fundamentally distorts public policy, leads to the misallocation of resources, harms the private sector and private sector development and particularly hurts the poor" (TI 2002).

TI is building coalitions with regional international institutions and actors to combat corruption. At the national level, TI is also working to build coalitions among all societal groups to strengthen governmental integrity systems.

TI is also having an impact in monitoring performance at the multinational corporate level. "Transparency International's rise has coincided with many companies' discovering that they need to improve their image for being socially responsible in many countries. That has helped bolster the organization's fortunes and make it an important player in the global anti-corruption battle" (Crawford 2003, p. 1).

With its broad international reach and media access, TI is yet another important global force for pushing governments and multinational corporations to be more accountable, and to produce tangible results for their stakeholders.

Source: TI 1997, 2002.

---

condition for debt relief—and similar to the MDGs—recipient governments must be able to monitor, evaluate, and report on reform efforts and progress toward poverty reduction. For instance, Uganda made progress in M&E and qualified for enhanced HIPC relief. In other cases, however, lack of capacity in building and maintaining results-based M&E systems has been a particular problem for participating HIPC countries such as Albania, Madagascar, and Tanzania.

- **International Development Association (IDA) funding.** Under the IDA 13 replenishment negotiations—which resulted in the largest donor contribution ever (about US$23 billion)—39 donors based their support for 79 of the world's poorest countries specifically on results. Explicit outcome indicators were formulated to track results toward goals, especially in health, education, and private sector development.

IDA now has in place a Performance-Based Allocation system that has helped to better target donor resources to countries with good policies and institutions—in short, good governance. Tighter links are being achieved between performance and donor resource allocations. The assessments and resulting allocations are increasingly being integrated in the country dialogue.

With IDA 13, an initiative was also launched to put into place a comprehensive system to measure, monitor, and manage for development results. The system ties into current initiatives and is aligned with measurement systems established by IDA's borrowers under their National Poverty Reduction Strategy Papers, as well as their work toward achieving the MDGs. Efforts are also underway to ensure that this approach has wide acceptance and is coordinated with other actions being taken by the donor community (IDA 2002).

- **World Trade Organization membership.** Other pressures come from the new rules of the game that have emerged with globalization, where demands for reduction of trade barriers have increased, and where financial capital and private sector interests demand a stable investment climate, the rule of law, and protection of property and patents before investing in a given country.

  The WTO, successor to the General Agreement on Tariffs and Trade (GATT), is one such example. Created in 1995, the WTO facilitates the free flow of international trade. It has 147 members, and another 26 in the process of membership negotiations. Over three-quarters of WTO members are among the developing or least developed countries. Members must agree to comply with, and be monitored and evaluated against, a specific set of rules regarding reciprocity and equal treatment, transparency in trade and legal regimes, reduction of trade barriers, adoption of intellectual property rights legislation, and commitment to environmental protection.

- **European Union enlargement.** The European Union (EU) has experienced five separate enlargements during its history, growing from 6 to 25 member countries. The EU is and will be engaged in negotiations with additional countries on their accession applications to join the EU. Aspiring countries must meet three

basic criteria for accession: stable, democratic institutions and respect for human rights and minority protections; a functioning
market economy capable of dealing with competitive pressures
within the EU; and the ability to meet membership obligations
associated with the political, economic, and monetary union. In
this context, the EU monitors potential members' progress with
respect to adopting, implementing, and applying EU legislation.
National industries must also meet EU norms and standards.

• **EU Structural Funds.** EU Structural Funds have been used to
  support and assist the socioeconomic development of the less-
  developed regions of EU member states. In an attempt to
  achieve greater socioeconomic cohesion within the EU, Structural Funds have been used to redistribute funds to the poorer
  regions. Beneficiary regions have been required to establish a
  monitoring and evaluation process. As the EU enlarges, the
  Structural Funds will also be extended to include the lesser-
  developed regions of new members, thereby drawing them into
  the evaluation system as well.

National Poverty Reduction Strategy Approach

The Multilateral Development Banks (MDBs) have established strategies and approaches for sustainable development and poverty reduction. These initiatives also involve setting goals, choosing indicators,
and monitoring and evaluating for progress against these goals.

• National Poverty Reduction Strategies. The HIPC initiative is
  also tied to National Poverty Reduction Strategies. In 1999, the
  international development community agreed that National
  Poverty Reduction Strategies should be the basis for concessional
  lending and debt relief.
      "Poverty Reduction Strategy Papers describe a country's
  macroeconomic, structural and social policies and programs to
  promote growth and reduce poverty, as well as associated external financing needs. PRSPs are prepared by governments through
  a participatory process involving civil society and development
  partners . . . " (World Bank 2003b).
      National Poverty Reduction Strategies must in turn be linked
  to agreed-upon development goals over a three year period—
  with a policy matrix and attendant sets of measurable indicators,
  and a monitoring and evaluation system by which to measure

progress. Specifically, "a PRSP will define medium and long-term goals for poverty reduction outcomes (monetary and nonmonetary), establish indicators of progress, and set annual and medium-term targets. The indicators and targets must be appropriate given the assessment of poverty and the institutional capacity to monitor. . . . a PRSP would [also] have an assessment of the country's monitoring and evaluation systems . . . " (World Bank 2003b).

Thus, countries vying to become part of HIPC must commit to a process that involves accountability and transparency through monitoring, evaluation, and achievement of measurable results.

- Comprehensive Development Framework. The Comprehensive Development Framework (CDF) consists of four basic principles: a long-term, holistic development framework; results orientation; country ownership; and country-led partnership. The CDF and National Poverty Reduction Strategies are mutually reinforcing; both also stress accountability for results.

  The adoption and application of the CDF—a systemic, long-term (generally 10 year) approach to development involving all stakeholders—has also resulted in pressures for the monitoring and evaluation of stakeholder participation and of economic development progress. The CDF includes in a country's national development strategy a clear delineation of medium- and long-term poverty reduction goals, with indicators to measure progress, thereby ensuring that policies are well designed, effectively implemented, and duly monitored.

  For example, stakeholders such as NGOs that have become involved in the process are looking for ways to monitor their own performance in terms of the National Poverty Reduction Strategy and the National Development Plan. The National Development Plan is now being implemented in a number of countries, and it is hoped that the approach will yield valuable information on setting baselines and measuring development outcomes. For example, the National Development Plan is a major force for developing results-based M&E in the Kyrgyz Republic.

  A recent assessment of the CDF found that "Further research and exchange of experience among recipient countries are needed on how to build up country-owned monitoring and evaluation systems . . . " (World Bank 2003a, p. 4).

Internal Initiatives and Forces for Change

Governments are also facing increasing calls for reform from internal stakeholders, for example, to demonstrate accountability and transparency, devise fair and equitable public policies, and deliver tangible goods and services in a timely and efficient manner. Pressures may come from government officials, parliament, opposition parties, program managers and staff, citizens, businesses, NGOs, civil society, and the media.

- Decentralization, deregulation, commercialization and privatization. The move toward various reforms, such as decentralization, deregulation, commercialization, or privatization, in many countries has increased the need for monitoring and evaluation at regional and local levels of government. The need for monitoring also has increased as new nongovernmental service providers (such as NGOs, the private sector, and civil society groups) have begun taking over some of the public sector functions that were normally provided by governments in the past.

  As such initiatives are undertaken, there will be a continuing need to monitor and evaluate performance at different governmental and nongovernmental levels, as well as among new groups of stakeholders. For example, Colombia, Chile, and Indonesia are all undergoing fiscal decentralization, and are looking to build and extend evaluation responsibilities down to the local level.

  Although some governments may be diminishing their roles in providing public goods and services, they will still have a need to monitor and evaluate the impact of their policies and programs—regardless of who implements them.
- Changes in government size and resources. There are many internal pressures on governments to downsize and reform themselves. Governments are experiencing budgetary constraints that force them to make difficult choices and tradeoffs in deciding on the best use of limited resources. The pressures to do more with less—and still demonstrate results—have grown. Governments are increasingly recognizing the need to build and sustain results-based M&E systems to demonstrate performance.

There is a vast array of national, multilateral, and international forces, initiatives, and stakeholders calling on governments to be more accountable and transparent, and to demonstrate results. If developing countries in particular are to join the globalization caravan and reap the benefits, they will need to meet specific requirements, standards, and goals. Results-based M&E systems can be a powerful public management instrument in helping them measure performance and track progress in achieving desired goals.

PART 2

Results-Based M&E—A Powerful Public Management Tool

This section examines the power of measuring performance (box i.iv), the history and definitions of M&E, the differences between traditional implementation-based M&E and the newer results-based M&E systems, and the complementary roles of monitoring and evaluation. This section also explores the many applications of results-based M&E. The technical, organizational—and especially political—challenges involved in building a results-based M&E system are also addressed. Finally, the ten-step model to designing, building, and sustaining such systems, with some comments about how to approach ensuring sustainability of such systems in a given country, is introduced.

There is tremendous power in measuring performance. The ancient Egyptians regularly monitored their country's outputs in grain and livestock production more than 5,000 years ago. In this sense, monitoring and evaluation is certainly not a new phenomenon. Modern governments, too, have engaged in some form of traditional monitoring and evaluation over the past decades. They have sought to

---

Box i.iv
The Power of Measuring Results

- If you do not measure results, you cannot tell success from failure.
- If you cannot see success, you cannot reward it.
- If you cannot reward success, you are probably rewarding failure.
- If you cannot see success, you cannot learn from it.
- If you cannot recognize failure, you cannot correct it.
- If you can demonstrate results, you can win public support.

Source: Adapted from Osborne & Gaebler 1992.

track over time their expenditures, revenues, staffing levels, resources, program and project activities, goods and services produced, and so forth.

Governments have many different kinds of tracking systems as part of their management toolkits. Every government needs the three-legged stool of good human resource systems, financial systems, and accountability systems. But they also need good feedback systems. A results-based M&E system is essentially a special public management tool governments can use to measure and evaluate outcomes, and then feed this information back into the ongoing processes of governing and decisionmaking.

Monitoring and Evaluation: What Is It All About?

Credible answers to the "so what" question address the accountability concerns of stakeholders, give public sector managers information on progress toward achieving stated targets and goals, and provide substantial evidence as the basis for any necessary mid-course corrections in policies, programs, or projects.

Building an M&E system essentially adds that fourth leg to the governance chair. What typically has been missing from government systems has been the feedback component with respect to outcomes and consequences of governmental actions. This is why building an M&E system gives decisionmakers an additional public sector management tool.

The OECD (2002a) defines monitoring and evaluation as follows:

Monitoring is a continuous function that uses the systematic collection of data on specified indicators to provide management and the main stakeholders of an ongoing development intervention with indications of the extent of progress and achievement of objectives and progress in the use of allocated funds (p. 27).

Evaluation is the systematic and objective assessment of an ongoing or completed project, program, or policy, including its design, implementation, and results. The aim is to determine the relevance and fulfillment of objectives, development efficiency, effectiveness, impact, and sustainability. An evaluation should provide information that is credible and useful, enabling the incorporation of lessons learned into the decisionmaking process of both recipients and donors (p. 21).

(See annex 6 for a complete OECD glossary of key terms in evaluation and results-based management.)

In juxtaposing these two definitions, it is immediately evident that they are distinct yet complementary. Monitoring gives information on *where* a policy, program, or project is at any given time (and over time) relative to respective targets and outcomes. It is descriptive in intent. Evaluation gives evidence of *why* targets and outcomes are or are not being achieved. It seeks to address issues of causality. Of particular emphasis here is the expansion of the traditional M&E function to focus explicitly on outcomes and impacts.

Evaluation is a complement to monitoring in that when a monitoring system sends signals that the efforts are going off track (for example, that the target population is not making use of the services, that costs are accelerating, that there is real resistance to adopting an innovation, and so forth), then good evaluative information can help clarify the realities and trends noted with the monitoring system. For example, "If annual performance information is presented by itself (in isolation) without the context and benefit of program evaluation, there is a danger of program managers, legislators . . . and others drawing incorrect conclusions regarding the cause of improvements or declines in certain measures . . . Simply looking at trend data usually cannot tell us how effective our government program interventions were" (ChannahSorah 2003, p. 7). We stress the need for good evaluative information throughout the life cycle of an initiative—not just at the end—to try and determine causality.

Table i.i highlights the different—yet complementary—roles that monitoring and evaluation play in M&E systems.

Monitoring can be done at the project, program, or policy levels. For example, in looking at infant health, one could monitor the project level by monitoring the awareness of good prenatal care in six targeted villages. At the program level, one could monitor to ensure that information on prenatal care is being targeted to pregnant women in a whole region of the country. At the policy monitoring level, the concern could be to monitor the overall infant morbidity and mortality rates for that same region.

Evaluation, like monitoring, may be conducted at the project, program, or policy level. To take an example of privatizing water systems, a project evaluation might involve the assessment of the improvement in water fee collection rates in two provinces. At the program level, one might consider assessing the fiscal management

Table i.i
Complementary Roles of Results-Based Monitoring
and Evaluation

Monitoring	Evaluation
• Clarifies program objectives	• Analyzes why intended results were or were not achieved
• Links activities and their resources to objectives	• Assesses specific causal contributions of activities to results
• Translates objectives into performance indicators and sets targets	• Examines implementation process
• Routinely collects data on these indicators, compares actual results with targets	• Explores unintended results
• Reports progress to managers and alerts them to problems	• Provides lessons, highlights significant accomplishment or program potential, and offers recommendations for improvement

of the government's systems, while at the policy level, one might evaluate different model approaches to privatizing public water supplies.

When we refer to evaluation in the context of an M&E system, we are not solely referring to the classical approach of determining attribution as embodied in the after-the-fact assessment of projects, programs, or policies. Impact evaluations do (or at least try to) address attribution. But we are viewing evaluation in a much broader context as a continuously available mode of analysis that helps program managers gain a better understanding of all aspects of their work—from design through implementation and on to completion and subsequent consequences. We will also discuss later in this handbook the notion that what managers increasingly need are streams of evaluation information, not additional discrete and episodic evaluation studies.

Evaluation has also been used for different purposes over the years. In the OECD countries, for example, early evaluations in the 1960s and 1970s studied ways of improving social programs. Later in the 1980s and 1990s, governments used evaluation to conduct budgetary management, for example, by examining ways to reduce expenditures and cut public programs. As noted earlier, efforts to develop M&E systems have spread to developing countries—many having been driven by the desire to meet specific donor requirements, international development goals, or, in some cases, both external and internal social and economic pressures.

Again, evaluation can be defined as an assessment, as systematic and objective as possible, of a planned, ongoing, or completed intervention. The aim is to determine the relevance of objectives, efficiency, effectiveness, impact, and sustainability so as to incorporate lessons learned into the decisionmaking process. Specifically, this kind of evaluation addresses: "why" questions, that is, what caused the changes being monitored; "how" questions, or what was the sequence or process that led to successful (or unsuccessful) outcomes; and "compliance and accountability" questions, that is, did the promised activities actually take place and as planned?

Key Features of Traditional Implementation-Focused and Results-Based M&E Systems

Traditional implementation-focused M&E systems are designed to address compliance—the "did they do it" question. Did they mobilize the needed inputs? Did they undertake and complete the agreed activities? Did they deliver the intended outputs (the products or services to be produced)? The implementation approach focuses on monitoring and assessing how well a project, program, or policy is being executed, and it often links the implementation to a particular unit of responsibility. However, this approach does not provide policymakers, managers, and stakeholders with an understanding of the success or failure of that project, program, or policy.

Results-based M&E systems are designed to address the "so what" question. So what about the fact that outputs have been generated? So what that activities have taken place? So what that the outputs from these activities have been counted? A results-based system provides feedback on the actual outcomes and goals of government actions.

Results-based systems help answer the following questions:

- What are the goals of the organization?
- Are they being achieved?
- How can achievement be proven?

Box i.v illustrates some of the key differences between traditional implementation-based M&E systems and results-based M&E systems.

Results-based monitoring is a continuous process of collecting and analyzing information to compare how well a project, program, or policy is being implemented against expected results.

Figure i.i illustrates the manner in which the monitoring and evaluation of national development goals will have to include not only the traditional implementation focus, but also a results focus. It also shows how results-based systems build upon and add to traditional implementation-focused systems.

We would note in figure i.i that by leaving the generation of outputs as an implementation effort rather than as a result, we are at some variance from the OECD glossary, which defines results as including outputs together with outcomes and impacts. We do this to stress the focus on answering the "so what" question. Building a school, paving a road, or training rural clinic workers does not, in our view, answer the "so what" question. These are outputs—and now one goes on to say "so what." What are the results of having this school building, this paved road, or these trained clinic workers?

As can be seen in figure i.i, monitoring progress toward national goals requires that information be derived in the logic model from all results levels, at different time frames, and for different stakeholder needs. A common strategy is to measure outputs (number of health professionals trained) but not improvements in performance (improved use of oral rehydration therapy [ORT] for managing childhood diarrhea). Improved institutional performance is assumed, but seldom documented. Without measured results, there is no way to document whether the effort is actually achieving the expected outcomes (improved use of ORT), and ultimately the associated national goal (reduction in child mortality).

So what does this mean in a governmental results-based M&E context? As governments seek to align the expenditure framework with policy outcomes, measuring the organization's performance in support of achieving outcomes is important. The efficiency of service delivery, the quality of program and policy implementation, and the effective management of resources are just a few examples. In the

---

Box i.v

Key Features of Implementation Monitoring versus Results Monitoring

Elements of Implementation Monitoring
(traditionally used for projects)

- Description of the problem or situation before the intervention
- Benchmarks for activities and immediate outputs
- Data collection on inputs, activities, and immediate outputs
- Systematic reporting on provision of inputs
- Systematic reporting on production of outputs
- Directly linked to a discrete intervention (or series of interventions)
- Designed to provide information on administrative, implementation, and management issues as opposed to broader development effectiveness issues.

Elements of Results Monitoring
(used for a range of interventions and strategies)

- Baseline data to describe the problem or situation before the intervention
- Indicators for outcomes
- Data collection on outputs and how and whether they contribute toward achievement of outcomes
- More focus on perceptions of change among stakeholders
- Systemic reporting with more qualitative and quantitative information on the progress toward outcomes
- Done in conjunction with strategic partners
- Captures information on success or failure of partnership strategy in achieving desired outcomes.

Source: Adapted from Fukuda-Parr, Lopes, and Malik 2002, p. 11.

Philippines, for instance, the government is at the early stages of defining organizational level indicators for major outcomes against which expenditure decisions can be made (World Bank 2001e).

Many Applications for Results-Based M&E

There are many and growing applications for results-based M&E. As the needs for accountability and demonstrable results have grown, so have the uses and applications for results-based M&E systems.

Project, Program, and Policy Applications Results-based M&E systems have been successfully designed and used to monitor and evaluate at all levels—project, program, and policy. Information and data

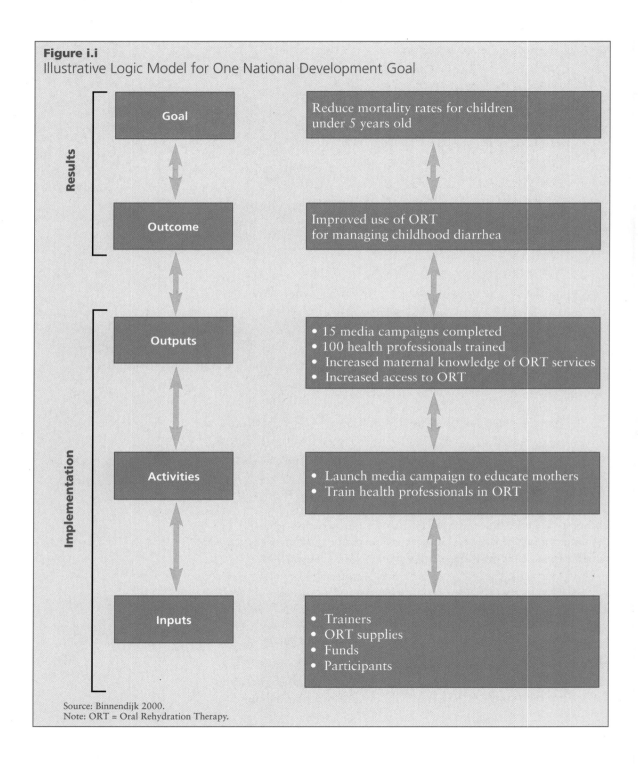

Figure i.i
Illustrative Logic Model for One National Development Goal

Results

Goal — Reduce mortality rates for children under 5 years old

Outcome — Improved use of ORT for managing childhood diarrhea

Implementation

Outputs
- 15 media campaigns completed
- 100 health professionals trained
- Increased maternal knowledge of ORT services
- Increased access to ORT

Activities
- Launch media campaign to educate mothers
- Train health professionals in ORT

Inputs
- Trainers
- ORT supplies
- Funds
- Participants

Source: Binnendijk 2000.
Note: ORT = Oral Rehydration Therapy.

can be collected and analyzed at any and all levels to provide feedback at many points in time. In this way, the information can be used to better inform key decisionmakers, the general public, and other stakeholders.

Monitoring and evaluation can and should be evident throughout the life cycle of a project, program, or policy, as well as after completion. M&E—with its continuing streams of data and feedback—has added value at every stage from design through implementation and impact. "The specific information will also be different at each level, the complexity of collecting data will be different, the political sensitivity on collecting the data may change, and the uses of the information may change from one level to another" (Kusek and Rist 2001, p. 17).

Internal and External Applications M&E can also be conducted at local, regional, and national levels of government. So whether one thinks of M&E in relation to levels of administrative complexity (project to program to policy) or geographically, the applications are evident—though they need not be identical. Again, the specific indicators may necessarily be different, as the stakeholders' needs for information will also be different for each level of government.

It should also be noted that a functioning M&E system provides a continuous flow of information that is useful both internally and externally. The internal uses come into play as the information from the M&E system is used as a crucial management tool for the public sector manager in achieving results and meeting specific targets. Information on progress, problems, and performance are all key to a public manager striving to achieve results. Likewise, the information from an M&E system is important to those outside the public sector who are expecting results, wanting to see demonstrable impacts from government action (and tax monies), and hoping to build trust in a government that is striving to better the life of its citizens.

Fundamentally, the M&E system aids in thinking about and clarifying goals and objectives. Governments and stakeholders can also use M&E systems for formulating and justifying budgetary requests. In contrast to the earlier implementation-based approach, results-based M&E focuses attention on achieving outcomes important to the organization and its internal and external stakeholders.

M&E systems can help identify potentially promising programs or practices. They can also identify unintended—but perhaps useful—

project, program, and policy results. Conversely, M&E systems can help managers identify program weaknesses and take action to correct them. An M&E strategy can be used to diminish fear within organizations and governments, and can instead devise ways of instilling an open atmosphere in which people can learn from mistakes, make improvements, and create knowledge along the way.

Knowledge Capital Good M&E systems are also a source of knowledge capital. They enable governments and organizations to develop a knowledge base of the types of projects, programs, and policies that are successful, and, more generally, what works, what does not, and why. M&E systems can also provide continuous feedback in the management process of monitoring and evaluating progress toward a given goal. In this context, they promote organizational learning.

Broad public access to information derived from results-based M&E systems is also important in aiding economic development both within and between countries. "Access to information is an essential component of a successful development strategy. If we are serious about reducing global poverty, we must liberate the access to information and improve its quality" (Stiglitz and Islam 2003, p. 10).

Transparency and Accountability M&E systems can also aid in promoting greater transparency and accountability within organizations and governments. Beneficial spillover effects may also occur from shining a light on results. External and internal stakeholders will have a clearer sense of the status of projects, programs, and policies. The ability to demonstrate positive results can also help garner greater political and popular support.

There are organizational and political costs and risks associated with implementing results-based M&E systems. However, there are also crucial costs and risks involved in *not* implementing such systems.

Political and Technical Challenges to Building a Results-Based M&E System

There are a variety of political and technical challenges involved in building results-based systems. The political are often the most difficult to overcome.

The Political Side of M&E Implementing results-based M&E systems poses many political challenges in OECD and developing countries alike. Above all, it takes strong and consistent political leadership and will—usually in the form of a political champion—to institute such a system. Bringing results-based information into the public arena can change the dynamics of institutional relations, budgeting and resource allocations, personal political agendas, and public perceptions of governmental effectiveness. Strong, vested interests may also perceive themselves to be under attack. There may be counter-reformers within and outside the government who actively oppose such efforts. Thus, the role of a political champion is key to ensuring the institutionalization and sustainability of results-based M&E systems.

Results-based M&E systems are essential components of the governance structure—and are thus fundamentally related to the *political* and power systems of government. M&E systems provide critical information and empower policymakers to make better-informed decisions. At the same time, providing such information may lessen or otherwise constrain the number of options available to politicians—leaving them less room to maneuver in their policies.

In democracies, information on project, program, and policy results is increasingly essential and is expected in the normal course of government operations. It is assumed that such information can help and guide policymaking. However, M&E systems may pose special challenges for countries that have been previously ruled by centralized, authoritarian political regimes. Instituting M&E systems that will highlight outcomes—both successes and failures—and provide greater transparency and accountability may be especially challenging and even alien to such countries. It may require a longer time for the political class, citizenry, and culture to adapt and change.

Finally, one cannot build strong economies on weak governments. Results-based M&E systems can help strengthen governments by reinforcing the emphasis on demonstrable outcomes. Getting a better handle on the workings and outcomes of economic and governmental programs and policies can contribute to poverty reduction, higher economic growth, and the achievement of a wide range of development goals.

The Technical Side of M&E—Building Institutional Capacity

Designing and building a reporting system that can produce trustworthy, timely, and relevant information on the performance of government projects, programs, and policies requires experience, skill, and real institutional capacity. This capacity for a results-based

Many organizations would prefer to operate in the shadows. They do not want to publish data about their performance and outcomes. Instituting a results-based M&E system sheds light on issues of organizational performance. Not all stakeholders will be pleased to have such public exposure. This is just one of the ways in which M&E systems pose a political—more than a technical—challenge.

By comparison with the politics of instituting results-based M&E systems, technical issues are relatively less complex to address and solve.

reporting system has to include, at a minimum, the ability to successfully construct indicators; the means to collect, aggregate, analyze, and report on the performance data in relation to the indicators and their baselines; and managers with the skill and understanding to know what to do with the information once it arrives. Building such capacity in governments for these systems is a long-term effort.

Some developing countries currently lack the basic capacity to successfully measure inputs, activities, and outputs. But all countries will eventually need to be able to technically monitor and track at each level of the results-based M&E system—at the input, activity, output (implementation), outcome, and impact (goal) levels.

Statistical capacity is an essential component of building results-based M&E systems. Information and data should be valid, verifiable, transparent, and widely available to the government and interested stakeholders—including the general public. This may be difficult for some governments that would prefer not to disclose and share data for political reasons or to hide corruption.

Technically trained staff and managers, and at least basic information technology, are also a must. In some cases, donor-supported technical assistance and training will first be necessary for the country to produce a minimum of information and data, and start to build an M&E system. For example, a recent assessment found that capacity building for key national officials in results-based M&E and performance-based budgeting will be needed in the Arab Republic of Egypt (World Bank 2001c). In the case of Colombia, government officials have commissioned an external evaluation of major projects while simultaneously building internal evaluation capacity.

Sometimes a great deal of data are collected in a country, but there may not be much understanding of how to use the data. Collecting and dumping large amounts of data on managers is not helpful. Providing mounds of data and no analysis will not generate the information needed to improve programs.

How much information and data are enough? Obviously, decisionmakers seldom have all the information they need when they need it. This is a common dilemma with respect to managing in any organization. Even without perfect data, though, if the M&E system can provide some analytic feedback, it will help policymakers make more well-informed decisions.

Introducing the 10-Step Model for Building a Results-Based M&E System

Although experts vary on the specific sequence of steps in building a results-based M&E system, all agree on the overall intent. For example, different experts propose four- or seven-step models. Regardless of the number of steps, the essential actions involved in building an M&E system are to:

- Formulate outcomes and goals
- Select outcome indicators to monitor
- Gather baseline information on the current condition
- Set specific targets to reach and dates for reaching them
- Regularly collect data to assess whether the targets are being met
- Analyze and report the results.

Given the agreement on what a good system should contain, why are these systems not part of the normal business practices of government agencies, stakeholders, lenders, and borrowers? One evident reason is that those designing M&E systems often miss the complexities and subtleties of the country, government, or sector context. Moreover, the needs of end users are often only vaguely understood by those ready to start the M&E building process. Too little emphasis is placed on organizational, political, and cultural factors.

In this context, the 10-step model presented here (Figure i.ii) differs from others because it provides extensive details on how to build, maintain—and perhaps most importantly—sustain a results-based M&E system. It also differs from other approaches in that it contains a unique readiness assessment. Such an assessment must be conducted *before* the actual establishment of a system. The readiness assessment is, in essence, the foundation of the M&E system. Just as a building must begin with a foundation, constructing an M&E system must begin with the foundation of a readiness assessment. Without an understanding of the foundation, moving forward may be fraught with difficulties and, ultimately, failure. It is Step 1.

Throughout, the model highlights the political, participatory, and partnership processes involved in building and sustaining M&E systems, that is, the need for key internal and external stakeholders to be consulted and engaged in setting outcomes, indicators, targets, and so forth. Step 2 of the model involves choosing outcomes to monitor and evaluate. Outcomes show the road ahead.

Step 3 involves setting key performance indicators to monitor progress with respect to inputs, activities, outputs, outcomes, and impacts. Indicators can provide continuous feedback and a wealth of performance information. There are various guidelines for choosing indicators that can aid in the process. Ultimately, constructing good indicators will be an iterative process.

Step 4 of the model relates to establishing performance baselines—qualitative or quantitative—that can be used at the beginning of the monitoring period. The performance baselines establish a starting point from which to later monitor and evaluate results. Step 5 builds on the previous steps and involves the selection of results targets, that is, interim steps on the way to a longer-term outcome. Targets can be selected by examining baseline indicator levels and desired levels of improvement.

Monitoring for results, Step 6 of the model, includes both implementation and results monitoring. Monitoring for results entails collecting quality performance data, for which guidelines are given. Step 7 deals with the uses, types, and timing of evaluation.

Reporting findings, Step 8, looks at ways of analyzing and reporting data to help decisionmakers make the necessary improvements in projects, policies, and programs. Step 9, using findings, is also important in generating and sharing knowledge and learning within governments and organizations.

Finally, Step 10 covers the challenges in sustaining results-based M&E systems including demand, clear roles and responsibilities, trustworthy and credible information, accountability, capacity, and appropriate incentives.

The 10-step system can be used for projects, programs, and policies. Though visually it appears as a linear process, in reality it is not. One will inevitably move back and forth along the steps, or work on several simultaneously.

The use of such results-based M&E systems can help bring about major cultural changes in the ways that organizations and governments operate. When built and sustained properly, such systems can lead to greater accountability and transparency, improved performance, and generation of knowledge.

Where to Begin: Whole-of-Government, Enclave, or Mixed Approach

Governments around the world differ in their approaches to adopting results-based M&E systems. There are essentially three ap-

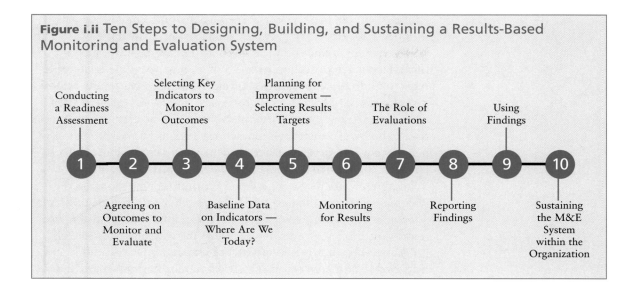

Figure i.ii Ten Steps to Designing, Building, and Sustaining a Results-Based Monitoring and Evaluation System

proaches. The first is the whole-of-government approach that was adopted in some of the early M&E pioneer countries. The whole-of-government approach involves a broad, comprehensive establishment of M&E across the government.

With the adoption of the MDGs, many developing countries are looking to design and implement comprehensive results-based M&E systems across many sectors and policies. Also, with the growing emphasis on results in international aid lending, more donor governments and institutions will likely provide support to developing countries to build broad M&E systems. There are trends among some donor agencies and governments to perform joint evaluations involving the recipient country as an active participant.

Often, different ministries are at different stages in their ability to take on the establishment of an M&E system. The whole-of-government strategy may not be able to move all ministries in tandem; there may be a need for sequencing among ministries in developing these systems. Many times innovations at one level will filter horizontally and vertically to other levels in the government.

Thus, the second approach is a more limited or enclave-focused one. Many countries—especially developing countries—may not yet be in a position to adopt such sweeping change in a comprehensive fashion. Other, more targeted approaches are available, such as beginning with the local, state, or regional governmental levels, or piloting M&E systems in a few key ministries or agencies.

Interestingly, some countries, such as Ireland, have adopted a third, blended approach to M&E. While some areas are comprehensively monitored and evaluated (projects financed by the EU Structural Funds, for example), other areas receive more sporadic attention. The government of Ireland has moved in the direction of a more comprehensive evaluation approach with respect to government expenditure programs (Lee 1999). The blended approach may also be a plausible alternative for some developing countries.

Piloting of M&E systems is often recommended, regardless of which approach is adopted. The best strategy to introduce an M&E system into a country is to first test a program in two or more pilot ministries. Albania, for example, is aligning a results-based M&E program with a newly implemented, medium-term expenditure framework, and pilot testing the effort in four key ministries. Egypt has selected six performance pilots to explore how performance-oriented budgeting could work before applying the approach to the government as a whole.

Yet a third strategy for applying a results-oriented program is a focus on a particular customer group. The government of Egypt wanted to improve its programs and services to advance women's issues. Each line ministry was expected to identify its current programs related to gender issues and assess the performance of the programs. In addition, the National Council for Women, a recently established government organization aimed at improving government support to women, was to identify a set of key performance indicators that the government could then track and monitor to achieve the established gender-related goals. It is the responsibility of the related ministries to track and monitor indicators for programs within their ministerial control, and to closely monitor and evaluate related government programs to achieve results (World Bank 2001c).

There is power in measuring performance. Results-based M&E systems are a powerful public management tool in helping governments and organizations demonstrate impacts and outcomes to their respective stakeholders, and to gain public support. Results-based systems are similar to traditional M&E systems, but move beyond them in their focus on outcomes and impacts—rather than simply ending with a focus on implementation, that is, inputs, activities, and outputs.

In sum, these systems have many applications, and can be used at the project, program, or policy level. There are many political, institutional, and technical challenges in building results-based M&E systems. Furthermore, countries should choose whether to adopt a whole-of-government approach in instituting such systems, or to begin by implementing an enclave approach at only one level in a government, or within a single ministry or small cluster of ministries. Experiences differ between developed and developing countries in how they have chosen to approach the design and construction of results-based M&E systems.

PART 3

M&E Experience in Developed and Developing Countries

This section provides some background information on experiences with results-based M&E systems in developed and developing countries. There is no one correct way to go about building such systems. Different countries—developed and developing alike—will be at different stages with respect to constructing M&E systems. Within countries, different ministries or levels of government may be at different stages of development in their M&E capacity. We will look at some of the special challenges facing developing countries as they try to build, operate, and sustain results-based M&E systems.

M&E Experience in Developed and OECD Countries

A large majority of the 30 OECD countries now have results-based M&E systems. Arriving there was neither an easy nor a linear process for them. They differ—often substantially—in their paths, approach, style, and level of development. According to a recent survey, Australia, Canada, the Netherlands, Sweden, and the United States have the highest evaluation culture rankings among OECD countries (Furubo, Rist, and Sandahl 2002).

The OECD countries have developed evaluation cultures and M&E systems in response to varying degrees of internal and external pressures. For example, France, Germany, and the Netherlands developed such a culture in response to both strong internal and external (mostly EU-related) pressures, while countries such as Australia, Canada, the Republic of Korea, and the United States were motivated mostly by strong internal pressures.

Interestingly, the pioneering OECD countries were motivated to

Building an effective M&E system is easier said than done. There are a number of systems that function well in developed countries, and fewer in developing countries. It is not that governments are not trying—many of them are. But creating such a system takes time, resources, and a stable political environment—and strong champions who do not become faint of heart.

adopt evaluation cultures mostly because of strong *internal* pressures. These countries were also instrumental in spreading the evaluation culture to other countries by disseminating evaluation ideas and information, and launching evaluation organizations, training institutes, networks, and consulting firms.

By contrast, many of the latecomer countries (for example, Italy, Ireland, and Spain) tended to respond to evaluation issues primarily because of strong *external* pressures. They were also heavily influenced by the evaluation culture of the pioneers, as well as the evaluation culture that has taken root in the international organizations with which their countries interact.

Boxes i.vi, i.vii, and i.viii give a brief overview of results-based M&E experiences in three OECD countries—Australia, France, and Korea. The motivations, approaches, and strategies differed in each case. Important conclusions and lessons can be drawn from these experiences.

Indications of Progress to Date in OECD Countries A recent OECD survey provides a useful overview of the extent to which a results-based focus has permeated and taken root in OECD country budgetary and management systems and practices. For example, "most governments today include performance information in their budget documentation and that information is subject to some form of audit in half of the countries. Though the current debate in the international public management and budgeting community on the distinction between outcomes and outputs is relatively new, the distinction between the two categories of results is used in most or all organizations in 11 out of 27 countries" (OECD 2002b, p. 12).

While substantial progress has been made in OECD countries on a number of fronts, there is still room for improvement. The OECD survey found "Only a limited number of countries link performance targets to expenditures for all government programs though around half of them have established links for some of their programs. A limited number of countries use performance targets without any linking to expenditure at all" (OECD 2002b, p. 12). Another weakness in OECD countries is that only "half of the countries reported that performance information is used for allocation purposes during the budget procedure but also that the use is confined to allocation within ministries and programs" (OECD 2002b, p. 12). Thus, while

Box i.vi

Australia's Whole-of-Government Model

Australia was one of the early pioneers in developing M&E systems, starting in 1987. The country had a number of intrinsic advantages conducive to building a sound evaluative culture and structure:

- Strong human, institutional, and management capacity in the public sector
- Public service known for integrity, honesty, and professionalism
- Well-developed financial, budgetary, and accounting systems
- A tradition of accountability and transparency
- Credible, legitimate political leaders.

A variety of factors contributed to Australia's success in building strong M&E systems. Initially, budgetary constraints prompted the government to look at ways of achieving better value for money. Australia also had two important institutional champions for evaluation—the Department of Finance and the Australian National Audit Office.

Australia chose to adopt a whole-of-government strategy. Such a strategy aims to bring all ministries on board—both the leading and the reluctant. The effort also had the support of cabinet members and key ministers who placed importance on using evaluation findings to better inform decisionmaking.

Australia's evaluation system evolved from one of tight, central controls imposed by the Department of Finance to a more voluntary and devolutionary principles-based approach. The latter approach has helped to increase evaluation commitment and ownership at the program level.

Today, monitoring and evaluation is left up to the individual departments and agencies. The formal M&E requirements have been relaxed considerably, and departments conduct M&E based on their own priorities. At the same time, departments are still required to report performance information in budget documents, and to report evaluation findings where available. Additionally, some evaluations continue to be mandated by the cabinet. The larger governmental departments are particularly active in commissioning formal evaluations and using the findings.

Source: Mackay 2002.

progress has been made in instituting results-based M&E systems and procedures in many OECD countries, much remains to be done.

Conclusions and Lessons from OECD Countries A number of factors contributed to the adoption of an evaluation culture in the pioneering countries in particular. Many of the earliest adopters of M&E systems were predisposed to do so because they had democratic

Box i.vii

France: Lagging Behind but Now Speeding Ahead in Governmental Reform

In contrast to other OECD countries, France was among the group that was slowest to move toward a results-based M&E system. Indeed, France even lagged behind many transition and developing economies. Various incremental reform efforts were attempted during the late 1980s and throughout the 1990s.

However, in 2001 the French government passed sweeping legislation—replacing the 1959 financial constitutional bylaw eliminating line-item budgeting, and instituting a new program approach. The new constitutional bylaw, which will be phased in over a five-year period (2001–2006), has two primary aims: reform the public management framework to make it results and performance-oriented; and strengthen parliamentary supervision. As former Prime Minister Lionel Jospin noted: "The budget's presentation in the form of programs grouping together expenditure by major public policy should give both members of Parliament and citizens a clear picture of the government's priorities and the cost and results of its action."

Approximately 100 to 150 programs were identified, and financial resources were budgeted against them. Every program budget that is submitted to parliament must have a statement of precise objectives and performance indicators. Public managers have greater freedom and autonomy with respect to the allocation of resources, but in return are held more accountable for results. Thus, the new budget process is completely results driven.

Future budget bills will include annual performance plans, detailing the expected versus actual results for each program. Annual performance reports are also included in budgetary reviews. Consequently, members of parliament have the ability to evaluate the performance of these governmental programs.

In line with the earlier observations about the political nature of M&E, this reform initiative altered some of the political and institutional relationships within the French government. In this context, parliament has been given increased budgetary powers. "Article 40 of the Constitution previously prohibited members of Parliament from tabling amendments that would increase spending and reduce revenue. They will now be able to change the distribution of appropriations among programs in a give mission." Parliament is able to vote on revenue estimates, appropriations for each mission, the limits on the number of state jobs created, and special accounts and specific budgets. In addition, the parliamentary finance committees have monitoring and supervisory responsibilities regarding the budget.

Source: Republique Française 2001.

Box i.viii
Republic of Korea: Well on the Road to M&E

In terms of public policy evaluation, the Korean government uses two approaches: a performance evaluation system introduced in 1962, and an audit and inspection system established in 1948. Performance evaluation has been carried out by organizations within or under the prime minister's office. Auditing and inspection are carried out by the Board of Audit, the supreme audit institution, and encompass auditing of public accounts and inspection of government agencies. The Board of Audit has grown and become stronger in recent years, and is now focusing on improvements in efficiency and transparency of audits and inspections.

The Asian economic crisis of the late 1990s brought about new changes in evaluation practices in the executive branch. "The new government in Korea asserted that the national economic crisis, caused by foreign exchange reserves, resulted from lack of efficiency of the public sector management. This assessment became an opportunity for reinventing government in Korea, which brought forth unprecedented restructuring of government organization as well as nongovernmental organization . . . " (Lee 2002, p. 194).

With respect to public sector evaluation in Korea, there are now eight different approaches in place:

- Institution evaluation, including evaluation of major policy measures, policy implementation capacity, and public satisfaction surveys of government services
- Evaluation of major programs and projects, including a select number of key projects, chosen according to importance to the ministry, consistency with government policies, and importance to the public
- Policy implementation capability evaluation, involving self-evaluation in the ministries, as well as an evaluation of an institution's ability to reform, innovate, and improve services
- Survey of public satisfaction with major policy measures and administrative services, polling public satisfaction with major government policies, programs, and services
- Special project evaluation, including, for example, state tasks and deregulation projects
- Ministries' internal evaluation or self-evaluation, including evaluations of major target policy measures and programs, and government innovation efforts by each ministry
- Evaluation of major policy measures and programs
- Evaluation of government innovation efforts by every ministry.

While Korea has made much progress in monitoring and evaluation, challenges remain. Cooperation and coordination between M&E institutions need strengthening. There has been excessive centralization of policy analysis and evaluation as well as audit and inspection. Korea still lacks sufficient numbers of professional and skilled personnel trained in M&E. Finally, more could be done to improve the effectiveness of post-evaluation proposals, which currently are not legally binding.

Source: Lee 2002.

political systems, strong empirical traditions, civil servants trained in the social sciences (as opposed to strict legal training), and efficient administrative systems and institutions. Indeed, building results-based M&E systems is primarily a political activity with some associated technical dimensions.

Countries with high levels of expenditure on education, health, and social welfare also adopted evaluation mechanisms that then spilled over into other areas of public policy. Evaluation must satisfy a need. "What is involved is a complex mixture of institutional preconditions, political culture, exposure to intellectual traditions, as well as sectoral concerns dominating the political discussion . . . " (Furubo, Rist, and Sandahl 2002, p.16).

Special M&E Challenges Facing Developing Countries

The challenge of designing and building a results-based M&E system in a developing country is difficult and not to be underestimated. The construction of such a system is a serious undertaking, and will not happen overnight. However, it is also not to be dismissed as being too complicated, too demanding, or too sophisticated for a developing country to undertake. All countries need good information systems so they can monitor their own performance—developing countries no less than others.

Developing countries building their own results-based M&E systems face challenges both similar to and different from those of developed countries. Demand for and ownership of such a system—the most basic requirement—may be more difficult to establish in developing countries. For example, a recent World Bank and African Development Bank study found that " . . . the key constraint to successful monitoring and evaluation capacity development in Sub-Saharan Africa is lack of demand. Lack of demand is rooted in the absence of a strong evaluation culture, which stems from the absence of performance orientation in the public sector" (Schacter 2000, p. 15). With respect to demand, then, a minimum of interested stakeholders and commitment is necessary for such a system to be established and take hold in any country—whether developed or developing.

In contrast to developed countries, developing countries may find it more challenging to do longer-term strategic economic, investment, and policy planning. Weak political will and institutional capacity may slow progress. Difficulties in interministerial cooperation and coordination can impede progress toward strategic planning, too. Indeed, lack of sufficient governmental cooperation and coordination can be a factor in both developed and developing countries.

Highly placed champions who are willing to assume the political risks in advocating results-based M&E are also needed—again emphasizing the political nature of building such systems. Sometimes they are present, as in the case of Egypt (Minister of Finance), Zambia (Secretary to the Cabinet), and the Kyrgyz Republic (Minister of Health), while in other instances, such as Bangladesh, they are lacking. The presence of a national champion can go a long way toward helping a country develop and sustain M&E systems.

Many developing countries are still struggling to put together strong, effective institutions. Some may require civil service reform, or reform of legal and regulatory frameworks. They are being supported by the international development community in improving many of these basic building blocks. Trying to build institutions, undertake administrative and civil service reforms, and revamp legal and regulatory codes—while at the same time establishing M&E systems—can be quite a challenge. However, it should be remembered that instituting M&E systems can help better inform and guide the government in undertaking needed reforms in all of these areas.

Developing countries must first have, or establish, a basic foundation—a traditional implementation-focused M&E system. Some developing countries are moving in this direction. Establishing a foundation requires basic statistical systems and data, as well as key budgetary systems. Data and information must be of appropriate quality and quantity. Developing countries—like developed ones—need to know their baseline conditions, that is, where they currently stand in relation to a given program or policy.

Capacity in the workforce is needed to develop, support, and sustain these systems. Officials need to be trained in modern data collection, monitoring methods, and analysis. This can be difficult for many developing countries. For example, there is a severe shortage of local capacity in Sub-Saharan African countries, compounded by the emigration of well-qualified people out of the region (Schacter 2000, p. 8).

Technical assistance and training for capacity and institutional development may be required. Donors are often willing to finance and support such activities, and share lessons of best practice.[2] At the

same time, donors should try to harmonize their evaluation requirements relative to recipient countries.

As part of the donor effort to support local capacity in developing
countries, donors are also moving to create development networks—
new computer on-line networks and participatory communities that
share expertise and information. " . . . [I]t can still be argued that
circumstances in Bangladesh, China, Costa Rica or Mali are unique
and distinct, and that the experience of one country will not necessarily translate to another. But once it is accepted that there is very
little generic development knowledge—that all knowledge has to be
gathered and then analyzed, modified, disassembled and recombined
to fit local needs—the source is immaterial. The new motto is: 'Scan
globally, reinvent locally'" (Fukuda-Parr, Lopes, and Malik 2002,
p. 18).

Developing countries will need to establish a political and administrative culture characterized by accountability and transparency, concern for ethics, and avoidance of conflicts of interest. Reformers need
to be aware, though, that any attempts to shed light on resource allocation and actual results through the adoption of an M&E system
may meet with political resistance, hostility, and opposition. In addition, given the nature of many developing country governments,
building an M&E system could lead to considerable reshaping of
political relationships.

Creation of a more mature M&E system requires interdependency,
alignment, and coordination across multiple governmental levels.
This can be a challenge because, in many developing countries, governments are loosely interconnected, and are still working toward
building strong administrative cultures and transparent financial systems. As a result, some governments may have only vague information about the amount and allocation of available resources, and
whether resources are, in fact, used for the purposes intended.
Measuring government performance in such an environment is
an approximate exercise.

Developed and developing countries alike are still working toward
linking performance to a public expenditure framework or strategy.
If these linkages are not made, there is no way to determine if the
budgetary allocations in support of programs are ultimately supporting a success or a failure. Furthermore, there would be no means of
providing feedback at interim stages to determine if fiscal adjust-

ments could be made to alter projects or programs, and thereby increase the likelihood of achieving the desired results.

Some developing countries are beginning to make progress in this area. For example, in the 1990s, Indonesia started to link evaluation to the annual budgetary allocation process. "Evaluation is seen as a tool to correct policy and public expenditure programs through more direct linkages to the National Development Plan and the resource allocation process" (Guerrero 1999, p. 5).

In addition, some developing countries—Brazil, Chile, and Turkey—have made progress with respect to linking expenditures to output and outcome targets. The government of Brazil also issues separate governmental reports on outcome targets (OECD 2002b).

Many developing countries still operate with two budget systems—one for recurrent expenditures and another for capital investment expenditures. Until recently, Egypt's Ministry of Finance oversaw the recurrent budget and the Ministry of Planning oversaw the capital budget. Consolidating these budgets within one ministry made it easier for the government to consider a results-based M&E system to ensure the country's goals and objectives will be met.

Attempting to institute a whole-of-government approach toward M&E—as in Australia, Canada, and the United States—may be too ambitious for some developing countries. Given the particular difficulties of establishing M&E systems in developing countries, adopting an enclave or partial approach, in which a few ministries or departments first pilot and adopt M&E systems, may be preferable. For example, in the Kyrgyz Republic, a 2002 readiness assessment recommended that the Ministry of Health—where some evaluation capacity already exists—be supported as a potential model for eventual government-wide implementation of a results-based M&E system (Kusek and Rist 2003).

M&E Experience in Developing Countries

Many developing countries have made progress toward instituting M&E. Keeping in mind the many challenges facing developing countries, boxes i.ix and i.x consider two examples: Malaysia and Uganda. Both countries have introduced new—albeit different—measures to the budgetary process to make it more transparent, accountable, and results focused.

The challenges facing developing countries are many. The countries' approaches may differ and it may require a considerable period of time to arrive at a results-based M&E approach. But experience around the world shows that the foundation for evaluation is being built in many developing countries. (See annexes 4 and 5 for more on developing country efforts with respect to M&E.)

Box i.ix

Malaysia: Outcome-Based Budgeting, Nation Building, and Global Competitiveness

Among developing countries, Malaysia has been at the forefront of public administration reforms, especially in the area of budget and finance. These reforms were initiated in the 1960s as part of an effort by the government to strategically develop the country. The public sector was seen as the main vehicle of development, consequently the need to strengthen the civil service through administrative reform was emphasized.

Budgetary reform focused on greater accountability and financial discipline among the various government agencies entrusted to carry out the socioeconomic development plans for the country. In addition to greater public sector accountability and improved budgetary system performance, the government undertook a number of additional reforms including improved financial compliance, quality management, productivity, efficiency in governmental operations, and management of national development efforts.

Most recently, Malaysia's budget reform efforts have been closely linked with the efforts at nation building and global competitiveness associated with Vision 2020—a program aimed at making Malaysia a fully developed country by the year 2020.

With respect to budgetary reform, Malaysia adopted the Program Performance Budgeting System (PPBS) in 1969 and continued to utilize it until the 1990s. The PPBS replaced line-item budgeting with an outcome based budgeting system. While agencies used the program-activity structure, in practice implementation still resembled the line item budgeting and an incremental approach.

In 1990, the government introduced the Modified Budgeting System (MBS) to replace the PPBS. Greater emphasis was placed on outputs and impact of programs and activities in government. Under PPBS, there were minimal links between outputs and inputs. Policies continued to be funded even when no results were being systematically measured.

The MBS approach was further modified in 2001, when the country embarked on another complementary reform by adopting a two-year budgeting system. The effect of this system will be known in several years time.

Although Malaysia has been at the forefront of public administration and budget reforms, these reform efforts have not been smooth or consistent over the years. Nonetheless, the MBS was a bold initiative on the part of the Malaysian government, demonstrating foresight, innovativeness, dynamism, and commitment to ensure value for money in the projects and policies being implemented.

Source: World Bank 2001b.

With the growing global movement to demonstrate accountability and tangible results, many more developing countries can be expected to adopt results-based M&E systems in the future. The international donor community's focus on development impact

---

Box i.x

Uganda and Poverty Reduction—Impetus toward M&E

"The government of Uganda has committed itself to effective public service delivery in support of its poverty-reduction priorities. The recognition of service delivery effectiveness as an imperative of national development management is strong evidence of commitment to results, which is also evident in several of the public management priorities and activities that are currently ongoing" (Hauge 2001, p. 16).

Over the past decade, Uganda has undergone comprehensive economic reform and has achieved macro-economic stabilization. Uganda developed a Poverty Eradication Action Plan (PEAP) in response to the Comprehensive Development Framework, and it is now incorporated into the Poverty Reduction Strategy Paper. The PEAP calls for a reduction in the absolute poverty rate from 44 percent (as of the late 1990s) to 10 percent by the year 2017.

Uganda was the first country to be declared eligible and to benefit from Highly Indebted Poor Country (HIPC) measures. Most recently, Uganda qualified for enhanced HIPC relief in recognition of the effectiveness of its poverty reduction strategy, consultative process involving civil society, and the government's continuing commitment to macroeconomic stability.

Uganda has introduced new measures to make the budget process more open and transparent to internal and external stakeholders. The government is modernizing its fiscal systems, and embarking on a decentralization program of planning, resource management, and service delivery to localities. The Ministry of Finance, Economic Planning and Development (MFPED) is also introducing output-oriented budgeting. In addition, government institutions will be strengthened and made more accountable to the public.

The country is still experiencing a number of coordination and harmonization difficulties with respect to M&E and the PEAP. "The most obvious characteristic of the PEAP M&E regime is the separation of poverty monitoring and resource monitoring, albeit both coordinated by the MFPED. The two strands of M&E have separate actors, reports and use different criteria of assessment. Financial resource monitoring is associated with inputs, activities and, increasingly, outputs, whereas poverty monitoring is based on analyzing overall poverty outcomes" (Hauge 2001, p. 6). Other M&E coordination issues revolve around the creation of a new National Planning Authority, and among the sector working groups.

Regarding future challenges and M&E, Uganda faces the task of keeping track of and learning from its progress toward poverty reduction via the PEAP/National Poverty Reduction Strategy. M&E cannot be isolated from the decisionmaking practices and incentives that underpin national development systems and processes.

Sources: Hauge 2001; World Bank 2002b.

Developing countries deserve good governance no less than other countries.

means that more donors will need to step in to ensure the necessary assistance for developing countries to implement such systems.

Instituting results-based M&E systems has been challenging for developed as well as developing countries—though developing countries face special difficulties. There is no one correct path or approach. Getting there takes commitment, effort, time, and resources. At the same time, one should continue to bear in mind that there are also costs to *not* instituting such systems and not responding to internal and external stakeholder calls for accountability, transparency, and results.

Chapter 1

Step 1: Conducting a Readiness Assessment

Figure 1.1

In the introduction we examined new challenges in public sector management—calls for increased public accountability, better governance, and demonstrable results. We introduced a new public management tool, the results-based monitoring and evaluation system, that can help policymakers respond to the increasing demands by NGOs; civil society; and national, multilateral, and international stakeholders for better performance. Finally, we reviewed the monitoring and evaluation experience in developed and developing countries, as well as the special challenges facing the developing world in building results-based M&E systems.

In this chapter, we turn to Step 1 of our 10-step model (figure 1.1)—the readiness assessment. This step is a unique addition to the many M&E models that currently exist because it provides an analytical framework to assess a given country's organizational capacity and political willingness to monitor and evaluate its goals, and develop a performance-based framework. This is a key step—unfortunately often missed or omitted—in helping developing countries, in particular, build their own results-based M&E systems.

Specifically, this chapter addresses: (a) the importance of conducting a readiness assessment; (b) the three main parts of the readiness assessment; (c) the eight key diagnostic areas that must be considered in any readiness assessment; (d) some examples of recent readiness assessments done in developing countries; and (e) lessons learned from these experiences. Annex I details a version of the readiness assessment step: "Assessing Results-Based Monitoring and Evaluation Capacity: An Assessment Survey for Countries, Development Institutions, and Their Partners" that countries can use for their own self-assessments.

PART 1

Why Do a Readiness Assessment?

Experts have devised a number of different models for building M&E systems, but often miss the complexities and nuances of the wider country context. The needs of the recipient country are often only vaguely understood by those experts trying to provide technical assistance. For all the good intentions to advance the design, creation, and use of results-based M&E systems, too little emphasis is placed on existing political, organizational, and cultural factors and contexts.

It will be a constant theme of this handbook that building a results-based M&E system is first and foremost a political activity with technical dimensions rather than vice versa.

Most of the existing models start by jumping straight into building a results-based M&E system—without even knowing where a given country stands in relation to a number of critical factors, including organizational roles, responsibilities, and capabilities; incentives and demands for such a system; ability of an organization to sustain systems; and so forth. There are a few models that pose key readiness questions. (See Mackay 1999 and World Bank 2003a.)

Most experts look at the "what" questions—what are the goals? what are the indicators?—and not the "why" questions: Why do we want to measure something? Why is there a need in a particular country to think about these issues? Why do we want to embark on building sustainable results-based M&E systems?

To answer these "why" questions, there is a considerable amount of preparatory work to do before the actual construction of a results-based M&E system. That preparatory work takes the form of the readiness assessment presented here. We will walk through, step-by-step, some of the important issues, concerns, and questions that should be addressed before embarking on building an M&E system.

Some might also pose the question: How does a readiness assessment differ from a needs assessment? Are they not the same thing? In fact, they are not. A needs assessment assumes that there is some fundamental, underlying question as to whether governments need such systems. A readiness assessment assumes that governments need to have these systems, and addresses whether governments are actually ready and able to move forward in building, using, and sustaining the systems. For example, what is the government's capability with respect to M&E in general? Does it simply measure outputs, or is the government in a position to move beyond measuring outputs to measuring outcomes? (It should also be remembered that studying organizational capacity is not enough. These are just a few of the key questions and concerns that only a readiness assessment can address and answer.) A readiness assessment provides the analytical framework for rating a country's ability to monitor and evaluate its progress in achieving designated development goals. It does this by assessing a country's current understanding, capacity, and use of existing monitoring and evaluation systems.

A readiness assessment is like constructing the foundation for a building. A good foundation provides support for all that is above it. It is below ground, not seen, but critical.

Three Main Parts of the Readiness Assessment

The readiness assessment is a diagnostic aid that will help determine where a given country[3] stands in relation to the requirements for establishing a results-based M&E system. It is composed of three main parts.

Incentives and Demands for Designing and Building a Results-Based M&E System   It is important to determine whether incentives exist—political, institutional, or personal—before beginning to design and build a results-based M&E system. There are five key questions related to incentives:

- What is driving the need for building an M&E system—legislative or legal requirements, citizen demand, donor requirements (National Development Plan, National Poverty Reduction Strategy, or others), or political or public sector reform?
- Who are the champions for building and using an M&E system—government, parliament, civil society, donors, others?
- What is motivating those who champion building an M&E sys-

tem—a political reform agenda, pressures from donors, a personal political agenda, or political directive?

- Who will benefit from the system—politicians, administrators, civil society, donors, citizens?
- Who will *not* benefit from building an M&E system—politicians, administrators, civil society, donors, citizens? Are there counterreformers inside or outside the political system?

Roles and Responsibilities and Existing Structures for Assessing Performance of the Government A readiness assessment will enable one to gauge the roles and responsibilities and existing structures available to monitor and evaluate development goals.

- What are the roles of central and line ministries in assessing performance?
- What is the role of parliament?
- What is the role of the supreme audit agency?
- Do ministries and agencies share information with one another?
- Is there a political agenda behind the data produced?
- What is the role of civil society?
- Who in the country produces data?
  - At the national government level, including central ministries, line ministries, specialized units or offices, including the national audit office
  - At the subnational or regional government level, including provincial central and line ministries, local government, NGOs, donors, and others
- Where in the government are data used?
  - Budget preparation
  - Resource allocation
  - Program policymaking
  - Legislation and accountability to parliament
  - Planning
  - Fiscal management
  - Evaluation and oversight.

Capacity Building Requirements for a Results-Based M&E System
The readiness assessment also includes a review of a country's current capacity to monitor and evaluate along the following dimensions: technical skills; managerial skills; existence and quality of data systems; available technology; available fiscal resources; and institu-

tional experience. This is an important part of the assessment in developing countries, because it can help identify any gaps in capacity needed to build and sustain results-based M&E systems.

Such an assessment also directs one to examine existing or possible barriers to building an M&E system, including a lack of fiscal resources, political will, political champion, expertise, strategy, or prior experience.

A number of key questions need to be considered:

- What are the skills of civil servants in the national government in each of the following five areas:
  - Project and program management
  - Data analysis
  - Project and program goal establishment
  - Budget management
  - Performance auditing?
- Is there any technical assistance, capacity building, or training in M&E now underway or that was done in the past two years for any level of government (national, regional, or local)? Who provided this help and under what framework or reform process?
- Are there any institutes, research centers, private organizations, or universities in the country that have some capacity to provide technical assistance and training for civil servants and others in performance-based M&E?

Now we will build on this material and explore the eight key areas covered by a readiness assessment in more detail.

PART 2

The Readiness Assessment: Eight Key Questions

The readiness assessment is a diagnostic tool that can be used to determine whether the prerequisites are in place for building a results-based M&E system. It is intended to assist and benefit individual governments, the donor community, and their many development partners involved in public sector reform.[4]

The readiness assessment provides a guide through the eight areas that must be considered and explored in determining a given country's or organization's ability and willingness to adopt and move forward with a results-based M&E system.

What Potential Pressures Are Encouraging the Need for the M&E System within the Public Sector and Why?

It is important to know where the demand for creating an M&E system is emanating from and why. Are the demands and pressures coming from internal, multilateral, or international stakeholders, or some combination of these? These requests will need to be acknowledged and addressed if the response is to be appropriate to the demand.

As noted in the introduction, internal demands may arise from calls for reforms in public sector governance and for better accountability and transparency. Anti-corruption campaigns may be a motivating force. Or political opponents may not trust the government's intentions or actions.

Externally, pressures may arise from the donor community for tangible development results for their investments. International organizations, such as the European Union, expect a feedback system on public sector performance via M&E for each of the accession countries. The competitive pressures of globalization may come into play, and the rule of law, a strong governance system, and clearly articulated rules of the game are now necessary to attract foreign investment. Financial capital and the private sector are looking for a stable, transparent investment climate, and protection of their property and patents, before committing to invest in a country. There are a multitude of pressures that governments may need to respond to, and these will drive the incentives for building a results-based M&E system.

Who Is the Advocate for an M&E System?

Champions in government are critical to the sustainability and success of a results-based M&E system. A highly placed government champion can be a strong advocate for more well-informed decision-making, and can help diffuse and isolate attacks from counterreformers who will have vested interests in averting the construction of such a system.

Within a given organization, there are individuals or groups who will likely welcome and champion such an initiative, while others may oppose or even actively counter the initiative. It is important to know who the champions are and where they are located in a government. Their support and advocacy will be crucial to the potential success and sustainability of the M&E system.

However, if the emerging champion is located away from the center of policymaking and has little influence with key decisionmakers, it will be difficult, although not impossible, to envision an M&E system being used and trusted. It will be hard to ensure the viability of the system under these circumstances. Viability is dependent upon the information being viewed as relevant, trustworthy, useable, and timely. M&E systems with marginally placed champions who are peripheral to the decisionmaking process will have a more difficult time meeting these viability requirements.

What Is Motivating the Champion to Support Such an Effort?

Constructing a results-based M&E system is an inherently political act entailing both political risks and benefits. On the risk side, producing information on government performance and strengthening accountability are not politically neutral activities. On the benefit side, champions may find rewards and recognition at the institutional and individual levels. Champions may be motivated by a sense of public responsibility. Champions may also find favor with parliaments, public and private stakeholders, civil society, and the international donor community by delivering on promises, being perceived as a reformer (a source of political capital), and demonstrating accountability and results.

Understanding political motivation is critical to understanding how an M&E system will be perceived by stakeholders, how and why certain persons or organizations will take the political risk while others will not, and what those championing such a system will need to defend the initiative and succeed.

Who Will Own the System? Who Will Benefit from the System? How Much Information Do They Really Want?

Politics is not the only factor often overlooked in building M&E systems. Frequently, a careful institutional assessment is not made—in particular, one that would reflect the real capacity of the users to actually create, utilize, and sustain the system.

A carefully done readiness assessment helps provide a good understanding of how to design the system to be responsive to the information needs of its users, determine the resources available to build and sustain the system, and assess the capacities of those who will both produce and use the information. Understanding these issues helps to tailor the system to the right level of complexity and completeness.

For a results-based M&E system to be effectively used, it should provide accessible, understandable, relevant, and timely information and data. These criteria drive the need for a careful readiness assessment prior to designing the system, particularly with reference to such factors as ownership of the system, and benefits and utility to key stakeholders. From a technical perspective, issues to be addressed include the capacity of the government or organization to collect and analyze data, produce reports, manage and maintain the M&E system, and use the information produced.

Thus, the readiness assessment will provide important information and baseline data against which capacity-building activities—if necessary—can be designed and implemented.

Furthermore, there is an absolute requirement to collect no more information than is required. Time and again, M&E systems are designed and are immediately overtaxed by too much data collected too often—without sufficient thought and foresight into how and whether such data will actually be used. Complexity and overdesign are constant concerns. There will also be a continuous erosion in the system that will need to be addressed. And stakeholders may try to pull the system in too many different directions at once. In short, little in the political arena remains the same. Keeping the M&E system up and running will demand vigilance and care (yet another reason why champions are necessary).

How Will the System Directly Support Better Resource Allocation and the Achievement of Program Goals?

Monitoring and evaluation is not an end unto itself. It is a tool to be used to promote good governance, modern management practices, innovation and reforms, and better accountability. When used properly, these systems can produce information that is trustworthy, transparent, and relevant. M&E systems can help policymakers track and improve the outcomes and impacts of resource allocations. Most of all, they help governments and organizations make more well-informed decisions and policies by providing continuous feedback on results.

Experience shows that the creation of a results-based M&E system often works best when linked with other public sector reform programs and initiatives, such as creating a medium-term public expenditure framework, restructuring public administration, or constructing a National Poverty Reduction Strategy. Linking the creation of M&E systems to such initiatives creates interdependencies and reinforcements that are crucial to the overall sustainability of the systems. The readiness assessment can provide a road map for determining whether such links are structurally and politically possible.

How Will the Organization, the Champions, and the Staff React to Negative Information Generated by the M&E System?

It is difficult to have a functioning M&E system in an organizational or political climate characterized by fear. M&E systems will inevitably (even if infrequently) produce data that may be embarrassing, politically sensitive, or detrimental to those in power. In a similar way, the information can also be detrimental to units and individuals in an organization. ("Punishing the messenger" is not an unknown occurrence in organizations.)

If it is clear from the readiness assessment that only politically popular or "correct" information will be allowed to emanate from the M&E system, the system is vulnerable and compromised from the beginning. It will not be seen as credible by those outside the organization. It will come to be seen as a hollow exercise. In such a political setting, it is important to build the system carefully and slowly. Finding units that will risk potentially detrimental information—including unfavorable information about their own performance—is perhaps the best that can be achieved. If such units are not present, there is little rationale or justification for proceeding further to design such a system. An emphasis on traditional implementation monitoring will have to suffice.

Governments willing to use performance information to make policy generally have achieved some level of democracy and openness. But even in these countries, there is often a reluctance to measure and monitor because of fears that the process will bring bad news to leadership and stakeholders alike. There are real political limitations to be recognized in building such systems.

A readiness assessment will help identify the barriers and obstacles—structural, cultural, political, or individual—in a given organization.

Not all barriers can be addressed simultaneously in the design of the system. However, not recognizing the presence of these barriers and addressing them as soon as possible creates the risk of a level of resistance greater and longer than may have been necessary. It is a strategic decision as to how much time and energy should be spent on removing barriers as opposed to using that same finite time and energy to strengthen champions and support emerging opportunities. We strongly lean toward the latter.

Where Does Capacity Exist to Support a Results-Based M&E System?

Performance data and information can be found in many places. The readiness assessment provides a useful guide to determining where such information and data can be found. For instance, are there any organizational units within the government that already have monitoring and evaluation capacity and that can undertake evaluations? What data systems can be found within, or are available to, the central and sector or line ministries of the government responsible for planning? This can include budget data, output data, outcome or impact data, performance audits, financial audits, project and program completion reports, and donor data information. Outside the government, NGOs, universities, research institutes, and training centers may also provide part of the necessary technical capacity to support a results-based M&E system.

How Will the M&E System Link Project, Program, Sector, and National Goals?

One of the main functions of the readiness assessment is to determine the opportunities for and risks of linking information across the government in an aligned fashion. In an ideal situation, project level performance data would be fed into and linked to program assessments that, in turn, would be linked to sectoral, regional, and national goals and targets. In other words, staff at each level would have a clear "line of sight" into, or understanding about, each of the other levels and how they relate to one another.

Results-based M&E at the project level that is not clearly aligned with program goals is not useful beyond the restricted information for a given project. Information must flow freely between levels to be truly useful. Each level must help inform the next level to achieve the desired results. It is important, as well, to ensure that within a level, there is a commitment to horizontally use and share information from the collection and analysis of data. The goal is to create an M&E system that is transparent and aligned from one level to the next. Information should flow up and down in a governmental system, rather than being collected, stored, and used at one level—but never shared across levels. A free flow of information can help ensure that policies, programs, and projects are linked and coordinated. Ultimately, the real question is whether the system can address the need at every level to be both producers and consumers of results-based information.

PART 3

Readiness Assessments in Developing Countries: Bangladesh, Egypt, and Romania

The readiness assessment can help governments, donors, and their partners address the challenges of the training, organizational capacity building, and sequencing of efforts that will be needed to design and construct results-based M&E systems. It provides the basis for an action plan to move forward in the country.

A readiness assessment should begin with a look at the data that are currently reported by traditional implementation-focused M&E systems, and whether public expenditure, financial, data, or procurement reviews have been done. Is the country moving toward economic, legal, and political reform; greater democracy and openness; more accountability and transparency? (Occasionally, one finds that several different diagnostic surveys are being undertaken simultaneously. In the Kyrgyz Republic in early 2002, for example, there was a Country Performance Portfolio Review, a Public Expenditure Review, and a Monitoring and Evaluation Review going on at the same time.) After reviewing where the country stands with regard to public management reforms, a country or field mission should then be undertaken.

While in the country, information is gathered in the field from key informants, including government officials, members of civil society, and NGOs. It is important to talk with ministers and a broad range of sector-level officials. One never knows where one will find a champion who is interested in having a performance-based data system that will enhance policymaking. Ideally, the readiness assessment should be undertaken by someone familiar with M&E capacity building.

Readiness Assessments: Three Developing Country Cases

Let us look now at three actual examples from the developing world—Bangladesh, Egypt, and Romania—to see how the readiness assessment can inform and shape efforts to build results-based M&E systems (boxes 1.1 through 1.3). We will also draw lessons from these experiences that may be applicable to other developing countries.

PART 4

Lessons Learned

What are the lessons that can be drawn from these three readiness assessment examples from the developing world?

Incentives and Demands for Designing and Building a Results-Based M&E System

It is most important to understand the situation in a given country in the eight areas outlined in the readiness assessment. Had the assessment not been conducted in Bangladesh, for example, efforts to design and build a results-based M&E system might have moved

Box 1.1

The Case of Bangladesh—Building from the Bottom Up

In the course of implementing the readiness assessment, Bangladesh posed a considerable challenge with respect to its readiness to design and build a results-based M&E system. In 2001, Bangladesh was ranked the most corrupt country of the 91 countries monitored by Transparency International, with the most corrupt public sector listed as the law enforcement agencies, followed by education, local government, and health. In 2002, Bangladesh was again listed as the most corrupt of the 102 countries monitored. Corrupt systems keep information out of the public domain—and this is a major obstacle to M&E.

The readiness assessment found no champion for M&E anywhere in the national government, including central and sector ministries. No reform initiatives could be identified that could create incentives for linking these reforms to the creation of an M&E system. Furthermore, there were no legal or regulatory requirements for the use of M&E that could be identified.

There were some monitoring systems in rural parts of the country for education, electrification, and food subsidies. There was also some evidence that NGOs and the donor community were actively monitoring for results of development projects, but this had not influenced the government to do the same. The Bangladesh Bureau of Statistics was found to be a strong state agency. If and when the government moves toward developing a results-based M&E system, the bureau could play a central role in the collection and analysis of data.

In terms of technical capability, the readiness assessment found weak capacity for M&E and minimal technical training capacity in universities and research centers. The assessment also indicated minimal organizational experience in the national government with respect to managing credible information systems.

As a result of the readiness assessment, we found that it was not realistic and feasible to introduce a results-based M&E system into the national government at that time. Strong political support and sustained institution capacity building will be needed before such an initiative can be undertaken.

There is hope on the horizon for Bangladesh. Subsequent to the readiness assessment, the government developed a National Poverty Reduction Strategy that will include M&E components. The readiness assessment recommended five strategies to donors and NGOs working in Bangladesh to strengthen some of their capacity and work in small, targeted ways.

Source: World Bank 2002c.

Box 1.2

The Case of Egypt—Slow, Systematic Moves toward M&E

One of the most important components of assessing a country's readiness to introduce results-based M&E is whether a champion can be found who is willing to take on ownership of the system. Conducting the readiness assessment uncovered significant interest in Egypt on the part of many senior government officials for moving toward a climate of assessing performance. The president himself has called for better information to support economic decisionmaking.

The Minister of Finance was found to be a key champion for the government of Egypt's move to a results focus. This minister was well versed in the international experience of other countries, such as Malaysia and OECD member countries. The minister underscored the importance of giving increased attention to improving the management of public expenditures by moving forward with a set of pilots to demonstrate how results-based M&E could be used to better manage budgetary allocations. The Minister of Finance will play a key leadership role in any effort to introduce results-based M&E in Egypt.

A number of other senior officials were identified who could play important roles. The First Lady of Egypt, who chairs the National Council for Women, is developing a system to monitor and evaluate efforts across many ministries to enhance the status and condition of women. However, for an M&E effort to be successful and sustainable, there must be a "buy-in" (or a sense of ownership) from line ministers who are responsible for resource expenditures and overseeing the implementation of specific programs. The team found interest in monitoring and evaluation for results on the part of several line ministers, including the Minister of Electricity and Energy, and the Minister of Health.

The readiness assessment also revealed a high level of capacity in Egypt to support the move toward a results-based strategy. A number of individuals with evaluation training were identified at the University of Cairo, the American University of Cairo, and private research organizations. In addition, the Central Agency for Public Mobilization and Statistics, and the Cabinet Information Decision Support Center have key roles in collecting, analyzing, and disseminating data to be used by both government and nongovernment researchers and policymakers.

A key criterion for a successful shift toward results is the development of a well-communicated and executable strategy. The diagnostic identified a fragmented strategy for moving the effort forward. A set of pilots had tentatively been identified, yet there were few, if any, criteria for establishing these as performance pilots. Nor was there a management structure set up within the government to effectively manage the overall effort. The Minister of Finance, however, had begun to define an approach that, if implemented, would provide the necessary leadership to move the effort forward. The minister was definite in his desire to move slowly and to nurture the pilots, learning along the way.

The results of this readiness assessment suggest that the government of Egypt is prepared to take ownership of the effort and to systematically and slowly begin to introduce the concepts of results management. Visible capacity exists that can be drawn upon to sustain the effort. Significantly, there is obvious political support to provide the necessary leadership. (The complete Egypt Readiness Assessment can be found in annex II.)

Source: World Bank 2001c.

Box 1.3

The Case of Romania—Some Opportunities to Move toward M&E

Romania is in negotiations with the European Union to gain accession, and hopes to become a member by 2007. The government has a clear political commitment to reform, and has developed a medium-term economic strategy. Romania also has a work force skilled in data collection and use. In this sense, it is ahead of many other developing and transition economies.

At the same time, though, Romania continues to suffer from the communist legacy in a number of ways, such as a continued central planning mentality in some parts of the government, weak governmental institutions, few government officials trained in modern public management principles and practices, and an inexperienced civil society with no tradition of actively participating in the business of government.

The readiness assessment revealed other barriers to moving toward M&E. These included a lack of understanding within Romania's public sector as to what is entailed in the development of a performance-oriented management culture, and conflicts with other overall government priorities.

Romania is conducting a set of budget performance pilots in which 5 agencies have been asked to submit a set of performance measures as an annex to the annual budget. The pilot program began with 5 governmental agencies, moving to 8 in the following year, 13 in the year thereafter, and finally to all agencies. At the time of the readiness assessment, the government was still in the pilot phase with a new budget that included 13 pilots.

The pilots that focused on allocating funds to agencies based on performance indicators were largely ignored by government managers and not taken seriously by the parliament. However, the pilots did represent a focal point for learning how to develop appropriate performance indicators to monitor the effectiveness of the annual budget. The Minister of Finance appears to be a strong champion of the effort, and could provide the necessary political leadership to initiate and sustain a larger results-based management effort.

Two additional potential champions were identified, including the Minister of Justice and a counselor to the prime minister. Both are leading efforts to improve management in the Romanian government, and they recognize the importance of reporting on the success of strategies.

The government's commitment to move toward M&E is supported by a framework of new laws, the move toward EU accession, and rising expectations on the part of civil society. For example, one change in the legal framework includes a set of laws assisting a drive toward e-administration. This initiative could be a potential vehicle for improving government transparency and providing civil society with results of the government's reform program. Developing e-administration can be a potent instrument for government accountability.

Finally, the readiness assessment suggests a number of opportunities to support the introduction of results-based M&E. The ongoing performance budgeting effort and other government reforms could provide a significant focus on, and catalyst for, results. There is also sufficient high level political leadership to jump-start M&E within at least three pilot areas: budget, anticorruption, and poverty reform.

Source: World Bank 2001d.

forward in an environment that had few of the necessary preconditions for M&E. Similarly, in both Egypt and Romania, the readiness assessment provided vital information regarding likely entry points for designing and building a results-based M&E system that had the benefit of strong champions and a larger reform environment.

There must be an acknowledged and publicized mandate for moving toward a results-oriented climate prior to introducing programs. As noted earlier, this can come about as a result of internal or external initiatives and forces. For example, the mandate might include a budget management reform law, EU accession, pressure from a concerned citizenry, the need to reduce burdensome civil service payrolls, or a desire to make good on political promises.

A sustained source of demand for performance information should be encouraged and supported, putting the government on notice that it will need to demonstrate results—that is, governments will need to demonstrate that the policies and programs being implemented are meeting expectations. Governments need prodding to ensure that reporting results becomes a regular and routine activity.

A successful results-based M&E system must have sustained leadership. While it is important to have good program managers overseeing the implementation of government programs and projects, there must also be strong political support at the very highest levels of government. The country, through its government, must be in the driver's seat in developing these systems to ensure ownership. Without a strong, well placed champion who is willing to take on the ownership of a results-based M&E system, the system will not be built or used.

Roles and Responsibilities and Existing Structures for Assessing Government Performance

High turnover among government officials represents a challenge to building M&E systems. Frequent personnel changes in ministries make it difficult to identify and keep working with champions. This might be another reason to look for additional champions in civil society, NGOs, or in parliament.

In many developing countries, different ministries and parts of government are going to be at different stages in their ability to monitor and evaluate. One should not necessarily assume that the whole government will be moving in tandem. There inevitably will be some sequencing and staggering with respect to building M&E systems. The readiness assessment can serve as a guide through the political system, and help identify the ability level of government ministries and agencies to monitor and evaluate. One should focus on nurturing those parts of the government that are in a position to move faster toward developing an M&E culture.

Clear links between the budget and other resource allocation decisions are also necessary in making the shift to a results-based culture.

In most governments, there is more than one agency working on a particular program. The readiness assessment can help identify overlaps among agencies so that overall program performance can be more effectively and efficiently measured and achieved. In effect, the readiness assessment can be a guide toward brokering differences between agencies doing the same or similar tasks.

Government policymakers need to be in communication and work in partnership with those responsible for information gathering and dissemination—particularly in areas such as the MDGs. Separate universes of political action, support, and capacity building will not work. The M&E system needs to be integrated into the policy arena of the MDGs so that it will be clear to all stakeholders why it is important to collect data, how the information will be used to inform the efforts of the government and civil society to achieve the MDGs, and what information needs to be collected.

Capacity Building Requirements for a Results-Based M&E System

Policy and management decisions should be based on reliable information. Bangladesh, Egypt, and Romania—like so many developing countries—lack sufficient capacity and many of the necessary resources for building M&E systems. This is not an insurmountable obstacle. Expertise, strategy, and experience can be acquired with time and money. However, lack of political will and champions will impede any move toward an M&E culture.

The country must eventually have its own capacity to design, implement, and use a results-based M&E system. It is not enough to acquire skills such as social research, public management, statistics, or data management via consulting contracts from the international community. These skills must, in some way, come to reside within the country—and be available for contributing to a program of regularly assessing the performance of government. If these skills are not present in sufficient quantities, a concerted capacity-building program is necessary.

Countries will need to build the capacity to implement pockets of innovation that can serve as beginning practices or pilot programs. The ability to test and pilot will become particularly important when we examine the selection of key performance indicators in chapter 3.

One of the challenges in designing and building M&E systems is that there are so many different donors often asking the government to report on the same development goal. The readiness assessment can be used as a tool for donor coordination of M&E systems, and attendant capacity- and institution-building activities. Such coordination can help the country make the best use of donor resources, in particular by avoiding the pitfalls of duplication, underfunding, or mismatch of priorities.

The challenges of designing and building a results-based M&E system in a developing country are not to be underestimated. The construction of such a system is a serious undertaking and will not happen overnight. However, it is also not to be dismissed as too complicated, demanding, or sophisticated for a developing country to initiate. All countries need good information systems so they can monitor their own performance—developing countries no less than others. Consequently, assisting developing countries in achieving this capacity merits the time and attention of country officials and their development partners.

Chapter 2

Step 2: Agreeing on Outcomes to Monitor and Evaluate

Figure 2.1

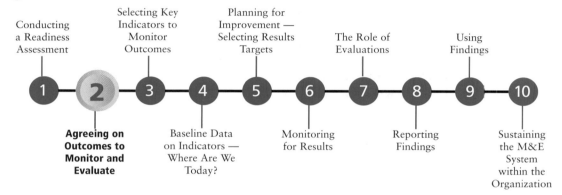

Setting goals is part of the governmental decisionmaking process at every level. All governments have goals—although not all have M&E capacity. Assuming that a country or organization is in fact in a position to move forward in building a results-based M&E system, the next step is to choose and agree on the outcomes (derived from the goals) to monitor and evaluate (figure 2.1). Knowing where you are going before you get moving is key.

Specifically, this chapter addresses (a) the importance of outcomes; (b) issues to consider in choosing outcomes to monitor and evaluate; (c) the importance of building a participatory and consultative process involving main stakeholders; and (d) the overall process of setting and agreeing on outcomes. Examples for consideration and discussion are also included.

The Importance of Outcomes

At the outset, it is important to distinguish between goals and outcomes. Goals are generally long term, such as the MDGs that were reviewed earlier. From goals we move to outcomes, which, in the MDG example, are of intermediate time frame (five to ten years). From outcomes we derive targets that are generally short-range—in the MDG context, about one to three years.

Why is it important to emphasize outcomes at this stage? Why not move directly to setting indicators? Because establishing outcomes will illustrate what success looks like. By contrast, indicators are only relevant when they measure against an objective. Thus, measuring indicators will show the progress made toward reaching the intended objectives.

Decisionmakers and stakeholders are positioned to make the intended outcomes of governmental action as explicit as possible. One cannot set indicators before determining outcomes because it is the *outcomes*—not the indicators—that will ultimately produce the benefits. Outcomes will demonstrate whether success has been achieved. In short, outcomes will show which road to take.

Setting outcomes is essential in building a results-based M&E system. Building the system is basically a deductive process in which inputs, activities, and outputs are all derived and flow from the setting of outcomes. Indicators, baselines, and targets (covered in subsequent chapters), all crucial elements of the performance framework, are derived from and based on the setting of outcomes.

Issues to Consider in Choosing Outcomes to Monitor and Evaluate

What are the strategic priorities? What are the desired outcomes? These are the questions that every organization, every level of government, and the interested parties in civil society can be asking—of themselves and others. We focus in the following primarily on how this relates to the national government.

Every country has finite budgetary resources and must set priorities. Consequently, it is important to keep the following distinction in mind: One budgets to outputs and manages to outcomes.

There are many issues to consider in choosing outcomes to monitor and evaluate. For example, outcomes could be linked to international economic development and lending issues, including a National Poverty Reduction Strategy, a National Development Plan, the HIPC Initiative, or the MDGs.

If there is an EU accession plan for the country, decisionmakers need to examine a host of socioeconomic and political benchmarks,

Outcomes are usually not directly measured, only reported on.

and articulate specific desired outcomes to meet them, to formally join this important regional bloc.

At the country level, there could already be some stated national, regional, or sectoral goals. Also, political and electoral promises may have already been made that specify improved governmental performance in a given area. In addition, there may be citizen polling data indicating particular societal concerns. Parliamentary actions and authorizing legislation are other areas that should be examined in determining desired national goals. There may also be a set of simple goals for a given project or program, or for a particular region of a country. From these goals, specific desired outcomes can be determined.

It should be noted that developing countries may face special challenges in formulating national outcomes. Developing countries may find it difficult to set governmental priorities for some of the reasons referred to earlier, including lack of political will, lack of planning and analytical capacity, or a weak central agency. At the same time, though, every government needs to have goals, and there are ways of building a national consensus and developing the necessary capacity to set priorities and determine desired outcomes. This entails launching a participatory process involving key stakeholders. Donor assistance with institution and capacity building can also help jump-start the technical and analytical process of formulating desired national outcomes.

The Importance of Building a Participatory and Consultative Process Involving Main Stakeholders

When choosing outcomes, do not travel the road alone.

Setting goals in isolation leads to a lack of ownership on the part of the main internal and external stakeholders. Likewise, when choosing outcomes, it is crucial to build a participatory and consultative process involving the stakeholders. The participatory process should start with the development of goals and continue with setting outcomes and building an indicator system. (Indicators cannot be simply turned over to technicians, because the political apparatus has to be consulted and has to agree on both goals and indicators. We will elaborate on this in Step 3, setting indicators).

The new realities of governance, globalization, aid lending, and citizen expectations require an approach that is consultative, cooperative, and committed to consensus building. The voices and views of stakeholders should be actively solicited. Engaging key stakeholders in a participatory manner helps to build consensus and gain a commitment to reaching the desired outcomes.

The Overall Process of Setting and Agreeing upon Outcomes

You need to know where you are going, why you are going there, and how you will know when you get there. There is a political process involved in setting and agreeing upon desired outcomes. Each part is critical to the success of achieving stakeholder consensus with respect to outcomes.

Identify Specific Stakeholder Representatives

Who are the key parties involved around an issue area (health, education, and so forth)? How are they categorized, for example, NGO, government, donor? Whose interests and views are to be given priority?

Identify Major Concerns of Stakeholder Groups

Use information gathering techniques such as brainstorming, focus groups, surveys, and interviews to discover the interests of the involved groups. Numerous voices must be heard—not just the loudest, richest, or most well-connected. People must be brought into the process to enhance and support a democratic public sector.

Translate Problems into Statements of Possible Outcome Improvements

It should be noted that formulating problems as positive outcomes is quite different from a simple reiteration of the problem. An outcome-oriented statement enables one to identify the road and destination ahead. We encourage outcomes to be framed positively rather than negatively (figure 2.2). Stakeholders will respond and rally better to positive statements, for example, "We want improved health for infants and children," rather than "We want fewer infants and children to become ill." Positive statements to which stakeholders can aspire seem to carry more legitimacy. It is easier to gather a political consensus by speaking positively to the desired outcomes of stakeholders.

Disaggregate to Capture Key Desired Outcome

Outcomes should be disaggregated sufficiently to capture only one improvement area in each outcome statement. A sample outcome might be to "increase the percentage of employed people." To know whether this outcome has been achieved, the goal needs to be disaggregated to answer the following:

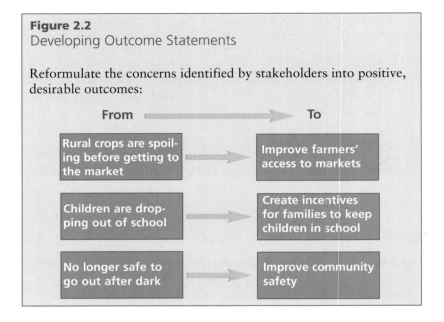

Figure 2.2
Developing Outcome Statements

Reformulate the concerns identified by stakeholders into positive, desirable outcomes:

From ➡ To

Rural crops are spoiling before getting to the market	Improve farmers' access to markets
Children are dropping out of school	Create incentives for families to keep children in school
No longer safe to go out after dark	Improve community safety

- For whom?
- Where?
- How much?
- By when?

We need to disaggregate this outcome by examining increased employment in terms of a target group, sector, percentage change, and timeframe. For instance, the disaggregated outcome may be to "increase employment among youth in the rural sector by 20 percent over the next four years." Only by disaggregating the outcome and articulating the details will we know if we have successfully achieved it.

Simplifying and distilling outcomes at this point also eliminates complications later when we start to build a system of indicators, baselines, and targets by which to monitor and evaluate. By disaggregating outcomes into subcomponents, we can set indicators to measure results.

Develop a Plan to Assess How a Government or Organization Will Achieve These Outcomes

When one monitors using the traditional implementation-based tools of inputs, activities, and outputs, the need to be clear about outcomes is much less apparent. Managers would gather inputs, assign activities, and wait for outputs. But the shortcoming of this approach is that completing all of the activities and outputs is not the same thing as achieving the desired outcomes. The sum of all activities may or may not mean that desired outcomes have resulted. A list of tasks and activities does not measure results. Even if all activities were completed within a given timeframe, the desired outcome has not necessarily been achieved.

This is not to say that activities are unimportant. The actions needed to manage and implement programs, use resources, and deliver government services are crucial to the process. They are necessary—just not sufficient.

It is best to first reach an agreement on strategic priorities and outcomes, and then use them to drive resource allocations and activities.

Being busy is not the same thing as attaining results.

Examples and Possible Approaches

What is involved in the actual process of choosing outcomes? The example below illustrates one scenario that may be helpful.

Situation	After broadly based consultations with key stakeholders, a president has set some important national and sector goals for inclusion in a five-year economic development plan. The prime minister has in turn been asked by the president to translate these goals into a set of outcomes that can be achieved—and demonstrate progress toward the strategic vision.
Actions	The prime minister asks the Minister of Finance to lead a 10-week effort to identify desired outcomes.
	The Minister of Finance forms a task group that includes representatives of the country's stakeholder groups.
Stakeholders included	Government, civil society, donors.
Reason included	To build consensus for the process.
Three key responsibilities	The finance minister gives the new task group three key responsibilities: (a) to identify specific stakeholder representatives; (b) to identify major concerns of each stakeholder group; and (c) to translate the list of concerns into a list of positive and desirable outcomes to achieve.

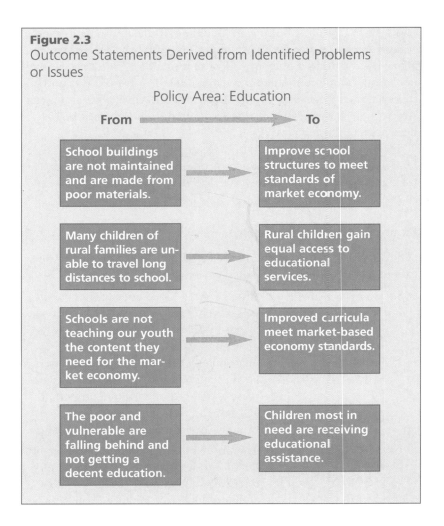

Figure 2.3
Outcome Statements Derived from Identified Problems or Issues

Policy Area: Education

From ➡ To

School buildings are not maintained and are made from poor materials.	Improve school structures to meet standards of market economy.
Many children of rural families are unable to travel long distances to school.	Rural children gain equal access to educational services.
Schools are not teaching our youth the content they need for the market economy.	Improved curricula meet market-based economy standards.
The poor and vulnerable are falling behind and not getting a decent education.	Children most in need are receiving educational assistance.

Translating problems into positive outcome statements is critical to the process. One must begin with the problems in a given country, then reformulate these concerns into a set of desirable outcomes. In other words, issues and problems need to be recast into a set of solutions. Figures 2.3 and 2.4 provide practical examples to illustrate the process, both correctly (figure 2.3) and incorrectly (figure 2.4).

Now consider the importance of capturing only a single outcome in each outcome statement. (This will become critical when we turn to indicators later in Step 3.) Figure 2.4 contains four examples of how NOT to construct outcome statements. The statements list mul-

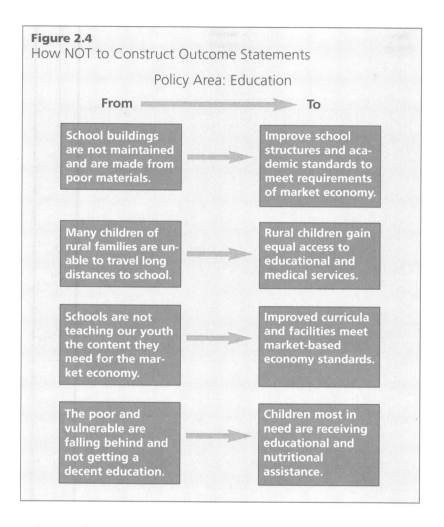

Figure 2.4
How NOT to Construct Outcome Statements

Policy Area: Education

From ➡ To

From	To
School buildings are not maintained and are made from poor materials.	Improve school structures and academic standards to meet requirements of market economy.
Many children of rural families are unable to travel long distances to school.	Rural children gain equal access to educational and medical services.
Schools are not teaching our youth the content they need for the market economy.	Improved curricula and facilities meet market-based economy standards.
The poor and vulnerable are falling behind and not getting a decent education.	Children most in need are receiving educational and nutritional assistance.

tiple areas for improvement, complicating the later process of setting indicators.

In the examples in figure 2.4 there should be two separate outcome statements while presently they are combined. The first, for example, should read "improve school structures to meet requirements of market economy," and the second: "improve academic standards to meet requirements of market economy." Likewise, the second statement also contains two outcomes, and should read instead as "rural children gain equal access to educational services," and "rural children gain access to medical services." The third state-

Figure 2.5
Developing Outcomes for One Policy Area

Example: Education

Outcomes	Indicators	Baselines	Targets
1. Nation's children have better access to preschool programs			
2. Primary school learning outcomes for children are improved			

ment should contain two outcomes: "improve curricula to meet market-based standards," and: "improve facilities to meet market-based standards." Finally, the fourth statement can also be translated into two outcomes: "children most in need are receiving educational assistance," and: "children most in need are receiving nutritional assistance."

Choosing outcomes is the first step in building the performance matrix. Figure 2.5 provides examples of possible educational development outcomes. Indicators, baselines, and targets will all flow from this initial step of establishing outcomes. As we move through the steps of the model in subsequent chapters, we will look at how to set indicators, baselines, and targets.

We have examined the critical importance of setting outcomes, the issues involved in choosing outcomes to monitor and evaluate, and the importance of building a participatory and consultative political process that includes the main stakeholders. We have identified the sequence of steps for setting outcomes, along with some guidelines for developing outcome statements that can be measured through a set of indicators. We turn next to Step 3, selecting key performance indicators to monitor outcomes.

Chapter 3

Step 3: Selecting Key Performance Indicators to Monitor Outcomes

Figure 3.1

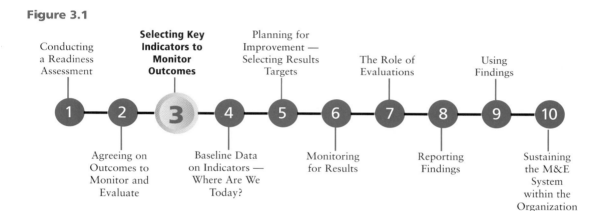

How will we know when we have achieved our desired outcomes? After examining the importance of setting achievable and well-defined outcomes, and the issues and process involved in agreeing upon those outcomes, we turn next to the selection of key indicators (figure 3.1). Outcome indicators are not the same as outcomes. Indicators are the quantitative or qualitative variables that provide a simple and reliable means to measure achievement, to reflect the changes connected to an intervention, or to help assess the performance of an organization against the stated outcome. Indicators should be developed for all levels of the results-based M&E system, meaning that indicators are needed to monitor progress with respect to inputs, activities, outputs, outcomes, and goals. Progress needs to be monitored at all levels of the system to provide feedback on areas of success and areas in which improvement may be required.

Outcome indicators help to answer two fundamental questions: "How will we know success or achievement when we see it? Are we moving toward achieving our desired outcomes?" These are the questions that are increasingly being asked of governments and organizations across the globe. Consequently, setting appropriate indicators to answer these questions becomes a critical part of our 10-step model.

Developing key indicators to monitor outcomes enables managers to assess the degree to which intended or promised outcomes are being achieved. Indicator development is a core activity in building a results-based M&E system. It drives all subsequent data collection, analysis, and reporting. There are also important political and methodological considerations involved in creating good, effective indicators.

This chapter specifically considers: (a) indicators required for all levels of the results-based M&E system; (b) translating outcomes into outcome indicators; (c) the "CREAM" of good performance indicators; (d) the use of proxy indicators; (e) the pros and cons of using predesigned indicators; (f) constructing indicators and tracking performance information; and (g) setting indicators using experience from developing countries.

Indicators Are Required for All Levels of Results-Based M&E Systems

Setting indicators to measure progress in inputs, activities, outputs, outcomes, and goals is important in providing necessary feedback to the management system. It will help managers identify those parts of an organization or government that may, or may not, be achieving results as planned. By measuring performance indicators on a regular, determined basis, managers and decisionmakers can find out whether projects, programs, and policies are on track, off track, or even doing better than expected against the targets set for performance. This provides an opportunity to make adjustments, correct course, and gain valuable institutional and project, program, or policy experience and knowledge. Ultimately, of course, it increases the likelihood of achieving the desired outcomes.

Translating Outcomes into Outcome Indicators

When we consider measuring "results," we mean measuring outcomes, rather than only inputs and outputs. However, we must translate these outcomes into a set of measurable performance indicators. It is through the regular measurement of key performance indicators that we can determine if outcomes are being achieved.

For example, in the case of the outcome "to improve student learning," an outcome indicator regarding students might be the change in student scores on school achievement tests. If students are continually improving scores on achievement tests, it is assumed that their overall learning outcomes have also improved. Another example is the outcome "reduce at-risk behavior of those at high risk of contracting HIV/AIDS." Several direct indicators might be the measurement of different risky behaviors for those individuals most at risk.

As with agreeing on outcomes, the interests of multiple stakeholders should also be taken into account when selecting indicators. We previously pointed out that outcomes need to be translated into a set of measurable performance indicators. Yet how do we know which indicators to select? The selection process should be guided by the knowledge that the concerns of interested stakeholders must be considered and included. It is up to managers to distill stakeholder interests into good, usable performance indicators. Thus, outcomes should be disaggregated to make sure that indicators are relevant across the concerns of multiple stakeholder groups—and not just a single stakeholder group. Just as important, the indicators have to be relevant to the managers, because the focus of such a system is on performance and its improvement.

If the outcome is to improve student learning, then one direct stakeholder group is, of course, students. However, in setting up a results system to measure learning, education officials and governments might also be interested in measuring indicators relevant to the concerns of teachers and parents, as well as student access to schools and learning materials. Thus, additional indicators might be the number of qualified teachers, awareness by parents of the importance of enrolling girls in school, or access to appropriate curriculum materials.

This is not to suggest that there must be an indicator for every stakeholder group. Indicator selection is a complicated process in which the interests of several relevant stakeholders need to be considered and reconciled. At a minimum, there should be indicators that directly measure the outcome desired. In the case of improving student learning, there must be an indicator for students. Scores on achievement tests could be that particular indicator.

What is the ideal number of indicators for any one outcome? The minimum number that answers the question: "Has the outcome been achieved?"

With the addition of outcome indicators (figure 3.2), we can expand on the performance framework for educational development outcomes introduced in the previous chapter.

Figure 3.2
Developing a Set of Outcome Indicators for a Policy Area

Example: Education

Outcomes	Indicators	Baselines	Targets
1. Nation's children have better access to preschool programs	1. Percent of eligible urban children enrolled in preschool education 2. Percent of eligible rural children enrolled in preschool education		
2. Primary school learning outcomes for children are improved	1. Percent of Grade 6 students scoring 70% or better on standardized math and science tests		

The "CREAM" of Good Performance Indicators

The "CREAM" of selecting good performance indicators is essentially a set of criteria to aid in developing indicators for a specific project, program, or policy (Schiavo-Campo 1999, p. 85). Performance indicators should be clear, relevant, economic, adequate, and monitorable. CREAM amounts to an insurance policy, because the more precise and coherent the indicators, the better focused the measurement strategies will be.

Clear	Precise and unambiguous
Relevant	Appropriate to the subject at hand
Economic	Available at a reasonable cost
Adequate	Provide a sufficient basis to assess performance
Monitorable	Amenable to independent validation

If any one of these five criteria are not met, formal performance indicators will suffer and be less useful[5].

Performance indicators should be as clear, direct, and unambiguous as possible. Indicators may be qualitative or quantitative. In establishing results-based M&E systems, however, we advocate beginning with a simple and quantitatively measurable system rather than inserting qualitatively measured indicators upfront.

Quantitative indicators should be reported in terms of a specific number (number, mean, or median) or percentage. "Percents can also be expressed in a variety of ways, e.g., percent that fell into a particular outcome category . . . percent that fell above or below some targeted value . . . and percent that fell into particular outcome intervals . . . " (Hatry 1999, p. 63). "Outcome indicators are often expressed as the number or percent (proportion or rate) of something. Programs should consider including *both* forms. The number of successes (or failures) in itself does not indicate the rate of success (or failure)—what was not achieved. The percent by itself does not indicate the size of the success. Assessing the significance of an outcome typically requires data on both number and percent" (Hatry 1999, p. 60).

"Qualitative indicators/targets imply qualitative assessments . . . [that is], compliance with, quality of, extent of and level of . . . .Qualitative indicators . . . provide insights into changes in institutional processes, attitudes, beliefs, motives and behaviors of individuals" (U.N. Population Fund 2000, p. 7). A qualitative indicator might measure perception, such as the level of empowerment that local government officials feel to adequately do their jobs. Qualitative indicators might also include a description of a behavior, such as the level of mastery of a newly learned skill. Although there is a role for qualitative data, it is more time consuming to collect, measure, and distill, especially in the early stages. Furthermore, qualitative indicators are harder to verify because they often involve subjective judgments about circumstances at a given time.

Qualitative indicators should be used with caution. Public sector management is not just about documenting *perceptions* of progress. It is about obtaining objective information on *actual* progress that will aid managers in making more well-informed strategic decisions, aligning budgets, and managing resources. Actual progress matters because, ultimately, M&E systems will help to provide information back to politicians, ministers, and organizations on what they can realistically expect to promise and accomplish. Stakeholders, for their part, will be most interested in actual outcomes, and will press to hold managers accountable for progress toward achieving the outcomes.

Every indicator has cost and work implications. In essence, when we explore building M&E systems, we are considering a new M&E system for every single indicator. Therefore, indicators should be chosen carefully and judiciously.

Performance indicators should be relevant to the desired outcome, and not affected by other issues tangential to the outcome.

The economic cost of setting indicators should be considered. This means that indicators should be set with an understanding of the likely expense of collecting and analyzing the data.

For example, in the National Poverty Reduction Strategy Paper (PRSP) for the Kyrgyz Republic, there are about 100 national and subnational indicators spanning more than a dozen policy reform areas. Because every indicator involves data collection, reporting, and analysis, the Kyrgyz government will need to design and build 100 individual M&E systems just to assess progress toward its poverty reduction strategy. For a poor country with limited resources, this will take some doing. Likewise, in Bolivia the PRSP initially contained 157 national-level indicators. It soon became apparent that building an M&E system to track so many indicators could not be sustained. The present PRSP draft for Bolivia now has 17 national-level indicators.

Indicators ought to be adequate. They should not be too indirect, too much of a proxy, or so abstract that assessing performance becomes complicated and problematic.

Indicators should be monitorable, meaning that they can be independently validated or verified, which is another argument in favor of starting with quantitative indicators as opposed to qualitative ones. Indicators should be reliable and valid to ensure that what is being measured at one time is what is also measured at a later time—and that what is measured is actually what is intended.

Caution should also be exercised in setting indicators according to the ease with which data can be collected. "Too often, agencies base their selection of indicators on how readily available the data are, not how important the outcome indicator is in measuring the extent to which the outcomes sought are being achieved" (Hatry 1999, p. 55).

Figure 3.3 is an additional checklist for assessing proposed indicators.

The Use of Proxy Indicators

"Better to be approximately correct than precisely wrong."

(Anon.)

You may not always be precise with indicators, but you can strive to be approximately right. Sometimes it is difficult to measure the outcome indicator directly, so proxy indicators are needed. Indirect, or proxy, indicators should be used only when data for direct indicators are not available, when data collection will be too costly, or if it is

---

Figure 3.3
Checklist for Assessing Proposed Indicators

Outcome to be measured: _____
Indicator selected: _____

Is the indicator . . .

1. As direct as possible a reflection of the outcome itself? _____
2. Sufficiently precise to ensure objective measurement? _____
3. Calling for the most practical, cost-effective collection
   of data? _____
4. Sensitive to change in the outcome, but relatively
   unaffected by other changes? _____
5. Disaggregated as needed when reporting on the
   outcome? _____

Source: United Way of America 1996.

---

not feasible to collect data at regular intervals. However, caution should be exercised in using proxy indicators, because there has to be a presumption that the proxy indicator is giving at least approximate evidence on performance (box 3.1).

For example, if it is difficult to conduct periodic household surveys in dangerous housing areas, one could use the number of tin roofs or television antennas as a proxy measure of increased household in-

---

Box 3.1
Indicator Dilemmas

The Chicago Museum of Science and Industry—a large, cavernous museum with many monumental-size exhibits, including an entire submarine and a coal mine—wanted to conduct a study to determine which exhibitions were of greatest interest to its visitors. They found that it was impossible to count how many visitors viewed every exhibit, so they decided to use a proxy indicator. They did this by determining where they needed to replace floor tiles most often. And where did they find the floor tiles most in need of replacement? In front of the exhibit of hatching baby chicks.

Source: Webb et al., 1966.

come. These proxy indicators might be correctly tracking the desired outcome, but there could be other contributing factors as well; for example, the increase in income could be attributable to drug money, or income generated from the hidden market, or recent electrification that now allows the purchase of televisions. These factors would make attribution to the policy or program of economic development more difficult to assert.

The Pros and Cons of Using Predesigned Indicators

Predesigned indicators are those indicators established independently of an individual country, organization, program, or sector context. For example, a number of development institutions have created indicators to track development goals, including the following:

- MDGs
- The United Nations Development Programme's (UNDP's) Sustainable Human Development goals
- The World Bank's Rural Development Handbook
- The International Monetary Fund's (IMF's) Financial Soundness Indicators.

The MDGs contain eight goals, with attendant targets and indicators assigned to each. For example, Goal 4 is to reduce child mortality, while the target is to reduce by two-thirds the under-five mortality rate between the years 1990 and 2015. Indicators include (a) under-five mortality rate; (b) infant mortality rate; and (c) proportion of one-year-old children immunized against measles. (For a complete list of MDG indicators, see annex 3.)

The UNDP created the Human Development Index (HDI) in 1990 as a way of measuring human progress and the quality of life in all countries of the world. "The HDI constitutes the first comprehensive attempt to measure achievements in development from a human perspective, expressed in terms of numerical indicators that permit inter-country and inter-temporal comparisons . . . The index also provides an initial working tool that could be further developed and refined, and that could guide country efforts to establish relevant databases" (UNDP 2001).

More specifically, "[t]he UNDP's Human Development Index measures a country's achievements in three aspects of human development: longevity, knowledge, and a decent standard of living. Longevity is measured by life expectancy at birth; knowledge is measured by a combination of the adult literacy rate and the combined gross primary, secondary, and tertiary enrollment ratio; and standard of living, as measured by GDP per capita" (UNDP 2001).

The World Bank's Rural Development Indicators Handbook, based on the World Development Indicators, defines and disseminates international statistics on a broad set of rural indicators for rural well-being, improvement in the rural economy, development of rural markets, improvement of accessibility and communication, sustainable management of the resource base, and policy and institutional framework. Specific indicators include, for example, rural population below the poverty line, agricultural gross domestic product, agricultural exports, paved roads, potential arable land, and local tax revenue.

Thus, the Rural Development Indicators Handbook helps to develop a common approach to monitoring and evaluating progress both within and across countries using a common, clearly defined set of indicators. The Handbook also contains a Rural Score Card—a composite indicator that can be used, for example, to assess a country's overall progress (or lack thereof) toward achievement of rural poverty reduction (World Bank 2000).

In light of regional financial crises in various parts of the world, the IMF is in the process of devising a set of Financial Soundness Indicators. These are indicators of the current financial health and soundness of a given country's financial institutions, corporations, and households. They include indicators of capital adequacy, asset quality, earnings and profitability, liquidity, and sensitivity to market risk (IMF 2003).

On a more general level, the IMF also monitors and publishes a series of macroeconomic indicators that may be useful to governments and organizations. These include output indicators, fiscal and monetary indicators, balance of payments, external debt indicators, and the like.

There are a number of pros and cons associated with using predesigned indicators:

Pros:
- They can be aggregated across similar projects, programs, and policies.

- They reduce costs of building multiple unique measurement systems.
- They make possible greater harmonization of donor requirements.

Cons:
- They often do not address country specific goals.
- They are often viewed as imposed, as coming from the top down.
- They do not promote key stakeholder participation and ownership.
- They can lead to the adoption of multiple competing indicators.

There are difficulties in deciding on what criteria to employ when one chooses one set of predesigned indicators over another.

Predesigned indicators may not be relevant to a given country or organizational context. There may be pressure from external stakeholders to adopt predesigned indicators, but it is our view that indicators should be internally driven and tailored to the needs of the organization and to the information requirements of the managers, to the extent possible. For example, many countries will have to use some predesigned indicators to address the MDGs, but each country should then disaggregate those goals to be appropriate to their own particular strategic objectives and the information needs of the relevant sectors.

Ideally, it is best to develop indicators to meet specific needs while involving stakeholders in a participatory process. Using predesigned indicators can easily work against this important participatory element.

Constructing Indicators

It will take more than one try to develop good indicators. Arriving at a final set of appropriate indicators will take time.

Constructing indicators takes work. It is especially important that competent technical, substantive, and policy experts participate in the process of indicator construction. All perspectives need to be taken into account—substantive, technical, and policy—when considering indicators. Are the indicators substantively feasible, technically doable, and policy relevant? Going back to the example of an outcome that aims to improve student learning, it is very important to make sure that education professionals, technical people who can construct learning indicators, and policy experts who can vouch for the policy relevance of the indicators, are all included in the discussion about which indicators should be selected.

Indicators should be constructed to meet specific needs. They also need to be a direct reflection of the outcome itself. And over time, new indicators will probably be adopted and others dropped. This is to be expected. However, caution should be used in dropping or modifying indicators until at least three measurement have been taken.

Taking at least three measurements helps establish a baseline and a trend over time. Two important questions should be answered before changing or dropping an indicator: Have we tested this indicator thoroughly enough to know whether it is providing information to effectively measure against the desired outcome? Is this indicator providing information that makes it useful as a management tool?

It should also be noted that in changing indicators, baselines against which to measure progress are also changing. Each new indicator needs to have its own baseline established the first time data are collected for it. (The topic of setting baselines is covered in further detail in chapter 4.)

In summary, indicators should be well thought through. They should not be changed or switched often (and never on a whim), as this can lead to chaos in the overall data collection system. There should be clarity and agreement in the M&E system on the logic and rationale for each indicator from top level decisionmakers on to those responsible for collecting data in the field.

Performance indicators can and should be used to monitor outcomes and provide *continuous feedback and streams of data* throughout the project, program, or policy cycle. In addition to using indicators to monitor inputs, activities, outputs, and outcomes, indicators can yield a wealth of performance information about the process of and progress toward achieving these outcomes. Information from indicators can help to alert managers to performance discrepancies, shortfalls in reaching targets, and other variabilities or deviations from the desired outcome.

Thus, indicators provide organizations and governments with the opportunity to make midcourse corrections, as appropriate, to manage toward the desired outcomes. Using indicators to track process and progress is yet another demonstration of the ways that a results-based M&E system can be a powerful public management tool.

"The central function of any performance measurement process is to provide regular, valid data on indicators of performance outcomes."

(Hatry 1999, p. 17)

Setting Indicators: Experience in Developing Countries

More and more developing countries—and even regions—are beginning to set indicators to track progress toward their development goals. Boxes 3.2 through 3.4 review experiences in the Africa region, Sri Lanka, and Albania.

Box 3.2

The Africa Region's Core Welfare Indicators

Efforts are underway throughout the Africa region to create the basic statistical and technical building blocks of M&E systems. Among these building blocks are the core indicators surveys that have been conducted in a number of African countries, including Ghana, Malawi, Mozambique, Nigeria, and Lesotho. The Core Welfare Indicators Questionnaire (CWIQ) was created jointly by the World Bank, the UNDP, and UNICEF to monitor development objectives through the use of leading indicators in general, and social indicators in particular. "Leading indicators are indicators which give advance warning of a future impact, whose emergence may be delayed or difficult to measure" (http://www4.worldbank.org/afr/stats/pdf/cwiq.pdf).

Specifically, the CWIQ helps governments collect indicators related to household well-being, and indicators of access to, usage of, and satisfaction with basic services on an annual basis.

CWIQ features include the following:

- A fixed set of core questions with flexible modules
- Quick data entry and validation
- Simple reporting
- Large sample
- Short questionnaire
- Easy data collection.

"The CWIQ is not a complicated survey. It incorporates a package of features, which, when taken together, ensure wide coverage and a rapid turnaround time" (www.worldbank.org/afr/stats/pdf/ghcoreinds.pdf).

The CWIQ also " . . . provides key social indicators for different population subgroups—within and across countries; [acts as] . . . an instrument for monitoring changes in key social indicators over time; and provides countries with a simple tool that produces rapid results" (World Bank p. 1).

At the same time, using the CWIQ does not prohibit in any way participant countries from also developing their own specific socioeconomic indicators.

For an example of a completed CWIQ, go to http://www.worldbank.org/afr/stats/pdf/ghcoreinds.pdf, which contains the Core Welfare Indicators for Ghana (http://www4.worldbank.org/afr/stats/pdf/cwiqloop.pdf).

Source: World Bank.

Box 3.3
Sri Lanka's National Evaluation Policy

The government of Sri Lanka's National Evaluation Policy seeks to: (a) create an evaluation culture and to use evaluations to manage for results; (b) promote evaluation through capacity building with respect to staff, institutions, tools, and methodologies; (c) enable learning of lessons from past experiences; (d) improve the design of development policies and programs through integration of evaluating findings; and (e) establish accountability, transparency, and good governance.

As part of the evaluation policy, the government is mandating the use of performance indicators for all policy, program, and project preparation initiatives. For this purpose, the government is encouraging partnerships with civil society organizations (for example, the Sri Lanka Evaluation Association) and NGOs to introduce participatory evaluations in the public sector. The government is also encouraging universities and public sector training institutions to include evaluation modules to share knowledge on evaluation techniques and methodologies.

Also see annex 4: The Sri Lanka National Development Plan for Monitoring and Evaluation.

Source: Sri Lanka Evaluation Association and
Ministry of Public Development and Implementation 2003.

To the extent possible, indicators should be developed based on the particular needs of a given country or organization. " . . . [T]he appropriate choice of performance indicators differ for different countries, times, and sectors. The only valid general rule is, therefore, when performance measurement is appropriate and cost-effective, performance should be assessed according to that combination of output, outcome and process indicators that are realistic and suitable for the specific activity, sector, country, and time" (Schiavo-Campo 1999, pp. 80–81).

Again, developing good indicators inevitably takes more than one try, and arriving at the final set of indicators will take time.

What we are ultimately building is a performance framework to provide countries and organizations with the means to develop strategies, set outcomes, build indicators, establish baselines, and set targets. This process will help guide the best use of budgets, resources, and personnel to achieve the desired outcomes.

Box 3.4
Albania's Three-Year Action Plan

Monitoring and evaluation systems—both implementation and performance-based—will be developed and used by the government of Albania to provide feedback on major programs constituting the Three-Year Action Plan (including all major strategic initiatives currently underway in Albania's public sector: the National Strategy for Social and Economic Development [NSSED]; the Medium-Term Expenditure Framework; the Stabilization and Association Agreement; the Anti-Corruption Action Plan; and the Strategy for Decentralization and Local Autonomy). The government has assigned the Coordination Department within the Council of Ministers to oversee and coordinate implementation monitoring of the Three-Year Action Plan. Similar responsibilities for NSSED performance monitoring will be assigned to the NSSED Department within the Ministry of Finance.

The Ministry of Finance is expected to oversee the overall performance and implementation management by the 12 line ministries covered by the NSSED. Responsibilities include: (a) procedures for setting indicators that will be tracked and reported on; (b) instructions to the line ministries on how to select indicators; (c) processes for selecting indicators to ensure they measure results that key stakeholders care about; and (d) procedures clarifying how information is to be collected against the indicators to ensure verification and reporting consistency.

Progress is also being made in the Education Ministry, which recently developed a draft NSSED progress monitoring matrix. A new M&E unit has also been established within the Education Ministry, including six representatives of different departments. A variety of education indicators will be developed in connection with the government's Growth and Poverty Reduction Strategy, Poverty Reduction Support Credit, Education Project, and Education for All, initiatives. Education indicators include, among others, school attendance by educational level, teacher salaries, share of GDP spent on education, pupil-teacher ratio, percentage of the teaching force that meets ministry standards for qualified teachers, average class size, education completion rates overall, and education rates disaggregated for rural and poor families.

More generally, the Albanian government has basic statistical capacity (although there is room for improvement), and recently established a policy analysis unit. The government also has the indicators in place with respect to the MDGs.

Source: World Bank 2002a.

The following are examples of indicators at various levels:

Box 3.5 provides some useful examples of program and project level indicators.

Box 3.6 provides an example of an outcome and some possible indicators.

Box 3.5

Program and Project Level Results Indicators: An Example
from the Irrigation Sector

Project name	Strengthening irrigation in a specific country area
Project goals	Improve agricultural productivity Raise farm income.
Indicators	
Outcome indicators	New area under irrigation Higher yield Increased production Increased farm income.
Output indicators	Construction of 10 new irrigation schemes Reconstruction of five old irrigation schemes Twenty-five farmer training sessions.

Source: Adapted from IFAD 2002, p.19.

Box 3.6

Outcome: Increased Participation of Farmers in Local Markets

Possible outcome indicators

• Percent change in annual revenue
• Percent change in amount of spoiled crops
• Percent change in crop pricing due to competition
• Percent change in agricultural employment.

Chapter 4

Step 4: Setting Baselines and Gathering Data on Indicators

Figure 4.1

After working through the process of selecting key performance indicators to monitor outcomes, we turn next to Step 4 and the establishment of baseline data, that is, establishing where we are at present relative to the outcome we are trying to achieve (figure 4.1). One cannot project performance into the future (set targets) without first establishing a baseline. The baseline is the first measurement of an indicator. It sets the current condition against which future change can be tracked. For instance, it helps to inform decisionmakers about current circumstances before embarking on projecting targets for a given program, policy, or project. In this way, the baseline is used to learn about current or recent levels and patterns of performance. Importantly, baselines provide the evidence by which decisionmakers are able to measure subsequent policy, program, or project performance.

This chapter specifically covers: (a) establishing baseline data on indicators; (b) building baseline information; (c) identifying data sources for indicators; (d) designing and comparing data collection methods; (e) the importance of conducting pilots; and (f) data collection, using some developing country experiences.

Establishing Baseline Data on Indicators

Establishing baselines is the third part of the performance framework. Baselines are derived from outcomes and indicators.

We would note in beginning this examination of baselines that establishing baselines is not an exotic idea. We gauge our personal performance against our own baseline data in our own lives. For example, we check our blood pressure against what we have had at one time in the past, track our capacity to exercise against our performance when we first began to exercise, and keep an eye on our weight against an earlier weight.

A performance baseline is information—qualitative or quantitative—that provides data at the beginning of, or just prior to, the monitoring period. The baseline is used as a starting point, or guide, by which to monitor future performance. Baselines are the first critical measurement of the indicators.

Figure 4.2 contains an example of baseline data for a particular policy area. It builds on the performance framework introduced in

Figure 4.2
Developing Baseline Data for One Policy Area

Example: Education

Outcomes	Indicators	Baselines	Targets
1. Nation's children have better access to preschool programs	1. Percent of eligible urban children enrolled in preschool education 2. Percent of eligible rural children enrolled in preschool education	1. In 1999, 75 percent of children ages 3–5 2. In 2000, 40 percent of children ages 3–5	
2. Primary school learning outcomes for children are improved	1. Percent of Grade 6 students scoring 70% or better on standardized math and science tests	1. In 2002, 75 percent scored 70 percent or better in math, and 61 percent scored 70 percent or better in science	

chapter 1. (We will complete the framework when we discuss Step 5, Setting Targets.)

The challenge is to obtain adequate baseline information on each of the performance indicators for each outcome. This can quickly become a complex process. It is important to be judicious in the number of indicators chosen, because each indicator will need data collection, analysis, and reporting systems behind it.

Building Baseline Information

There are eight key questions that should be asked in building baseline information for every indicator. (These questions continue to apply in subsequent efforts to measure the indicator.)

1. What are the sources of data?
2. What are the data collection methods?
3. Who will collect the data?
4. How often will the data be collected?
5. What is the cost and difficulty to collect the data?
6. Who will analyze the data?
7. Who will report the data?
8. Who will use the data?

So, for each indicator, we will need to complete table 4.1.

The statistical systems in developed countries frequently can deliver precise information for all three stages of traditional implementation monitoring—inputs, activities, and outputs. However, develop-

Table 4.1
Building Baseline Information

Indicator	Data source	Data collection method	Who will collect data?	Frequency to collect	Cost and difficulty to collect	Who will analyze data?	Who will report data?	Who will use data?
1								
2								
3								

ing countries generally have less sophisticated systems. The data systems may not be available and may vary with respect to precision. Some countries will know with reasonable precision how many rural children are in school, while others will have only rough estimates. Other developing countries may know the utilization rates of hospital beds, and some may not.

The selected performance indicators, and the data collection strategies used to track those indicators, need to be grounded in the realities of what data systems are in place, what data can presently be produced, and what capacity exists to expand the breadth and depth of data collection and analysis.

Identifying Data Sources for Indicators

Every indicator constitutes its own miniature M&E system, so the first consideration in starting to build the information system for that indicator is what sources of information potentially can supply the relevant data.

A number of issues need to be considered when identifying data sources. Can the data source be accessed in a practical fashion? Can the data source provide quality data? Can the data source be accessed on a regular and timely basis? Is primary data collection from the information source feasible and cost effective?

Sources are who or what provide data—not the method of collecting data.

It is important to collect only the data that is intended to be used. After all, performance information should be a management tool— and there is no need to collect information that managers are not going to use. "As a rule of thumb, only collect baseline information that relates directly to the performance questions and indicators that you have identified. Do not spend time collecting other information" (IFAD 2002, Section 5, p. 32).

Data sources for indicators can be primary or secondary. Primary data are collected directly by the organization concerned, and may include administrative, budget, or personnel data; surveys; interviews; and direct observation. Secondary data have been collected by other outside organizations, and are gathered for purposes other than those of the organization concerned. Examples of secondary data include survey data collected by another agency (UNDP or UNESCO [United Nations Educational, Scientific and Cultural Organization], for example), financial market data, or demographic health survey data.

There are pros and cons associated with the use of secondary data to establish performance trends on indicators. On the positive side, secondary data can be more cost efficient. Secondary data may also be used in instances when it is not practical or possible to collect primary data frequently, as in the case of large scale and expensive household surveys.

However, for a variety of reasons, secondary data must be used with caution. Secondary data will have been gathered with other organization goals or agendas in mind. Other questions arise in using secondary data as well: Are the data valid? Are they reliable? How often are the data collection instruments validated? Furthermore, using secondary data means using someone else's data to report progress and success in moving toward *your* own desired outcomes. Are you as a manager comfortable with this arrangement, given all the advantages and disadvantages of doing so?

Examples of sources of actual data may include administrative records (written or computerized) from government and nongovernment organizations; interviews and surveys with client target groups, program officials, and service providers; reports from trained observers; and mechanical measurements and tests.

An increasing understanding of the need for streams of information, not discrete studies that are episodic and spaced out over time, is emerging in public sector organizations throughout the world. Managers are looking for information—whether on policy strategies, utilization of health clinics, farming methods, or migration patterns—that they can trust and use in real time. Waiting for months or even a year or more for studies to be completed is not helpful. The new approach to building results-based M&E systems is increasingly toward building those systems that provide more or less continuous information streams.

Designing and Comparing Data Collection Methods

Over time, internal organizational capacity for data collection and analysis can and should be built, as it is a key component in establishing a sustainable M&E system.

If the sources of data are known, what will be the strategies and instruments for data collection? Decisions will need to be made regarding how to obtain the necessary data from each source, how to prepare the data collection instruments to record the information appropriately, what procedures to use (surveys versus interviews, for example), how often to access the data sources, and so forth.

The government might also contract externally to use existing capacity at universities and research centers for data collection efforts. Data collection can also be purchased from private sector providers.

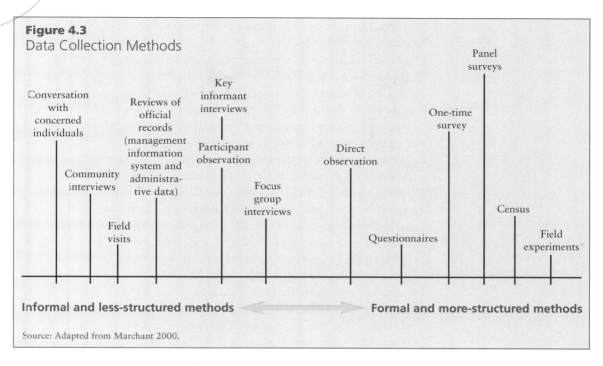

Figure 4.3
Data Collection Methods

Conversation with concerned individuals

Reviews of official records (management information system and administrative data)

Key informant interviews

Panel surveys

One-time survey

Community interviews

Participant observation

Direct observation

Focus group interviews

Census

Field visits

Questionnaires

Field experiments

Informal and less-structured methods ←—————→ **Formal and more-structured methods**

Source: Adapted from Marchant 2000.

However, any strategy that involves the long-term purchase of data collection from nongovernment vendors has certain vulnerabilities and is likely to be more expensive.

Figure 4.3 illustrates some of the possible methods of collecting data. There is no correct answer as to which method is best. It will depend on a given organization's resource availability, access, needs, time constraints, and so forth. It will also depend on the needs of the user of the information. For example, there may be questions about how much precision is actually needed by a given user in light of tradeoffs of cost and time.

A combination of data collection strategies might work best in building the information system to support tracking each indicator. For example, an organization could choose to have only a few indicators and draw on data collection strategies from different places along the continuum. There is no one right approach to the selection of data collection strategies. A number of contingencies help to frame what is possible and what can be afforded.

It is worth some time to understand the implications of choosing one collection strategy in comparison to other options. To just decide in an ad hoc, off-hand way to use surveys, or to conduct multiple focus groups, or to undertake a household survey, is to create possibly critical problems later on.

Table 4.2 is an illustrative comparison of four major data collection methods along four dimensions. It highlights some of the tradeoffs among different strategies. Before any decisions are made on the strategies to deploy, it is important to check with the users. Try and determine their level of comfort with the tradeoffs and with the sorts of performance information they will be receiving.

Data collection strategies necessarily involve some tradeoffs with respect to cost, precision, credibility, and timeliness. For example, the more structured and formal methods for collecting data generally tend to be more precise, costly, and time consuming. If data are needed frequently and on a routine basis to inform management decisionmaking, it may be preferable to adopt less precise, more unstructured, and inexpensive data collection strategies.

From the beginning, we have noted that the 10-step model in this handbook is not strictly linear and sequential. As they build performance systems, organizations will need to go back and forth among the steps. The development and fine tuning of the system will continue, and the information needs of users will change—requiring new indicators, new baseline data, and so forth. The result is that there needs to be a certain degree of adaptability and flexibility in the system to identify new data sources, new collection techniques, and new ways of reporting.

The Importance of Conducting Pilots

Piloting of indicators and the information requirements behind them should be done—period. It is extremely risky to move to full implementation of an indicator system at any level in a government, or even an individual organization, before thorough testing of the data sources, collection and analysis strategies, and means of reporting.

The pilot is a means of learning what works and what does not. It is a way of making small mistakes early rather than big mistakes later. A pilot alerts managers that there are some indicators for which data do not exist, or for which data are too costly, time consuming, or complex to obtain. This is crucial information to have as the baseline is established. The pilot might demonstrate that it would be easier to set an indicator on the basis of existing secondary data that are already being collected across an organization or government as opposed to creating a new indicator that needs its own M&E system.

Table 4.2

Comparison of Major Data Collection Methods

Characteristic	Data collection method			
	Review of program records	Self-administered questionnaire	Interview	Rating by trained observer
Cost	Low	Moderate	Moderate to high	Depends on availability of low-cost observers
Amount of training required for data collectors	Some	None to some	Moderate to high	Moderate to high
Completion time	Depends on amount of data needed	Moderate	Moderate	Short to moderate
Response rate	High, if records contain needed data	Depends on how distributed	Generally moderate to good	High

Source: United Way of America 1996.

The use of existing data systems can be quite helpful in the early stages of building a results-based M&E system. It is important to "[r]ecognize that an existing data collection system may offer a partial route, at a minimum, for collecting some of the needed data, possibly at a reduced cost. [There may be] an opportunity . . . for using parts of an existing data set by selecting, adding, or modifying data elements . . . Design a sample—based on an existing data collection system, new collection procedures, or a combination of the two—and extrapolate to the universe" (Wye 2002, p. 31).

The pilot is the correct time to step back and look at any proposed indicators as they relate to data collection strategies. If every indicator will require costly data collection methods, some rethinking of the indicators is necessary. One should choose indicators that will yield the best information at the lowest cost. This is an opportunity to start to rationalize and prioritize the set of indicators. There will be continuing pressure from stakeholders to include more indicators, but it is better to have fewer indicators than a multitude of them.

For example, the Comprehensive Development Framework in the Kyrgyz Republic mentioned earlier initially included a list of nearly 100 national indicators—each entailing explicit data collection

---

Box 4.1
Albania's Strategy for Strengthening Data Collection Capacity

The government of Albania is embarking on a number of policy initiatives, such as the Growth and Poverty Reduction Strategy, that will require good information for policymakers as they move forward in the design, implementation, and evaluation of socioeconomic programs. The government, with the help and support of some international donors, is seeking to improve the country's data practices to produce reliable statistical information on a regular basis to measure and monitor poverty, inequality, and other social indicators. Specifically, the project will assist the government in four areas: (a) data collection; (b) data processing and analysis; (c) data dissemination and usage; and (d) survey organization and administration.

With respect to data collection, the project will provide technical assistance and hands-on training to enhance capacity at the Albanian Institute of Statistics (INSTAT). The goal is to help INSTAT to regularly produce a number of surveys, such as the Living Standards Measurement Survey, a Population and Household Census, Household Budget Surveys, and annual Labor Force Surveys. Additional work is being planned with several line ministries to do poverty mapping.

Regarding data processing and analysis, the project will support improvements in the efficiency and use of information, as well as support for institutional capacity to process household-level information. Technical assistance and hands-on training in the areas of data entry, cleaning, and editing will also be provided to help ensure the quality and timeliness of the information generated. The areas of data analysis include use of statistical and Geographic Information Systems software, poverty analysis methodology, collection and analysis of panel data, household survey techniques, and questionnaire development, sampling, and poverty mapping.

Data dissemination and usage will be supported with the aim of fostering a participatory process for generation of statistical information. Capacity building will be directed at both producers and users of statistical household information. A data users group will be formed and will be chaired by INSTAT. The users group will contain representatives from line ministries, donors, and NGOs. A comprehensive strategy will be developed to publish and disseminate results.

Finally, survey organization and administration will be supported by the project in the form of a review of INSTAT organization, with a particular focus on those INSTAT units directly engaged in household survey work. The review will assess options for strengthening INSTAT's organizational capacity to manage and administer regular household surveys, and will develop a related staffing plan. The review will also assess the internal organizational procedures for administering the survey, including lines of managerial and financial subordination, and will develop a package of related internal administrative procedures.

Source: World Bank 2002d.

strategies for measuring them. For each of these indicators, one must consider the seven key questions on data collection and management. Obviously, so many indicators can be difficult to track, and will be a drain on the resources of a developing country. Reducing the number of indicators is surely preferable in such a case.

Data Collection: Two Developing Country Experiences

Boxes 4.1 and 4.2 provide examples of data collection in two developing countries. The government of Albania is working to build capacity and to reform data practices. The government of Lebanon is joining the IMF data system to align its data collection and statistical system with IMF and international standards.

Establishing baseline data on indicators is crucial in determining current conditions and in measuring future performance against the starting point. Subsequent and continuous measurements from the baseline will provide important directional or trend data, and can help decisionmakers determine whether they are on track in achieving the desired outcomes over time. But making the decisions on the performance information data to collect, how to collect and analyze it, and how to report it are all important. Pilots can help frame the decisions.

Use existing information and data systems whenever possible—so long as they are trustworthy, fit the information needs, and are accessible over time.

> **Box 4.2**
> Lebanon: Joining the IMF Data System
>
> The government of Lebanon is making an effort to bring its statistical data collection up to international standards. It recently joined the General Data Dissemination System (GDDS) of the IMF. "The purposes of the GDDS are to: encourage member countries to improve data quality; provide a framework for evaluating needs for data improvement and setting priorities . . . ; and guide member countries in the dissemination to the public of comprehensive, timely, accessible, and reliable economic, financial and socio-demographic statistics . . . [It] is built around four dimensions—data characteristics, quality, access and integrity—and is intended to provide guidance for the overall development of macroeconomic, financial, and socio-demographic data" (IMF 2002).
>
> "'Lebanon's membership in the International Monetary Fund's data system is expected to help boost good governance in the country. . . . By selecting the GDDS as a framework to develop the country's national statistical systems, the authorities have underscored their commitment to improving the production of economic and socio-demographic data . . . this will help increase international recognition of Lebanon's commitment to better statistics,' the director of statistics for the IMF said . . . " (The Daily Star 2003). The statistics will be posted and available to the public in three languages on the Lebanese Central Bank Web site, and will be updated regularly by the Central Bank and the line ministries.
>
> Sources: *The Daily Star* 2003; IMF 2002.

Chapter 5

Step 5: Planning for Improvement—Selecting Results Targets

Figure 5.1

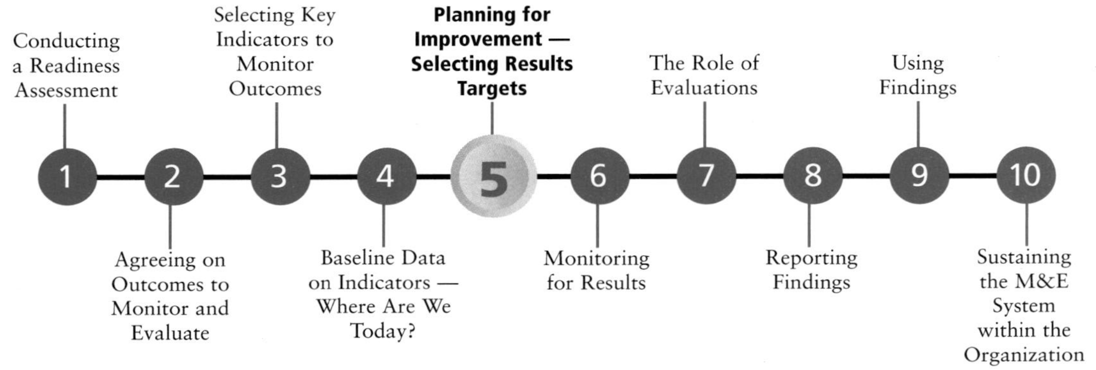

Figure 5.1

Conducting a Readiness Assessment — 1

Agreeing on Outcomes to Monitor and Evaluate — 2

Selecting Key Indicators to Monitor Outcomes — 3

Baseline Data on Indicators — Where Are We Today? — 4

Planning for Improvement — Selecting Results Targets — 5

Monitoring for Results — 6

The Role of Evaluations — 7

Reporting Findings — 8

Using Findings — 9

Sustaining the M&E System within the Organization — 10

After gathering baseline data on indicators, the next step is to establish results targets—what can be achieved in a specific time toward reaching the outcome (figure 5.1). Identifying the expected and desired level of project, program, or policy results requires the selection of specific performance targets.

Target setting is the final step in building the performance framework. It, in turn, is based on outcomes, indicators, and baselines. The reasoning process is a deductive one, flowing back from the desired outcomes.

This chapter will address (a) a definition of targets; (b) factors to consider when selecting indicator targets; (c) examples of targets related to development issues; and (d) the overall performance-based framework.

Definition of Targets

A target is " . . . a specified objective that indicates the number, timing and location of that which is to be realized"[6] (IFAD 2002,

Figure 5.2
Identifying Desired Level of Results Requires Selecting
Performance Targets

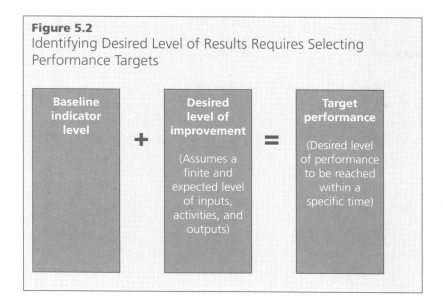

Baseline indicator level	**+**	Desired level of improvement	**=**	Target performance
		(Assumes a finite and expected level of inputs, activities, and outputs)		(Desired level of performance to be reached within a specific time)

p. A-11). In essence, targets are the quantifiable levels of the indicators that a country, society, or organization wants to achieve by a given time. For example, one target might be "all families should be able to eat two meals a day, every day, by 2005."

One method to establish targets is to start with the baseline indicator level, and include the desired level of improvement (taking into consideration available resources over a specific time period, for example, 24–36 months), to arrive at the performance target. In so doing, the starting point will be known, as will the available resources to make progress toward that target over a particular period of time. This will give the target performance.

The formula in figure 5.2 shows the process for devising performance targets.

Factors to Consider When Selecting Performance Indicator Targets

There are a number of important factors to consider when selecting performance indicator targets. One factor is the importance of taking baselines seriously. There must be a clear understanding of the baseline starting point; for example, an average of the last three years' performance, last year's performance, average trend, data over the past six months, and so forth. In other words, previous

"The baseline is the situation before a program or activity begins; it is the starting point for results monitoring. The target is what the situation is expected to be at the end of a program or activity . . . A thorough analysis of the key factors influencing a development problem complements the development of baseline data and target setting."

(UNDP 2002, pp. 66–67)

Targets are based on known resources (financial and organizational) plus a reasonable projection of the available resource base over a fixed period of time.

Targets are interim steps on the way to an outcome and eventually to a longer-term goal.

performance should be considered in projecting new performance targets. One might observe how an organization or policy has performed over the previous few years before projecting future performance targets.

Another consideration in setting targets is the expected funding and resource levels—existing capacity, budgets, personnel, funding resources, facilities, and the like—throughout the target period. This can include internal funding sources as well as external funding from bilateral and multilateral donors. Targets should be feasible given all of the resource considerations as well as organizational capacity to deliver activities and outputs.

Most targets are set annually, but some could be set quarterly. Others could be set for longer periods. However, setting targets more than three to four years forward is not advisable. There are too many unknowns and risks with respect to resources and inputs to try to project target performance beyond three to four years. In short, be realistic when setting targets.

The political nature of the process also comes into play. Political concerns are important. What has the government or administration promised to deliver? Citizens have voted for a particular government based on articulated priorities and policies that need to be recognized and legitimized in the political process. Setting targets is part of this political process, and there will be political ramifications for either meeting or not meeting targets.

Setting realistic targets involves the recognition that most desired outcomes are longer term, complex, and not quickly achieved. Thus, there is a need to establish targets as short-term objectives on the path to achieving an outcome.

So how does an organization or country set longer-term, strategic goals to be met perhaps 10 to 15 years in the future, when the amount of resources and inputs cannot be known? Most governments and organizations cannot reliably predict what their resource base and inputs will be 10 to 15 years ahead. The answer is to set interim targets over shorter periods of time when inputs can be better known or estimated. "Between the baseline and the . . . [outcome] there may be several milestones [interim targets] that correspond to expected performance at periodic intervals" (UNDP 2002, p. 66).

For example, the MDGs have a 15-year time span. While these long-term goals are certainly relevant, the way to reach them is to set targets for what can reasonably be accomplished over a set of three-to four-year periods. The aim is to align strategies, means, and inputs to track progress toward the MDGs over shorter periods of time with a set of sequential targets. Targets could be sequenced: target one could be for years one to three; target two could be for years four to seven, and so on.

Flexibility is important in setting targets because internal or external resources may be cut or otherwise diminished during budgetary cycles. Reorientation of the program, retraining of staff, and reprioritization of the work may be required. This is an essential aspect of public management.

If the indicator is new, be careful about setting firm targets. It might be preferable to use a range instead. A target does not have to be a single numerical value. In some cases it can be a range. For example, in 2003, one might set an education target that states "by 2007, 80 to 85 percent of all students who graduate from secondary school will be computer literate."

It takes time to observe the effects of improvements, so be realistic when setting targets. Many development and sector policies and programs will take time to come to fruition. For example, environmental reforestation is not something that can be accomplished in one to two years.

Finally, it is also important to be aware of the political games that are sometimes played when setting targets. For example, an organization may set targets so modest or easily achieved that they will surely be met. Another game that is often played in bureaucracies is to move the target as needed to fit the performance goal. Moving targets causes problems because indicator trends can no longer be discerned and measured. In other cases, targets may be chosen because they are *not* politically sensitive.

Each indicator is expected to have only one target over a specified time frame.

Examples of Targets Related to Development Issues

Box 5.1 presents two examples of targets related to development issues. One should work toward setting a specific target by identifying the concerned groups, the objective, and the timeframe by which the target is to be achieved. In each case the target will be just the first of several sequential sets of targets needed to reach the outcome. Furthermore, each sequential target is set from the baseline data established in the previous step.

Targets should specify what is being tracked, the expected amount

> **Box 5.1**
> Examples of Development Targets
>
> **1. Goal: Economic Well-Being**
>   Outcome target: By 2008, reduce the proportion of
>   people living in extreme poverty by 20 percent against
>   the baseline.
>
> **2. Goal: Social Development**
>   Outcome target: By 2008, increase the primary education
>   enrollment rate in the Kyrgyz Republic by 30 percent
>   against the baseline.

of change or improvement, and a timeframe by which the target will
be achieved.

The Overall Performance-Based Framework

The completed matrix of outcomes, indicators, baselines, and targets
becomes the performance framework. It defines outcomes and plans
for the design of a results-based M&E system that will, in turn, begin
to provide information on whether interim targets are being achieved
on the way to the longer-term outcome.

Figure 5.3 illustrates the completed performance framework for a
national education development policy area. The traditional implementation dimensions of inputs, activities, and outputs also need targets, as they always have; we are emphasizing here that now outcomes need targets as well.

The performance framework becomes the basis for planning—
with attendant implications for budgeting, resource allocation,
staffing, and so forth. The framework can and should be a relevant
guide to managers. It should be frequently consulted and considered
during the process of managing toward the desired outcomes.

These performance frameworks have broad applicability, and can
be usefully employed as a format for national poverty reduction
strategies, as well as framing project, program, and policy outcomes.

Performance targeting is critical to the process of reaching outcomes. The formula for arriving at the target performance is a simple
one involving baseline indicator levels and desired levels of improvement over a specified period of time. A participatory, collaborative
process with relevant stakeholders and partners is also key.

Figure 5.3
Developing Targets for One Policy Area

Example: Education

Outcomes	Indicators	Baselines	Targets
1. Nation's children have better access to preschool programs	1. Percent of eligible urban children enrolled in preschool education 2. Percent of eligible rural children enrolled in preschool education	1. In 1999, 75 percent of children ages 3–5 2. In 2000, 40 percent of children ages 3–5	1. By 2006, 85 percent of children ages 3–5 2. By 2006, 60 percent of children ages 3–5
2. Primary school learning outcomes for children are improved	1. Percent of Grade 6 students scoring 70% or better on standardized math and science tests	1. In 2002, 75 percent scored 70 percent or better in math, and 61 percent scored 70 percent or better in science	1. By 2006, 80 percent scoring 70 percent or better in math and 67 percent scoring 70 percent or better in science

Chapter 6
Step 6: Monitoring for Results

Figure 6.1

PART 1

After selecting targets and completing the performance-based framework, we are now ready to use the information to monitor for results (figure 6.1). This chapter describes putting together a system to get the necessary data to better inform the decisionmaking process. The resulting data will provide evidence on performance and flag any changes that may be needed for a given project, program, or policy.

This chapter focuses on how a results-based M&E system is, most importantly, a system to help government (or any organization) better manage resources. It now becomes relevant to review the need to manage inputs as well as outputs and outcomes. Managers use a variety of organizational tools to manage inputs, including budgets, staffing plans, and activity plans. A results-based M&E system needs to align with annual plans and other work plans of the organization to become a true results-oriented system.

Figure 6.2
Sample Gant Chart

Task — Phase I	Duration	Start	Finish
1. Recruit personnel	14 days	6/1	6/14
2. Assign project roles and responsibilities	3 days	6/15	6/17
3. Visit sites	14 days	6/18	7/2
4. Analyze data	10 days	7/3	7/12
5. Draft report	10 days	7/13	7/22

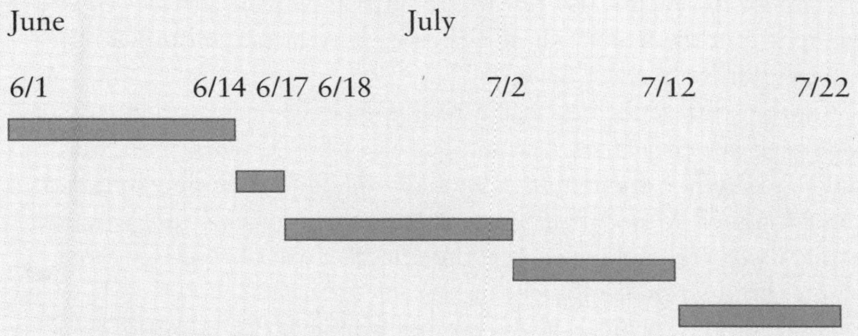

June   July

6/1   6/14 6/17 6/18   7/2   7/12   7/22

Source: Authors' data 2004.

But a results-based system is not the same as monitoring against a set of annual work plans. Monitoring work plans, however, is very much the way a manager traditionally would assess how well a project, program, or policy is being implemented. In this traditional approach, a manager's first step might be to identify activities and assign responsibilities. Often, a manager might employ the use of an activity chart or Gant chart which is, in essence, a to-do list of activities plotted against a specific time line, showing start and due dates for each item, and who will be responsible for which activities. A typical Gant chart is shown in figure 6.2.

A Gant chart is a management tool used to track activities and outputs. However, this management tool does not show whether desired results are actually being achieved. Completing all activities mapped in such a chart does not mean that the organization is achieving its desired goals or outcomes.

Moreover, focusing on activities and outputs does not mean that individuals within the organization are not working hard. In many cases, individuals are busy and keeping focused day in and day out. But focused on what? A results-based M&E system focuses the organization on achieving outcomes, and manages to each indicator, as we have established in earlier chapters. An activity-based management system focuses the organization on working against a set of identified activities, without aligning these activities to outcomes, making it difficult to understand how the implementation of these activities results in improved performance. Be careful not to fall into the trap of equating being busy with being effective.

Activities are crucial. They are the actions taken to manage and implement programs, use resources, and deliver the services of government. But the sum of these activities may or may not mean the outcomes have been achieved.

Another difference between a results-based system and an activities-based system is that, with an activities-based work plan, one looks at whether the activities were completed in a timely and appropriate manner. Monitoring systems, however, demonstrate whether results have been achieved. It is the effective use of resources that counts, not just their efficient use.

This chapter considers (a) key types and levels of monitoring; (b) links between implementation monitoring and results monitoring; (c) key principles in building a monitoring system; (d) the needs of every monitoring system; (e) the data quality triangle; (f) analyzing performance data; (g) achieving results through partnership; and (h) pretesting data collection instruments and procedures.

Key Types and Levels of Monitoring

As figure 6.3 indicates, there are two key types of monitoring—implementation monitoring and results monitoring. Both are important in tracking results.

Figure 6.4 provides examples of results monitoring at the policy, program, and project levels.

Implementation monitoring tracks the means and strategies (that is, those inputs, activities, and outputs found in annual or multiyear work plans) used to achieve a given outcome. These means and strategies are supported by the use of management tools, including budgetary resources, staffing, and activity planning.

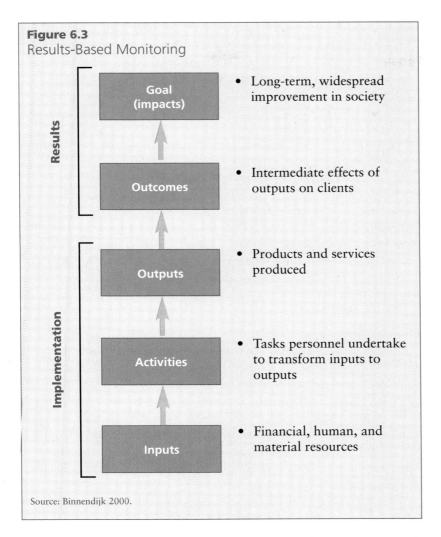

Figure 6.3
Results-Based Monitoring

- **Goal (impacts)** — • Long-term, widespread improvement in society
- **Outcomes** — • Intermediate effects of outputs on clients
- **Outputs** — • Products and services produced
- **Activities** — • Tasks personnel undertake to transform inputs to outputs
- **Inputs** — • Financial, human, and material resources

Results
Implementation

Source: Binnendijk 2000.

It should also be noted that there is an interaction between means and strategies (inputs, activities, and outputs) and outcome targets. Targets are set according to what the means and strategies potentially can yield.

We have spent much of this handbook examining results-based monitoring and evaluation. But implementation—how well outputs are achieved using available inputs and activities—also needs to be measured. Next, the alignment of the outputs with the results the organization hopes to achieve over time needs to be examined. This

Figure 6.4
Examples of Results Monitoring

	Infant Health	Girls Education
Policy monitoring	Decreasing infant mortality rates	Increasing girls educational attainment
Program monitoring	Clinic-based prenatal care is being used by pregnant women	Number of girls in secondary schools completing math and and science courses
Project monitoring	Information on good prenatal care provided in six targeted villages	Number of girls in four urban neighborhoods completing primary education

brings us closer to the concept of performance budget frameworks.

A performance budget framework is an expenditure planning system that assumes good macroeconomic and fiscal management, sector priority setting, and program performance management. Budgets are developed according to funds available for a given budget year, with managers stating outputs they will achieve over that budget year. A medium-term budget incorporates the idea that three one-year budgets should be used to achieve desired targets or outcomes. Thus, performance-based budgets budget to outputs, but also help officials manage to outcomes.

Boxes 6.1 and 6.2 review results-monitoring efforts in Mexico and Brazil.

The lessons we can draw from these various experiences include the following:

- If a strong link is to be forged between performance monitoring and resource allocation, a single unit must be responsible for both.
- If performance is intended to influence management, a single unit must be responsible for carrying out activities and monitoring performance.
- The units responsible for performance monitoring, management, and resource allocation must coincide for accountability to be

---

Box 6.1

Results Monitoring in Mexico

Mexico has separate planning and budget processes. A National Development Plan is prepared every six years, roughly coterminous with the president's term of office. Objectives, policies, and performance targets are set through this process. Programs (the mode for achieving the objectives) derive from the plan. The annual budget process takes the objectives and programs as given. After determining annual resource constraints, funds are allocated to programs and projects. Performance information is incorporated into the annual budget documents—some 10,000 indicators primarily measuring performance relative to plan targets. But these performance measures are not used in agency management decisions, nor are they used in resource allocation decisions. The Office of the President does monitor these indicators, but follow-up is unclear, and there are no formal reviews. Performance is not built into pay either. Moreover, the program structure has changed annually over the past few years, suggesting it does not tie into an organizational structure or a program manager; therefore the accountability framework is weak.

Source: Dorotinsky 2003b.

---

possible, and to enable improvements in efficiency and effectiveness (or even to enable monitoring of efficiency or effectiveness).

Links between Implementation Monitoring and Results Monitoring

Figure 6.5 depicts how outcomes and targets link to annual work plans, as well as the continuous flow of information up and down the system. Annual work plans are the means and strategies that are used by the organization to use inputs effectively to achieve outputs and, ultimately, outcomes and impacts. We learned in chapter 5 that every target is an interim effort on the way to achieving an outcome. Thus, a means and strategy should be implemented to help achieve every target.

The example of children's morbidity in figure 6.6 illustrates the links between means and strategies, target, outcome, and impact, that is, the specific links between implementation monitoring and results monitoring. In this example, one target—reducing the incidence of gastrointestinal disease by 20 percent over three years—has been identified to help reach the outcome of improving children's health. A manager would next identify an annual strategy aimed at reducing the incidence of gastrointestinal disease by the targeted amount. In

Box 6.2
Results Monitoring in Brazil

Countries struggle to integrate performance information and management oversight—to have performance information actually used in decisionmaking. Some attempt to monitor actual performance relative to prior baseline performance or benchmarks, while others seek to monitor performance relative to predetermined targets or plans. The approach chosen, and vehicles for implementation, are influenced by the degree to which national planning and budgeting processes are integrated.

Brazil has a national plan separate from the budget process. The Ministry of Planning, Budget, and Management is responsible for developing the five-year plan (roughly coterminous with the presidential term of office). The planning process is used to set priorities, objectives, and performance targets. (Unlike in Mexico, the program structure is fixed, and covers all government activities. Also unlike Mexico, the national plan includes resource allocations for programs, by year, over the planning period.) But, given the fixed, multiyear nature of the plan, target resource allocations beyond the first year are highly uncertain. New administrations imprint their policies according to which programs they select as priority programs, with targets and resource allocations designated for the programs. For example, the Cordoso administration designated 80 priority programs.

A management information system was developed to tie program funding to performance information, focusing on performance relative to plan targets. Programs were defined supra-organizationally—cutting across ministries and implementing agencies—and program managers were appointed to manage the programs. However, the program managers had no formal authority, controlled no resources, and could not actually influence the activities in ministries that participated in their programs (except in a few cases where the head of a ministry activity was also designated the program manager). Under this structure, the activity manager cannot use program performance information to manage work, and program managers have no influence over actual management. There is a mismatch between authority and responsibility that prevents accountability.

In Brazil, performance information is not included in the formal budget documents, but the on-line database does allow partial matching of objectives, performance, and resources—marginal resources. In developing the program concept, Brazil created separate "programs" to encompass personnel expenses, so all other programs only contain the marginal cost of the activity.

Despite the structural flaws in the system, Brazil did try to stimulate management use of performance information. The planning office of the Ministry of Planning, Budget, and Management used the information system for quarterly performance updates. The planning office used this information to evaluate each priority program with respect to national plan targets and financial performance relative to a given year's budget. Programs performing poorly, or not likely to fully use that year's resources, would lose resources that would then be transferred to other priority programs deemed to be performing better. This was an attempt to use performance information for management and resource decisions, and give added imperative to performance improvement.

Source: Dorotinsky 2003b.

Figure 6.5
Links between Implementation Monitoring and Results Monitoring

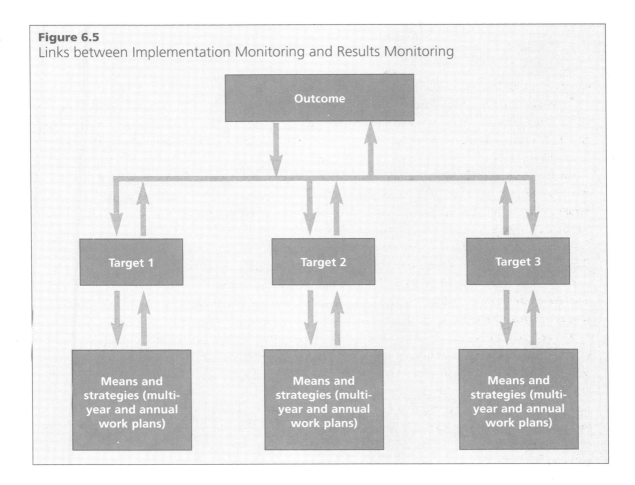

doing so, the manager would need to take into account the inputs available over three budget years, and decide how to plan the organization's work to achieve the stated target.

PART 2

Key Principles in Building a Monitoring System

There are a number of key principles involved in building a results-based monitoring system:

- There are results information needs at the project, program, and policy levels.
- Results information must move both horizontally and vertically in the organization (sometimes presenting a political challenge).

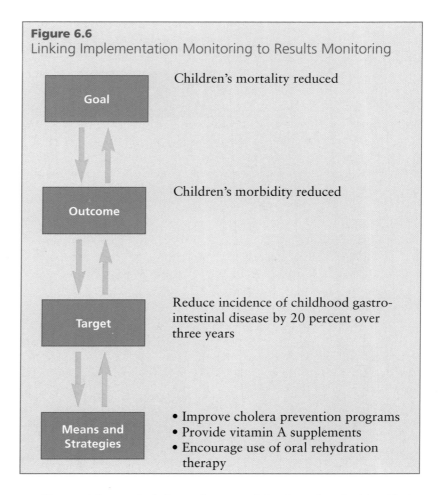

Figure 6.6
Linking Implementation Monitoring to Results Monitoring

Goal — Children's mortality reduced

Outcome — Children's morbidity reduced

Target — Reduce incidence of childhood gastro-intestinal disease by 20 percent over three years

Means and Strategies —
• Improve cholera prevention programs
• Provide vitamin A supplements
• Encourage use of oral rehydration therapy

- Demand for results information at each level needs to be identified.
- Responsibility at each level needs to be clear for

    1. What data are collected (source)
    2 When data are collected (frequency)
    3. How data are collected (methodology)
    4. Who collects data
    5. Who reports data
    6. For whom data are collected.

Performance information needs to move both horizontally and vertically within and between organizations. Horizontal sharing of information is crucial. People need to know and understand what information is being collected by their own organization and by other organizations. For instance, there might be one organization that is collecting data that would be suitable for another. In addition, if each organization starts its own information system, there may not be sufficient capacity to sustain all of the systems.

Many organizations find it difficult to share information horizontally. Information may move easily in a vertical manner within a system, but often there are strong political and organizational walls between one part of the system and another. Bureaucratic and political turf battles are often the cause. Also, bureaucratic incentives are almost always vertical; seldom are there incentives to share information horizontally.

Ideally, all concerned organizations and agencies need to coordinate and collaborate in sharing performance information, especially in those instances where there are intra-institutional partnerships developed to achieve specific targets.

It is important to be as clear and precise as possible in the answers to the six questions about responsibility for the system. If these six questions cannot be answered, there will likely be gaps and the system may falter. This is yet another reason to begin by piloting the initiation of a performance-based M&E system.

Achieving Results through Partnership

More and more partnerships are being formed to achieve development goals. Partnerships may be formed at the international and multilateral, regional, country, and governmental levels. Whatever the case, the same results-based monitoring system can be applied to partnership efforts, as illustrated in figure 6.7.

Given scarce resources and ambitious development objectives, development partners need to leverage resources to achieve the desired goal. Therefore, the means and strategies will be set by multiple partners. One must look beyond one's own organizational unit when considering available inputs. Partnerships may be created elsewhere in one's own organization or even with other organizations inside or outside the government.

When resources are cut or diminished, governments and organizations may need—or be forced to enter into—partnerships with others to reach goals that may be similar. Collaborations can include the for-

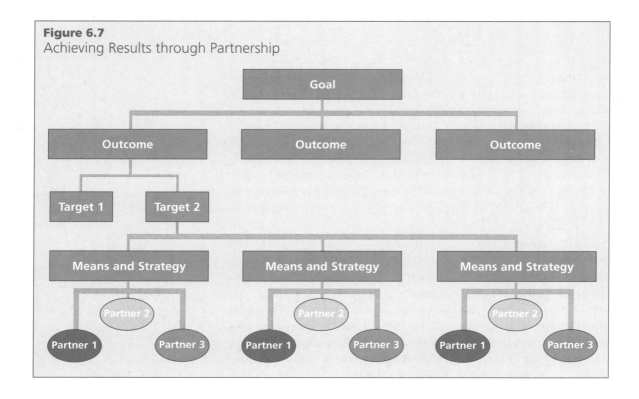

Figure 6.7
Achieving Results through Partnership

mation of partnerships with the private sector, NGOs, and the international donor community. By combining resources, outcomes are more achievable—even during times of input constraints.

Needs of Every Results-Based Monitoring System

Every monitoring system needs four basic elements: ownership, management, maintenance, and credibility (figure 6.8).

Ownership

Ownership can be thought of as the demand part of the equation. Ownership has to come from those at every level who use the system, and demand for performance information at each level needs to be identified. Stakeholder ownership of data at every level—national, regional, and local—is critical. If there are levels where people do not see the need for, or have a use for, the data collected, there will be

Figure 6.8
Every Monitoring System Needs

- Ownership
- Management
- Maintenance
- Credibility

problems with quality control and ownership. The feedback loop will be disrupted. Without ownership, stakeholders will not be willing to invest time and resources in the system. The system will ultimately degenerate, and the quality of data will decline.

A strong political champion can help to ensure ownership of the system. A champion is needed to stress that good performance data must be generated, shared, and properly reported.

Management

Who, how, and where the system will be managed is critical to its sustainability. Data collection can also be hampered by overlap of data coming from different agencies; duplication of data in ministries and the national statistical agency; time lags in receiving data, that is, data that are received too late to have an impact on the decisionmaking process; and people not knowing what data are available.

Maintenance

Maintenance of monitoring systems is essential, to prevent the systems from decaying and collapsing. It is important to know who will collect what kind of information and when, and to ensure that information is flowing horizontally and vertically in the system. Monitoring systems, like other government information systems (such as auditing or budgeting) must be continually managed.

Management and maintenance of M&E systems require creating the right incentives and providing sufficient financial, human, and technical resources for organizations, managers, and staff to carry out monitoring tasks. Individual and organizational responsibilities should be delineated, and a clear "line of sight" established—meaning that staff and organizations should understand their connections to common goals. Clear relationships need to be established between actions and results. Individuals and organizations need to understand how their specific tasks contribute to the big picture.

Good maintenance of monitoring systems should also take into account new advances in management and technology. Systems, procedures, or technologies may need upgrading and modernizing. Staff and managers should also be provided periodic training to keep their skills current.

Unless systems are well managed, they will deteriorate. Monitoring systems—like any other systems—require constant rebuilding, renewal, and strengthening through good management.

Credibility

Credibility is also essential to any monitoring system. Valid and reliable data help ensure the credibility of the system. To be credible, monitoring systems need to be able to report all data—both good and bad. If bad news, or information demonstrating failure to meet desired outcomes and targets, is deliberately not reported, the system will not be credible.

In some instances, political pressure may be brought to bear on national statistical offices to minimize bad news or not report certain data, for instance, HIV incidence, or infant mortality. If political constraints are such that no negative news or data can be reported, or the messenger is punished, the monitoring system will be compromised. In short, if people think information is politically motivated or tainted, they will not trust it and will not use it.

The Data Quality Triangle: Reliability, Validity, and Timeliness

A data collection system for all indicators (implementation and results) should possess three key criteria: reliability, validity, and timeliness (figure 6.9). To the extent that any of these criteria are absent, the credibility of the system will diminish. (See also Hatry 1999, p. 223.)

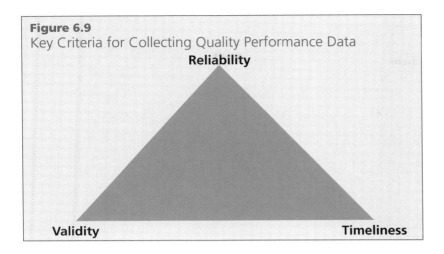

Figure 6.9
Key Criteria for Collecting Quality Performance Data

Reliability

Validity   Timeliness

Reliability is the extent to which the data collection system is stable and consistent across time and space. In other words, measurement of the indicators is conducted the same way every time (figure 6.10).

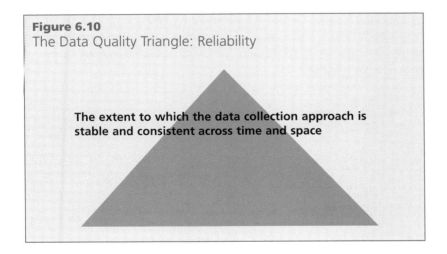

Figure 6.10
The Data Quality Triangle: Reliability

The extent to which the data collection approach is stable and consistent across time and space

Validity is important: indicators should measure, as directly and succinctly as possible, actual and intended performance levels (figure 6.11).

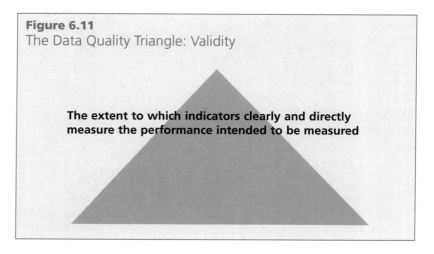

Figure 6.11
The Data Quality Triangle: Validity

The extent to which indicators clearly and directly measure the performance intended to be measured

Timeliness consists of three elements: frequency (how often data are collected); currency (how recently data have been collected); and accessibility (data availability to support management decisions) (figure 6.12). If the data are not available to decisionmakers when they need it, the information becomes historical data. Modern public management requires good and timely information. Real-time, continuous data that decisionmakers can use to lead and manage in their work environment is now essential. It makes little sense to manage in the public sector using essentially historical data that may be three, four, or even five years old.

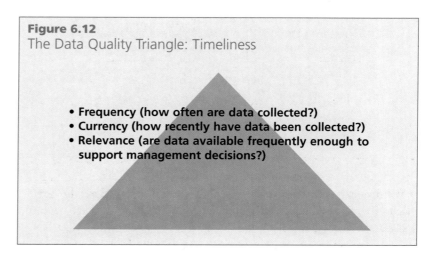

Figure 6.12
The Data Quality Triangle: Timeliness

• Frequency (how often are data collected?)
• Currency (how recently have data been collected?)
• Relevance (are data available frequently enough to support management decisions?)

Analyzing Performance Data

Performance findings should be used to help improve projects, programs, and policies. Analyzing and reporting data yields important, continuous information about the status of projects, programs, and policies. It can also provide clues to problems that arise during the course of implementation, and create opportunities to consider improvements in implementation strategies. The continuous stream of data can also provide significant information regarding trends and directions over time.

> *In analyzing and reporting data, the more frequent the data measurements over time, the more certain one can be of trends, directions, and results.*

The more often measurements are taken, the less guesswork there will be regarding what happened between specific measurement intervals (figure 6.13). More data points enable managers to track trends

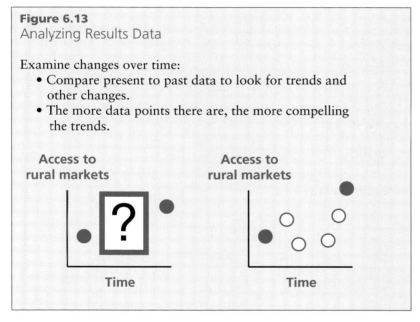

Figure 6.13
Analyzing Results Data

Examine changes over time:
- Compare present to past data to look for trends and other changes.
- The more data points there are, the more compelling the trends.

Access to rural markets ... Time

Access to rural markets ... Time

and understand project, program, and policy dynamics. The more time that passes between measurements, the greater the chance that events and changes in the system might happen that may be missed. For example, if there is a year between measurements, many things can happen and it may be more difficult to attribute causality. Did the indicator get better? Worse? Was there a straight-line progression or a wave?

Consequently, the monitoring system strategy should include a clear data collection and analysis plan detailing the following:

There is often an explicit tradeoff between measurement frequency and measurement precision. Cost and capacity also come into play in making decisions about how often and how precisely to measure indicators.

- Units of analysis (for example, school district, community hospital, village, region)
- Sampling procedures
- Data collection instruments to be used
- Frequency of data collection
- Expected methods of data analysis and interpretation
- Those responsible for collecting the data
- Data collection partners, if any
- Those responsible for analyzing, interpreting, and reporting data
- For whom the information is needed
- Dissemination procedures
- Follow-up on findings.

Pretesting Data Collection Instruments and Procedures

Pretesting or piloting data collection instruments and procedures is vital to building an effective monitoring system. Key points about pretesting include the following:

In short, do not move too quickly. Start on a small scale and pilot whenever possible.

- A data collection approach needs be be tested to find out how good it is.
- Pretesting provides a way to improve instruments or procedures—before data collection is fully under way.
- Avoiding pretesting *probably will* result in mistakes. The mistake could cost the organization a lot of time and money, and maybe its valued reputation with the public.
- If there is some ambiguity as to how data will be collected and what the data will look like, it is best to pilot several strategies, if possible.

If the monitoring system is to be a useful management tool, it needs to be manageable. Do not overload the system with too many indicators. Otherwise, too much time will be spent managing the system that produces the data, and not enough time will be spent using the data to manage.

For example, the first set of measurements will be the baseline—and it may not be exactly what should be measured. If the baseline is erroneous because the wrong (or incomplete) data are being collected—and targets have been set against this baseline—the monitoring system will be based on a faulty foundation.

In sum, monitoring for results entails both implementation monitoring and results monitoring. It involves the formation of partnerships to attain common outcomes. Every monitoring system needs ownership, management, maintenance, and credibility. Monitoring for results also calls for data collection and analysis of performance data. The key criteria for collecting quality performance data are reliability, validity, and timeliness. Finally, pretesting of data collection instruments and procedures is important in every monitoring system.

Chapter 7

Step 7: The "E" in M&E—Using Evaluation Information to Support a Results-Based Management System

Figure 7.1

The previous chapters of this handbook placed a strong emphasis on the monitoring function—the "M" in M&E. Building a monitoring system to continuously track performance is absolutely essential for managers. The monitoring system gives ongoing information (via select indicators) on the direction of change, the pace of change, and the magnitude of change. It can also identify unanticipated changes. All are critical to knowing whether policies, programs, and projects are moving in the intended direction.

We have also stressed that monitoring data do not give the basis for attribution and causality for change. These monitoring data also do not provide evidence of how changes are coming about—only that they are or are not occurring. Likewise, monitoring data, in and of themselves, cannot address the strengths and weaknesses in the design of the project, program, or policy. Consequently, to address these and other important questions regarding the generation of appropriate results, evaluation information is necessary—the "E" in M&E (figure 7.1).

We have defined evaluation as an assessment of a planned, ongoing, or completed intervention to determine its relevance, efficiency, effectiveness, impact, and sustainability. The intent is to incorporate lessons learned into the decisionmaking process.

It is appropriate that we now come to an examination of the evaluation function in M&E systems. We want to stress the complementarity of evaluation to monitoring. Each supports the other—even as each asks different questions and will likely make different uses of information and analyses. The immediate implication is that moving to a results-based M&E system requires building an information and analysis system with two components—monitoring and evaluation. Either alone, in the end, is not sufficient.

There are several complementarities of monitoring and evaluation. First is sequential complementarity, in which monitoring information can generate questions to be subsequently answered by evaluation— or the reverse, with evaluation information giving rise to new areas or domains of monitoring to be initiated. Second is information complementarity, in which both monitoring and evaluation can use the same data, but pose different questions and frame different analyses. Third is interactional complementarity, in which managers are using monitoring and evaluation in tandem to help direct their initiatives.

It is important to emphasize here that the evaluation function in the M&E system significantly expands and moves beyond what is understood as the traditional after-the-fact approach to evaluation. Evaluation is not restricted to assessing causes and changes after an intervention or initiative is over. The after-the-fact approach is restrictive because this type of evaluation information does not feed back into the ongoing management of the government organizations and units aimed at achieving public sector results. The emphasis on after-the-fact evaluations as the means to strive for the definitive answers on attribution and causality necessarily precludes real-time uses of evaluation by public sector managers.

What follows is not a "how to" on designing and conducting evaluations. There are many textbooks and handbooks that can take a reader through the step-by-step process of an evaluation— from design, methods selection, data collection and analysis, to reporting and dissemination. One electronic source for this material and guidance comes in 12 modules from the International Program in Development Evaluation Training (IPDET) and can be found at http://www.worldbank.org/oed/ipdet/ (World Bank 2001a).

The emphasis is on how the development of an evaluation capacity in government supports a results-based management approach and the uses managers can make of evaluation information. Good evaluative information can provide answers to a broad range of questions relevant to performance and the achievement of outcomes. We will identify a number of these questions as well as the evaluation strategies available to answer them.

Uses of Evaluation

The emphasis on building sources of ongoing evaluation information versus sporadic and individual evaluation studies spaced out over generally lengthy periods is deliberate. M&E systems need to provide government officials with useful and timely information to manage and guide government resources and interventions. The value of an evaluation comes from its use.

Pragmatic Uses of Evaluation

While the evaluation literature is replete with long and technical discussions of different types and categories of use, this material will be bypassed. Instead, we will go to a pragmatic list of six uses that government managers can make of evaluation information.

Help Make Resource Allocation Decisions Evaluation information can inform managers on what policies or programs have been more or less successful in terms of their outcomes and thus what level of resources they might merit. Likewise, evaluation information can help guide decisions on whether the results of pilot efforts suggest expanding, redesigning, or even dropping the initiative altogether.

Help Rethink the Causes of a Problem Frequently, policy and program interventions appear not to be having any notable consequences on an existing problem. While the absence of change may be attributable to either poor design or poor implementation, it may also be that the intervention is of no consequence because the problem is different than originally presumed. Evaluation information can raise the need for a re-examination of the presumed cause of a problem—and what alternative countermeasures might be needed.

Identify Emerging Problems Evaluation information can highlight issues that are not yet widespread, but may clearly require the attention of government officials, such as rising drop out rates in select groups of youth, the number of orphans whose parents have died from AIDS, or drug use among subteens.

Support Decisionmaking on Competing or Best Alternatives Often governments will approach a problem situation by piloting more than one strategy. For example, a government may try to address youth unemployment through in-school programs, special apprentice programs in the private sector, vouchers for employers who hire youth, and so forth. After each pilot has been in operation for some time, it will be easier to determine which has the more compelling evidence of success, and which merits more or less support.

Support Public Sector Reform and Innovation Evaluation information can provide evidence to citizens that reform efforts are working. For example, evidence that school improvements are being made, that corruption is being diminished, or that more of the rural poor are receiving health care can give credibility to government efforts. Reform efforts often lose momentum if there is no evidence of positive change.

Build Consensus on the Causes of a Problem and How to Respond Evaluation information can contribute to the discussions among government officials and important stakeholders about the causes of the conditions and how to create an appropriate response. The definition of a problem should precede any deployment of countermeasures to try and solve, or at least diminish, the problem. Evaluation information can provide evidence of causality, and evidence of the relevance and impact of previous responses.

To summarize this brief examination of the uses of evaluation information in an M&E system, government officials and their partners can use this information to focus on the broad political strategy and design issues ("are we doing the right things?"), on operational and implementation issues ("are we doing things right?"), and whether there are better ways of approaching the problem ("what are we learning?"). See box 7.1.

Using Evaluation to Answer Management Questions

Evaluations can also help answer eight different types of questions that managers frequently pose:

Box 7.1
Evaluation Provides Information on:

- Strategy: are the right things being done?
  — Rationale or justification
  — Clear theory of change

- Operations: are things being done right?
  — Effectiveness in achieving expected outcomes
  — Efficiency in optimizing resources
  — Client satisfaction

- Learning: are there better ways?
  — Alternatives
  — Best practices
  — Lessons learned

- Descriptive: Describe the content of the information campaign in country X for HIV/AIDS prevention. (Focuses on careful description of a situation, process, or event. Often used as the basis for a case study approach.)
- Normative or compliance: How many days during the year were national drinking water standards met? (Determines whether a project, program, or policy met stated criteria.)
- Correlational: What is the relation between the literacy rate and number of trained teachers in a locality? (Shows the link between two situations, or conditions, but does not specify causality.)
- Impact or cause and effect: Has the introduction of a new hybrid seed caused increased crop yield? (Establishes a causal relation between two situations or conditions.)
- Program logic: Is the sequence of planned activities likely to increase the number of years girls stay in school? (Assesses whether the design has correct causal sequence.)
- Implementation or process: Was a project, program, or policy to improve the quality of water supplies in an urban area implemented as intended? (Addresses whether implementation occurred as planned.)
- Performance: Are the planned outcomes and impacts from a policy being achieved? (Establishes links between inputs, activities, outputs, outcomes, and impacts.)

- Appropriate use of policy tools: Has the government made use of the right policy tool in providing subsidies to indigenous farmers to deploy a new agricultural technology? (Establishes whether the appropriate instruments were selected to achieve aims.)

The Timing of Evaluations

Evaluation information is relevant and helpful to government managers at all phases of management of policies, programs, and projects. The question of timing is easily answered: Any time there are concerns for which evaluation information can be useful is the time to gather evaluative information.

But it is necessary to go deeper in addressing when to deploy resources to gather evaluation information. Four instances follow that warrant evaluation information to support management decision-making. (We recognize there are others beyond these four, but these are illustrative of when we think evaluation information is essential.)

Divergence between Planned and Actual Performance

When regular measurements of key indicators suggest a sharp divergence between planned performance and actual performance, evaluation information can be crucial. Consider the graphs in figure 7.2.

In the graphs in figure 7.2 it is apparent that planned and actual performances are diverging. The manager needs to know why. "What is going on that either we are falling behind our planned performance so badly (left chart) or that we are doing so well that we are ahead of our own planning frame (right chart)?" Managers will recognize from their own experience that planned and actual performances are most often not identical, and some variation is to be

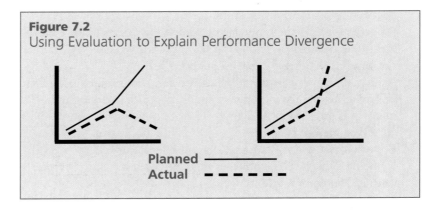

Figure 7.2
Using Evaluation to Explain Performance Divergence

Planned ————
Actual – – – – –

expected. But when that divergence is dramatic, sustained, and has real consequences for the policy, program, or project, it is time to step back, evaluate the reasons for the divergence, and assess whether new strategies are needed (in the case of poor performance), or learn how to take the accelerated good performance and expand its applications.

The Contributions of Design and Implementation to Outcomes

Evaluation information can help differentiate between the contributions of design and implementation to outcomes.

In figure 7.3, Square 1 is the best place to be—the design (a causal model of how to bring about desired change in an existing problem) is strong and the implementation of actions to address the problem is also strong. All managers, planners, and implementers would like to spend their time and efforts like this—making good things happen for which there is demonstrable evidence of positive change.

Square 2 generates considerable ambiguity in terms of performance on outcome indicators. In this situation there is a weak design that is strongly implemented—but with little to no evident results. The evidence suggests successful implementation, but few results. The eval-

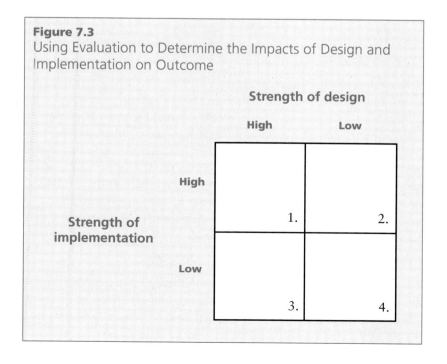

Figure 7.3
Using Evaluation to Determine the Impacts of Design and Implementation on Outcome

uative questions would turn to the strength and logic of the design. For example, was the causal model appropriate? Was it sufficiently robust that, if implemented well, it would bring about the desired change? Was the problem well understood and clearly defined? Did the proposed change strategy directly target the causes of the problem?

Square 3 also generates considerable ambiguity in terms of performance with respect to outcome indicators. In this situation there is a well-crafted design that is poorly implemented—again, with little to no evident results. This is the reverse situation of Square 2, but with the same essential outcome—no clear results. The evaluative questions focus on the implementation processes and procedures: Did what was suppose to take place actually take place? When, and in what sequence? With what level of support? With what expertise among the staff? The emphasis is on trying to learn what happened during implementation that brought down and rendered ineffective a potentially successful policy, program, or project.

Square 4 is not a good place to be. A weak design that is badly implemented leaves only the debris of good intentions. There will be no evidence of outcomes. The evaluation information can document both the weak design and the poor implementation. The challenge for the manager is to figure out how to close down this effort quickly so as to not prolong its ineffectiveness and negative consequences for all involved.

Resource Allocations

When resource allocations are being made across policies, programs, or projects, evaluation information can help managers analyze what is or is not working efficiently and effectively. The tradeoffs in budget and personnel allocations are many. Political conflicts among competing demands are real. Evaluation information can assist in the process, especially when the government is working to install a performance-based budget system. But it is also important and realistic to acknowledge that evaluation information cannot override and negate political, institutional, or personal agendas that inevitably come into play.

Conflicting Evidence of Outcomes

Evaluation information can help when similar projects, programs, or policies are reporting different outcomes. Comparable initiatives with clearly divergent outcomes raise the question of what is going on and where. Among the questions that evaluation information can address are the following: Are there strong variations in implementation that are leading to the divergence? Or do key individuals not understand the intentions and rationale of the effort, so are providing different guidance leading to essentially different approaches? Or, as a third possibility, are the reporting measures so different that the comparisons are invalid?

Types of Evaluations

Different types of evaluations are appropriate for answering different kinds of questions. There is no "one size fits all" evaluation template to put against the variety of questions. It is important for managers to have an understanding of what they want to know from evaluations. Likewise, it is important for those producing the evaluative information to understand what is needed by the manager. It is not beneficial for anyone involved to find themselves with a mismatch between the question asked and the information provided.

Figure 7.4 depicts seven broad evaluation strategies that can be used to generate evaluation information. Each is appropriate to specific kinds of evaluation questions, and each will be briefly reviewed. (Note that only one of these seven is the classic after-the-fact evaluation—the impact evaluation.)

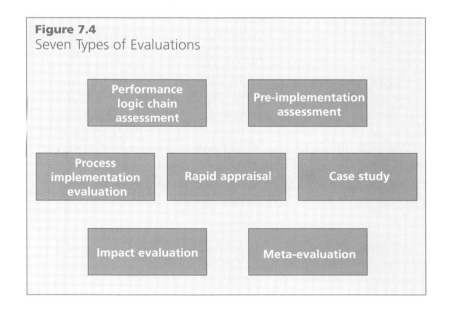

Figure 7.4
Seven Types of Evaluations

Performance logic chain assessment

Pre-implementation assessment

Process implementation evaluation

Rapid appraisal

Case study

Impact evaluation

Meta-evaluation

Performance Logic Chain Assessment

The performance logic chain assessment evaluation strategy is used to determine the strength and logic of the causal model behind the policy, program, or project. The causal model addresses the deployment and sequencing of the activities, resources, or policy initiatives that can be used to bring about a desired change in an existing condition. The evaluation would address the plausibility of achieving that desired change, based on similar prior efforts and on the research literature. The intention is to avoid failure from a weak design that would have little or no chance of success in achieving the intended outcomes.

In attempting to assess the present effort in comparison to past efforts, the evaluator could focus on the level of resources, timing, capacity of the individuals and organizations involved, level of expected outcomes, and so forth, to determine if the present strategy can be supported from prior experience. Likewise, in examining the research literature, the evaluator can find out if the underlying premises of the proposed initiative can be supported; for example, that increased awareness by citizens of government corruption through a public information campaign will lead to increased pressure from civil society for the government to combat and control the corruption.

Pre-Implementation Assessment

The pre-implementation assessment evaluation strategy addresses three standards that should be clearly articulated before managers move to the implementation phase. The standards are encompassed in the following questions: Are the objectives well defined so that outcomes can be stated in measurable terms? Is there a coherent and credible implementation plan that provides clear evidence of how implementation is to proceed and how successful implementation can be distinguished from poor implementation? Is the rationale for the deployment of resources clear and commensurate with the requirements for achieving the stated outcomes? The intention of such an evaluation approach is to ensure that failure is not programmed in from the beginning of implementation.

Process Implementation Evaluation

The focus of process implementation evaluation is on implementation details. What did or did not get implemented that was planned? What congruence was there between what was intended to be implemented and what actually happened? How appropriate and close to plan were the costs; the time requirements; the staff capacity and capability; the availability of required financial resources, facilities, and staff; and political support? What unanticipated (and thus unintended) outputs or outcomes emerged from the implementation phase? The implementation phase can be short or long. The emphasis throughout would be to study the implementation process. Managers can use this information to determine whether they will need to make any mid-course corrections to drive toward their stated outcomes.

This evaluation strategy is similar to monitoring. The added value is that the implementation is not just documented (monitored). In evaluating the implementation, unanticipated outcomes can be studied. Additionally, some of the more intangible aspects of implementation, such as political support, institutional readiness for change, and the trust in management to successfully lead a change effort, can be addressed. Finally, having some understanding of why the implementation effort is or is not on track gives a firm basis for initiating countermeasures, if needed.

Rapid Appraisal

Because we view M&E as a *continuous* management tool, rapid appraisals deserve special consideration here. Rapid appraisals can be invaluable to development practitioners in a results-based M&E system. They allow for quick, real-time assessment and reporting, providing decisionmakers with immediate feedback on the progress of a given project, program, or policy.

Rapid appraisal can be characterized as a multimethod evaluation approach that uses a number of data collection methods. These methods tend to cluster in the middle of the continuum presented in figure 4.3. "Rapid appraisal methodology . . . [can be thought of] in the context of the goal of applied research; that is, to provide timely, relevant information to decision-makers on pressing issues they face in the project and program setting. The aim of applied research is . . . to facilitate a more rational decision-making process in real-life circumstances" (Kumar 1993, p. 9).

There are five major rapid appraisal data collection methods: (a) key informant interviews; (b) focus group interviews; (c) community interviews; (d) structured direct observation; and (e) surveys. These methods are particularly useful in dealing with the following situations:

- When descriptive information is sufficient for decisionmaking
- When an understanding is required of the motivations and attitudes that may affect people's behavior, in particular the behavior of target populations or stakeholders in an intervention
- When available quantitative data must be interpreted
- When the primary purpose of the study is to generate suggestions and recommendations
- When the need is to develop questions, hypotheses, and propositions for more elaborate, comprehensive formal studies (Kumar 1993, pp. 21–22).

Rapid appraisals are highly relevant to the timely production of management-focused evaluation information.

As with any evaluation method, there are some strengths and weaknesses of rapid appraisals that should be taken into account. Rapid appraisals produce needed information on a quick and timely basis and are relatively low cost, especially in comparison with more formal, structured evaluation methods. Such appraisals can provide a quick turnaround to see whether projects, programs, and policies are basically on track. However, the reliability, credibility, and validity of rapid appraisals may be more open to question because of such factors as individual bias and preconceptions, and lack of quantitative data that can be easily replicated and verified. Likewise, it is difficult to aggregate the findings from multiple rapid appraisals, as each is relatively unique and the mix of methods varies from one application to another. On balance, though, rapid appraisals can make rapid reporting possible and help flag the need for continuous corrections.

Case Study

The case study is the appropriate evaluation strategy to use when a manager needs in-depth information to understand more clearly what happened with a policy, program, or project. Case studies imply a tradeoff between breadth and depth in favor of the latter. There are six broad ways that managers can draw on case study information to inform themselves: (a) case studies can illustrate a more general condition; (b) they can be exploratory when little is known about an area or problem; (c) they can focus on critical instances (high success or terrible failure of a program); (d) they can examine select instances of implementation in depth; (e) they can look at program effects that emerge from an initiative; and, finally, (f) they can provide for broader understanding of a condition when, over time, provide for broader understanding of a condition when, over time, the results of multiple case studies are summarized and a cumulative understanding emerges.

Impact Evaluation

An impact evaluation is the classic evaluation (though not only after the fact) that attempts to find out the changes that occurred, and to what they can be attributed. The evaluation tries to determine what portion of the documented impacts the intervention caused, and what might have come from other events or conditions. The aim is attribution of documented change. This type of evaluation is difficult, especially as it comes after the end of the intervention (so that if outcomes are to be evident, they will have had time to emerge). Obviously, the longer the time between the intervention and the attempt to attribute change, the more likely it is that other factors will interfere in either positive or negative ways to change the intended outcome, that the timeframe in which one was seeking to measure change is incorrect (too soon or too late), and that the outcome will become enveloped in other emerging conditions and be lost.

Another way of addressing the issue of attribution is to ask the counterfactual question, that is, what would have happened if the intervention had not taken place? Answering this question is difficult. But there are strategies for doing so, using both experimental and quasi-experimental designs. Use of random assignment and control or comparison groups are the basic means of addressing this question.

When possible, it is best to plan for impact evaluations before the intervention even begins. Determining which units will receive the intervention and which will not, and establishing baseline information on all units, are just two of the reasons for planning the impact evaluation prospectively.

Meta-Evaluation

If a number of evaluations have been conducted on one or similar initiatives, a meta-evaluation establishes the criteria and procedures for systematically looking across those existing evaluations to summarize trends and to generate confidence (or caution) in the cross-study findings. Meta-evaluation can be a reasonably quick way of learning "what do we know at present on this issue and what is the level of confidence with which we know it?" Leeuw and Cooksy

(2003) used a meta-evaluation approach to summarize findings from three evaluations from three development agencies—the Department for International Development (DIFD), the UNDP, and the World Bank.

Characteristics of Quality Evaluations

If managers are going to rely on information from an M&E system, they are right to question the quality and trustworthiness of the information they are getting. Poor, inaccurate, and biased information is of no use to anyone.

How is a manager to know if the information is worth considering? Without going into a detailed discussion of the many facets of data validity and reliability, and without expecting the manager to have mastered advanced statistics, there are six characteristics that can be considered (figure 7.5). An assessment across these six characteristics will not guarantee that the information is impeccable or that it is error free, but it will provide a checklist for a manager to use in forming an opinion on whether to use the information.

- Impartiality: The evaluation information should be free of political or other bias and deliberate distortions. The information should be presented with a description of its strengths and weak-

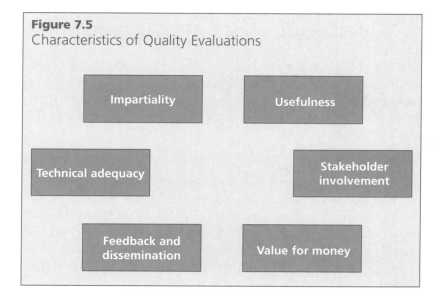

Figure 7.5
Characteristics of Quality Evaluations

Impartiality

Usefulness

Technical adequacy

Stakeholder involvement

Feedback and dissemination

Value for money

nesses. All relevant information should be presented, not just that which reinforces the views of the manager.

- Usefulness: Evaluation information needs to be relevant, timely, and written in an understandable form. It also needs to address the questions asked, and be presented in a form desired and best understood by the manager.
- Technical adequacy: The information needs to meet relevant technical standards—appropriate design, correct sampling procedures, accurate wording of questionnaires and interview guides, appropriate statistical or content analysis, and adequate support for conclusions and recommendations, to name but a few.
- Stakeholder involvement: There should be adequate assurances that the relevant stakeholders have been consulted and involved in the evaluation effort. If the stakeholders are to trust the information, take ownership of the findings, and agree to incorporate what has been learned into ongoing and new policies, programs, and projects, they have to be included in the political process as active partners. Creating a façade of involvement, or denying involvement to stakeholders, are sure ways of generating hostility and resentment toward the evaluation—and even toward the manager who asked for the evaluation in the first place.
- Feedback and dissemination: Sharing information in an appropriate, targeted, and timely fashion is a frequent distinguishing characteristic of evaluation utilization. There will be communication breakdowns, a loss of trust, and either indifference or suspicion about the findings themselves if: (a) evaluation information is not appropriately shared and provided to those for whom it is relevant; (b) the evaluator does not plan to systematically disseminate the information and instead presumes that the work is done when the report or information is provided; and (c) no effort is made to target the information appropriately to the audiences for whom it is intended.
- Value for money: Spend what is needed to gain the information desired, but no more. Gathering expensive data that will not be used is not appropriate—nor is using expensive strategies for data collection when less expensive means are available. The cost of the evaluation needs to be proportional to the overall cost of the initiative.

The emphasis in this chapter has been on the role that evaluation can and should play in the development of a results-based M&E system. Evaluation information can be relevant at all phases of a policy, program, or project cycle. Evaluation information can be useful to the needs of the public sector manager if it comes in a timely fashion, is appropriately presented, is technically adequate, addresses questions directly, and is trustworthy. Evaluation and monitoring are complementary and both are needed in a results-based management system.

Figure 7.6
Examples of Evaluation

	Privatizing water systems	Resettlement
Policy evaluations	Comparing model approaches to privatizing public water supplies	Comparing strategies used for resettlement of rural villagers to new areas
Program evaluations	Assessing fiscal management of government systems	Assessing the degree to which resettled village farmers maintain previous livelihood
Project evaluations	Assessing the improvement in water fee collection rates in two provinces	Assessing the farming practices of resettled farmers in one province

Examples of Evaluation at the Policy, Program, and Project Levels

Evaluation information can inform policymakers and program and project managers if their interventions are leading to desired results, and provide important clues as to why implementation strategies are or are not on track. Figure 7.6 presents the kind of information evaluation can provide for projects, programs or polices in two examples: water privatization systems and resettlement strategies.

Chapter 8

Step 8: Reporting the Findings

Figure 8.1

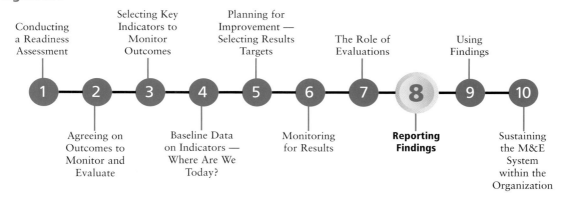

Performance information is to be used as a management tool. Thus, performance information is derived from both monitoring and evaluation. Both can provide critical, continuous, and real-time feedback on the progress of a given project, program, or policy.

Analyzing and reporting performance findings is a critical step because it determines what is reported, when it is reported, and to whom it is reported. This step also has to address the current technical capacity of the organization because it focuses on the methodological dimensions of accumulating, assessing, and preparing analyses and reports.

This chapter focuses specifically on reporting findings and addressing the following issues: (a) uses of monitoring and evaluation findings; (b) knowing the audiences and targeting the appropriate information to those audiences; (c) presentation of performance data in clear and understandable form; and (d) what happens if performance news is bad.

> *". . . [R]eporting is too often the step to which evaluators give the least thought."*
>
> (Worthen, Sanders, and Fitzpatrick 1997, p. 407)

The Uses of Monitoring and Evaluation Findings

Monitoring and evaluation reports can play many different roles, and the information produced can be put to very different uses:

- To demonstrate accountability—delivering on political promises made to citizenry and other stakeholders
- To convince—using evidence from findings
- To educate—reporting findings to help organizational learning
- To explore and investigate—seeing what works, what does not, and why
- To document—recording and creating an institutional memory
- To involve—engaging stakeholders through a participatory process
- To gain support—demonstrating results to help gain support among stakeholders
- To promote understanding—reporting results to enhance understanding of projects, programs, and policies.

Evaluation reports serve many purposes. The central purpose, however, is to "deliver the message"—inform the appropriate audiences about the findings and conclusions resulting from the collection, analysis, and interpretation of evaluation information. (Adapted from Worthen, Sanders, and Fitzpatrick 1997.)

Know and Target the Audience

"Some call this 'speaking truth to power,' but what good is speaking truth if power isn't listening? Unless we find more effective ways to help our audiences listen, all our good works are likely to go for naught. How we report our results is often the difference between creating a tiny ripple or making a proper splash."

(Wholey, Hatry, and Newcomer 1994, p. 549)

Know your audiences and how they want to see the information expressed. The interests, expectations, and preferred communications medium of the audience should be taken into account. A communications strategy should be developed that will address the following questions:

- Who will receive what information?
- In what format?
- When?
- Who will prepare the information?
- Who will deliver the information?

During the ongoing process of determining monitoring and evaluation findings, it is important to ensure that everyone is informed of progress, and that there are no surprises. If the information system is to provide continuous performance feedback as a management tool, continuous communication is also important to the process. Monitoring and evaluation results should be continuously disseminated to provide feedback to decisionmakers. Informal (phone, e-mail, fax, conversations) and formal (briefings, presentations, written reports) communications should be a part of the overall communications strategy.

Data should be presented in a short and crisp manner and be relevant to the target audience. Only the most important data should be presented. "A . . . report [on findings] obviously cannot be well targeted without clear definition of its audience(s) and the types of questions that audience is likely to raise about findings" (Worthen, Sanders, and Fitzpatrick 1997, p. 409).

If there are multiple audiences—those involved at the project, program, and policy levels—the data may have to be packaged and formatted differently according to the main interests and preferences of each audience. The communications strategy should take into account the challenges in communicating results to different stakeholders. Furthermore, "[c]lear the report with all key parties before it is formally presented. This will help to eliminate errors and will also ensure that many points are clarified informally without the embarrassment of confrontations [later on] . . . " (Valadez and Bamberger 1994, p. 437).

One can anticipate that there may be multiple uses of the performance findings. Think of this as concentric circles, that is, the target audience forms the inner circle, but there may be uses for the findings beyond the inner circle including those less directly concerned or affected. "Evaluators often limit the use of evaluation data to the questions . . . under investigation. The information collected may, and usually does, have meaning and use to others in the organization for purposes well beyond the intent of the original evaluation study" (Wholey, Hatry, and Newcomer 1994, p. 578). Consequently, one should also anticipate further dissemination of performance findings to a broader audience.

Typically, the higher up the chain of command, the less need there is for extensive detail and explanation; aggregated, succinct data relevant to the specific issue will be more appropriate. For this reason, personal briefings—especially to high-level officials—can be another effective means of communicating performance findings. Further down the managerial chain, it is more likely that more operational data will be desired.

Large "data dumps" of information are counterproductive. Know what the decisionmakers want and provide them with the necessary information in the format with which they are most comfortable. This may require tailoring information into the preferred format for each of the decisionmakers and end users.

Decisionmakers may be looking for some indications of action required in response to data findings. They will also be interested in available options (including costs, pros and cons, and the like) with respect to acting on performance findings throughout the monitoring and evaluation process.

Furthermore, it is important to highlight the implications of recommended actions throughout the monitoring and evaluation process. "Simply recommending that certain actions be taken is rarely sufficient. Officials will usually want a fuller understanding of the implications of their action. Wise evaluators anticipate this need and provide, whenever possible, best estimates (or perhaps a range of estimates) of both the costs and consequences of the recommendations" (Wholey, Hatry, and Newcomer 1994, p. 563). Continuous reporting on findings can and should also extend to guiding decisionmakers through implementation of recommendations.

In terms of follow-up and feedback, one could set up a political process to bring stakeholders and evaluators together to discuss findings, insights, alternative actions, and next steps. It would also be useful to " . . . obtain feedback periodically from major constituencies, such as elected officials, funders, and the public . . . regarding the usefulness and readability of performance reports. Use the feedback to help tailor future performance reports to the particular audience" (Hatry 1999, p. 154).

Report performance data in comparison to earlier data and to the baseline.

Comparisons of performance data over time are critical. Providing data for a specific quarter or year by itself is not useful. To distinguish trends, one needs to begin with baselines. Always report against the baseline and intermediate measurements to determine whether progress has been sustained, whether there was only a short spurt of improvement, or whether early improvements have all disappeared.

Comparing actual outcomes to targets is central to reporting results. Table 8.1 illustrates indicator baselines, current and target measurements, as well as percentage differences relative to expected outcomes.

Presentation of Performance Data in Clear and Understandable Form

It is important to report results data in comparison to earlier data and to the baseline. Comparisons over time are critical.

The following data can be reported:

- Expenditure or income—cost of, or return on, project, program or policy

Table 8.1

Outcomes Reporting Format: Actual Outcomes versus Targets

Outcome indicator	Baseline (percent)	Current (percent)	Target (percent)	Difference (percentage points)
Rates of hepatitis (N = 6,000)	30	25	20	−5
Percentage of children with improved overall overall health status (N = 9,000)	20	20	24	−4
Percentage of children who show four out of five positive scores on physical exams (N = 3,500)	50	65	65	0
Percentage of children with improved nutritional status (N = 14,000)	80	85	83	+2

Source: Sample data 2004.

- Raw numbers—early indications, rough projections, estimates, and so forth
- Percentages (for example, percentage of citizens served by a project)
- Statistical tests
- Organizational units
- Geographical locations
- Demographics
- Client satisfaction scales—high, medium, low.

Data should be presented in a simple, clear, and easily understandable format. Only the most important data should be presented. Acronyms and jargon should be avoided. A minimum of background information should be provided to establish the context. Major points should be stated up front. Findings and recommendations should be organized around key outcomes and their indicators. A separate appendix or report can be used to convey detailed data.

There are four dimensions of reporting: written summaries, executive summaries, oral presentations, and visual presentations.

Written Summaries

To be a useful management tool, the written summary should contain an introduction (including purpose of report, evaluation questions, program background, and program goals and objectives). The summary should contain a description of the evaluation (including evaluation focus, methodology, limitations of methodology, who performed the evaluation, and when the evaluation was performed). The report should present data on findings selectively and in an understandable manner; organize data around study questions, major themes or program components; and use charts and tables.

Conclusions should be clearly connected to evidence on performance. Evidence should be presented to support recommendations.

When planning the time needed to prepare the analysis and reporting format, leave plenty of time to revise. Having a knowledgeable outside reader review the findings and draft report can also be helpful.

Executive Summaries

Executive summaries should be short (one to four pages). Major findings and recommendations should be presented in bullet format. The summary can refer readers to the report or appendices for more details. The executive summary should contain a brief overview, including the background and purpose of the study. It should also include a brief description of major questions, issues, and research methods.

Oral Presentations

Oral presentations also can be used, either alone or in conjunction with a written report. In addition to rehearsing and getting feedback, one needs to consider the following in preparing for an oral presentation:

- Who is the audience?
- What should they remember from the presentation?
- How much time is there for the presentation?
- What are the available delivery resources?
- What handouts should be provided, if any?

Oral presentations—like written ones—should be simple, clear, and tailored to the audience. Complex language and detailed data should be avoided. Organization is also important: "Tell them what you will tell them; tell them; tell them what you told them." If possible, use an interactive format with the audience, and be prepared for questions.

Visual Presentations

Visual presentations—charts, graphs, and maps—are also helpful in highlighting key points and performance findings. They can illustrate directions and trends at a glance. There are a variety of charts (pie, flow, column, time series, scatter plot, bar, range, and so forth) and graphs (line, scatter, bar, pie, surface, pictograph, contour, histogram, area, circle, column) that should be considered in presenting data to the target audience.

The purpose of charts and tables is to describe, explore, tabulate, and compare. Charts and tables can provide impact and visual interest, encourage audience acceptance and memory retention, and show the big picture. Charts and tables should present data simply and accurately, and make the data coherent. They should engage the audience.

Tables are best used for presenting data, and highlighting changes, comparisons, and relationships. Charts are better for presenting the message. They are useful in depicting organizational structures, demonstrating flows, presenting data as symbols, conveying concepts and ideas, and presenting numerical data in visual form.

Effectively designed tables will have the following characteristics:

- Simplicity and accuracy
- Clearly labeled rows and columns with no abbreviations
- Percentages rounded to the nearest whole number
- Total numbers
- Source of the data.

Table 8.2 is an example of an effective table that could be used to demonstrate and report descriptive data.

Characteristics of effectively designed charts include the following:

- Easily read and appropriate for the delivery, using both upper and lower case (not all caps) and only a few type faces
- No busy patterns

"Visual presentations of evidence should be governed by principles of reasoning about quantitative evidence. For information displays, design reasoning must correspond to scientific reasoning. Clear and precise seeing becomes as one with clear and precise thinking."

(Tufte 2002, p. 53)

Table 8.2		
Sample Table for Reporting Descriptive Data		
Gender Differences in Voting		
Voted in last election	**Yes**	**No**
Men (N = 1,000)	75%	25%
Women (N =700)	55%	45%
Source: Sample data 2004.		

- Effective use of white space
- Simple
- Honest scales
- Message conveyed in title
- Sufficient data provided with chart so that message is clear
- Source of the data
- Supporting data in an appendix.

Effective charts enable policymakers and decisionmakers to quickly see the current status of a given project, program, or policy—including trends, directions, delays, problems, successes, and prospects. Charts should be used to provide informative and useful visual aids for continuous reporting of findings.

Whether in chart or table form, portraying information graphically is an important part of reporting. Figure 8.2 provides some guidance for the use of graphics.

Figure 8.2 contains examples of chart options for the continuous process of reporting findings.

There are many different reporting formats including written reports and displays. It is important to check with users and stakeholders for any preferences for data presentation. Be cautious not to use inappropriate graphs just because they may be popular.

What Happens If the M&E System Produces Bad Performance News?

"The value of information [often] decreases rapidly over time, so essential findings should be communicated as quickly as possible."

(Valadez and Bamberger 1994, p. 437)

One cannot manage by receiving only good news. A good performance measurement system is intended to surface problems—not just bring good news. This is another of the political aspects of results-based M&E systems. Reporting on bad news is a critical aspect of how one distinguishes success from failure. If the difference cannot be determined, it is likely that both failure and success are being rewarded by managers. A good performance system can serve as a kind of early warning system.

Performance reports should include explanations (if possible) about poor outcomes and identify steps taken or planned to correct problems (Hatry 1999). Messengers should not be punished for delivering bad news. Instilling fear of bringing forth bad news will not encourage reporting and use of findings.

Figure 8.2

Principles of Graphical Excellence

Edward Tufte teaches courses in statistical evidence and information design at Yale University. He is considered one of the major authorities on presenting information in a clear and accurate manner. Here are a few guidelines from his writing.

"Graphical excellence is the well-designed presentation of interesting data—a matter of *substance*, of *statistics*, and of *design*."

"Graphical excellence consists of complex ideas communicated with clarity, precision, and efficiency."

"Graphical excellence is that which gives to the viewer the greatest number of ideas in the shortest time with the least ink in the smallest space."

"Graphical excellence is nearly always multivariate."

"And graphical excellence requires telling the truth about the data."

Source: Tufte 2001, p. 51.

Sample Charts for Displaying Information

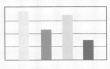 Line graph: trends over time

 Pie chart: parts of a whole

 Bar chart: percent distribution

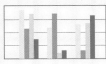 Cluster bar chart: comparing several items

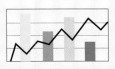 Combination chart

 Beware of too much of a good thing

Chapter 9
Step 9: Using the Findings

Figure 9.1

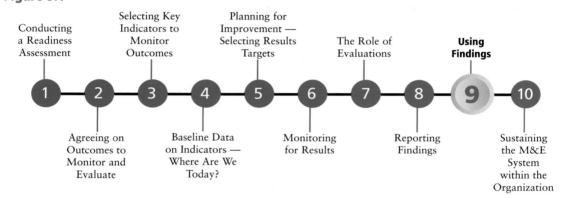

Using results-based findings will help inform the decisionmaking process.

After examining effective ways of reporting in the previous chapter, we turn now to the use of findings emanating from the results-based monitoring and evaluation system (figure 9.1). We will consider (a) the uses of performance findings; (b) additional benefits of using the findings—feedback, knowledge, and learning; and (c) strategies for sharing information.

Uses of Performance Findings

Using findings to improve performance is the main purpose of building a results-based M&E system. The main point of the M&E system is not simply to generate continuous results-based information, but to get that information to the appropriate users in a timely fashion so that the performance feedback can be used to better manage organizations and governments.

Findings can be used in a variety of concrete ways, as shown in box 9.1.

Box 9.1

Ten Uses of Results Findings

1. Respond to elected officials' and the public's demands for accountability
2. Help formulate and justify budget requests
3. Help make operational resource allocation decisions
4. Trigger in-depth examinations of what performance problems exist and what corrections are needed
5. Help motivate personnel to continue making program improvements
6. Formulate and monitor the performance of contractors and grantees
7. Provide data for special, in-depth program evaluations
8. Help provide services more efficiently
9. Support strategic and other long-term planning efforts (by providing baseline information and later tracking progress)
10. Communicate better with the public to build public trust.

Source: Hatry 1999.

With respect to helping formulate and justify budget requests, performance information can inform decisions that can lead to budgetary increases—or reductions. Projects, programs, and policies may be enhanced or expanded based on performance feedback; likewise, they may be cut or eliminated altogether. Managers also have the option of offering incentives (monetary and nonmonetary) to personnel for good performance or sanctions (such as poor employee or manager performance reviews) for performance that fails to meet expectations or falls short of intended outcomes.

In terms of motivating personnel, when civil servants are brought in as partners to the business of government, we see better implementation. Employees throughout the system begin to understand and become more enthusiastic about their contributions toward achievement of the desired goal when they have a "line of sight" between their own actions and the goal. In some OECD countries (Australia and France, for example), managers are given greater operational flexibility in exchange for enhanced accountability.

Australia provides an example regarding the performance of contractors and grantees. In Australia, there are actual performance contracts with agencies that specify that no annual budget funds will be allocated until contracts have been evaluated and results monitored.

Bringing stakeholders into cooperation with government generates trust.

In other cases, "If the agency contracts or provides grants to other organizations for services to customers, it can include outcome-based performance targets in the agreements and then compare outcomes against those targets" (Hatry 1999, p. 170). Rewards and penalties based on performance can also be delineated in such contracts.

If there are no data on which to base decisions, those decisions can be arbitrary. At the same time, decisionmakers always have the discretion to make their own decisions. However, better decisionmaking will result from taking the time to monitor, measure, and evaluate, and incorporate the findings into the decisionmaking process. An interesting corollary to this is that if one starts to ask for performance information, improved performance will result.

Other uses of results findings include identifying best practices, supporting economies of scale, avoiding overlap and duplication, and coordinating similar programs across agencies (Wye 2002, p. 49).

There are many examples of using findings. Boxes 9.2 and 9.3 illustrate some of the different uses of performance findings.

Additional Benefits of Using Findings: Feedback, Knowledge, and Learning

M&E systems provide important feedback about the progress, as well as the success or failure, of projects, programs, and policies throughout their respective cycles. These systems constitute a powerful, continuous public management tool that decisionmakers can use to improve performance, and demonstrate accountability and transparency with respect to results. One way to consider M&E feedback within the development context is as follows: "Evaluation feedback has been broadly defined as a dynamic process which involves the presentation and dissemination of evaluation information in order to ensure its application into new or existing development activities . . . feedback, as distinct from dissemination of evaluation findings, is the process of ensuring that lessons learned are incorporated into new operations" (OECD 2001, p. 60).

The use of M&E findings can promote knowledge and learning in governments and organizations. The new emphasis in the international aid community is more and more on local knowledge acquisition, not knowledge transfer from donor to recipient. What exactly do we mean by "learning" in a results-based monitoring and evaluation context? "Learning has been described as a continuous dynamic process of investigation where the key elements are experience,

Box 9.2

Using Performance Data to Track and Reduce Crime in New York City

Over the past decade, the New York City Police Department has used a special results-based M&E system to map the daily incidence of violent crime. "CompStat is a sophisticated performance measurement system that reorders an organization's day-to-day operations, as well as its overall orientation toward its core mission and goals. CompStat is based upon the compilation, distribution, and utilization of 'real time' data in order to allow field managers to make better-informed and more effective decisions" (O'Connell 2001, p. 6).

As former New York mayor Rudolph Giuliani noted, "We have 77 police precincts. Every single night they record all of the index crimes that have occurred in that precinct and a lot of other data. We record the number of civilian complaints. We record the number of arrests that are made for serious crimes and less serious crimes. It is all part of CompStat, a computer-driven program that helps ensure executive accountability. And the purpose of it is to see if crime is up or down, not just citywide, but neighborhood by neighborhood. And if crime is going up, it lets you do something about it now—not a year and a half from now when the FBI puts out crime statistics . . . Now we know about it today. And we can make strategic decisions accordingly" (O'Connell 2001, p. 9).

As a result, during a five year period, "New York City experienced a precipitous drop in the burglary rate (53 percent), a 54 percent drop in reported robberies, and an incredible 67 percent drop in the murder rate . . . These extraordinary achievements were realized in large part due to the department's innovative model of police management, known as CompStat" (O'Connell 2001, p. 8).

The overall result of using this real-time results-based system has been that "New York City now holds the undisputed title as the safest big city in the nation . . . " (NYC.gov 2003).

Sources: O'Connell 2001, NYC.gov 2003.

Box 9.3

U.S. Department of Labor—An Organization with a Mature, Functioning Results-Based M&E System

The U.S. Department of Labor (DOL) is an example of an organization that has a mature, functioning results-based M&E system. Its efforts were jump-started by the U.S. Government Performance Results Act of 1993 (see box 10.2).

The DOL established a mission, vision, strategic plan, and three main strategic goals: a prepared workforce; a secure workforce; and quality workplaces. Working from these three goals, the DOL then established three attendant outcomes for each of these larger strategic goals.

Strategic Goal:	1. A prepared workforce
Outcomes:	a. increase employment, earnings, and assistance
	b. increase the number of youth making a successful transition to work
	c. improve the effectiveness and information and analysis on the U.S. economy
Strategic Goal:	2. A secure workforce
Outcomes:	a. increase compliance with worker protection laws
	b. protect worker benefits
	c. increase employment and earnings for retrained workers
Strategic Goal:	3. Quality workplaces
Outcomes:	a. reduce workplace injuries, illnesses, and fatalities
	b. foster equal opportunity workplaces
	c. reduce exploitation of child labor, protect the basic rights of workers, and strengthen labor markets

Annual budgets are assigned for each of these strategic goals, and are later measured against actual budgetary outlays.

The DOL then holds biannual reviews on each of these goals and includes the following information:

Results:	The most recent results available for the performance outcome
Indicator:	The measures that will be used to assess progress toward performance goal accomplishment
Data Source:	The measurement systems that will be used to collect performance indicator data
Baseline:	The baseline year and baseline level against which progress will be evaluated
Comment:	Issues related to goal accomplishment, measurement systems, and strategies that provide a context or description of the performance goal or indicator.

Source: U.S. Department of Labor 2002.

knowledge, access and relevance. It requires a culture of inquiry and investigation, rather than one of response and reporting" (UNDP 2002, p. 77).

Knowledge and knowledge management are additional key components of using performance findings. New knowledge can be generated through the use of findings on a continuous basis. Knowledge management means capturing findings, institutionalizing learning, and organizing the wealth of information produced continually by the M&E system.

Results-based monitoring and evaluation systems and units have a special capacity to add to the learning and knowledge process. When used effectively, M&E systems can be an institutionalized form of learning and knowledge. "Learning must therefore be incorporated into the overall programming cycle through an effective feedback system. Information must be disseminated and available to potential users in order to become applied knowledge . . . Learning is also a key tool for management and, as such, the strategy for the application of evaluative knowledge is an important means of advancing toward outcomes . . . Outcomes present more variables around which learning can and must take place" (UNDP 2002, pp. 75–76).

Institutionalizing learning is important in governments and organizations. Policy and program evaluation should play a systematic instead of an ad hoc role in the process of organizational learning. A political environment needs to be created that encourages continuous reporting, as well as the use of results. This implies that a certain level of institutionalization has to occur before findings can be used in the management of government institutions. Emphasizing organizational learning as a means of enhancing organizational performance is a fruitful and promising area of engagement with the public sector.

Box 9.4 provides an example of how German aid agencies are moving increasingly in the direction of evaluation-based learning.

Many governments and organizations may yet be resistant to learning, internalizing, and sharing performance findings within and between ministries, organizations, agencies, and departments. There are a number of organizational, behavioral, and political challenges to be recognized. In box 9.5 we look at some of the obstacles to learning.

Good M&E systems can help to overcome these obstacles to learning. By producing a continual flow of feedback and data, M&E systems help decisionmakers manage more effectively. Organizational

"A monitoring and evaluation framework that generates knowledge, promotes learning and guides action is, in its own right, an important means of capacity development and sustainability of national results."

(UNDP 2002, p. 76)

Box 9.4

Signs of Improving Conditions for Evaluation-Based Learning in German Aid Agencies

- Germany's diversified development co-operation structure is now gradually moving towards greater *concentration* on particular issues, priority areas and countries. There is also a parallel trend towards greater decentralisation.
- German official aid agencies see themselves more than ever as *learning organisations,* and are beginning to restructure their management systems accordingly. *Evaluation systems* are intended to play a key part in this, and are being given greater priority and greater institutional independence.
- The *quality of evaluation* is improving. More sophisticated methods, more impact orientation and a greater number of broader-based evaluations (not confined to a single project) all offer the prospect that in future more of the knowledge will be generated that is needed for both quality improvement and conceptual advancement of development cooperation work, and for greater external accountability.
- Aid agencies themselves believe it is important to increase the extent to which they systematize and institutionalize their *feedback system* for evaluation-based learning and accountability."
- Aid agencies see a strong need to do more to promote the *internalization* of evaluation lessons, taking a more systematic and innovative approach. Some are currently appraising the inclusion of this in an overall system of knowledge management.
- . . . a substantial boost [has been given] to *horizontal learning* among German aid agencies in recent years.

Source: OECD 2001, p. 19.

---

cultures can be transformed through the use of M&E systems. There may be decreased pressures to spend as governments receive data that help them manage resource flows. M&E systems also provide built-in incentives to learn, pointing out directions, trends, successes, and problems.

Tunnel vision can be overcome as data on results shed light on areas previously unknown or not fully understood. The loss of institutional memory due to staff changes can also be minimized because M&E systems, when well maintained, produce a record of data over time. Finally, change can be managed more easily with continuous feedback.

Obstacles can also be overcome by understanding how governments and organizations learn and by identifying and overcoming the impediments. There are ways to encourage greater use of performance findings through learning and knowledge building among governments and organizations (box 9.6).

Box 9.5

Obstacles to Learning

The OECD has identified several obstacles that can prevent learning:

Organisational culture—some organisations have a culture where accountability tends to be associated with blame. This has the effect of discouraging openness and learning. In other [organizations], it is more acceptable to own up to mistakes and see these as opportunities for learning, recognizing that there is often as much to learn from poorly performing projects as there is from success stories.

Pressure to spend—learning takes time, and pressure to meet disbursement targets can lead to shortcuts being taken during project planning and approval stages, with lessons from previous experience being ignored or only selectively applied in the haste to get decisions through.

Lack of incentives to learn—unless there is proper accountability . . . built into the project cycle there may be little incentive to learn. This is particularly the case when staff or consultants shift from task to task, and have generally moved on long before the consequences of failure to learn are felt.

Tunnel vision—the tendency of some staff or operational units to get stuck in a rut, carrying on with what they know, even when the shortcomings of the old familiar approaches are widely accepted.

Loss of institutional memory—caused by frequent staff rotation or heavy reliance on short-term consultants, or by the weakening or disbanding of specialist departments.

Insecurity and the pace of change—if staff are insecure or unclear about what their objectives are, or if the departmental priorities are frequently shifting, this can have an adverse effect on learning.

The unequal nature of the aid relationship—which tends to put donors in the driving seat, thereby inhibiting real partnerships and two-way knowledge sharing.

Source: OECD 2001, pp. 20–21.

Box 9.6

Incentives for Learning, Knowledge Building, and Greater Use of Performance Findings

Governments and organizations can pro-actively encourage staff to learn, build knowledge, and use performance findings. Here are just a few examples:

- Develop guidance materials on the use of outcome information.
- Provide training in uses of outcome information for managers and other staff who can use outcome information.
- Hold regular 'How are we doing?' sessions with staff soon after each outcome report becomes available.
- Identify and reward offices, grantees, and facilities with good outcomes.
- Develop grant allocation guidelines that reward improved performance.
- Use the outcome data to identify successful ('best') practices within the agency . . .
- Use outcome data to identify common problems, and if possible, solutions.
- Use outcome information to identify needs for training for staff or technical assistance . . .
- Use outcome information to help prioritize use of resources.

Source: Hatry, Morley, Rossman, and Wholey 2003, pp. 16–17.

Strategies for Sharing Information

"Plan for communication as part of your M&E system from the outset" (IFAD 2002 pp. 6–7). A good communication strategy is essential for disseminating information and sharing it with key stakeholders. Results-based information should be shared with all internal and external stakeholders and interested parties. "*Active follow-up* [emphasis added] is necessary to implement recommendations . . . and to incorporate lessons learned in future decision-making processes . . . The more stakeholders are involved in planning the next steps, the more likely they are to follow through on implementing evaluation recommendations" (UNPF 2002). Information sharing strategies designed for and targeted to specific stakeholder groups can also be helpful. In this context, it helps to "[t]ry to adapt existing reporting requirements and resources to new uses and formats" (Wye 2002, p. 55).

Using results information can take passive and active forms (box 9.7).

Understanding the target audience is key. Communication strategies need to be tailored to suit a particular target audience—parliament, ministers, the media, the private sector, NGOs and civil society organizations, and the general public. "Disclosure of negative or controversial evaluation findings can obviously create difficulties for

---

Box 9.7

Active and Passive Approaches to Using Results Information

It is imperative that results information be used. Simply providing information to potential users within the government—managers and oversight agencies—is not enough. Even improved transparency through publication of performance information is not enough.

Countries have used different approaches to providing such an imperative, and generally fall into either active or passive groupings. More active measures include formal reviews (regularly scheduled meetings at which performance is assessed), senior management attention (either as the chair of the formal review or direct engagement in monitoring and following up on performance exceptions), nonmonetary rewards (generally public recognition with an award or honor). Many of these are blended for greater impact. Former U.S. Vice President Al Gore's "High-Impact Agency Initiative," and the U.K. Prime Minister's Office's six month performance reviews, are examples of active approaches.

Passive approaches include performance contracts (formal agreements between managers and staff on targets, implying a formal review at the end of the contract period), peer pressure (a scorecard of performance for each unit, made widely available so the units can be easily compared), public embarrassment or approval, or monetary incentives (hope of monetary benefit if performance improves or targets are achieved, either on an individual basis by tying senior management pay or bonuses to organizational performance, or on an overall basis by tying organization-wide pay or bonuses to organizational performance, or by trying to link the organization's budget to its performance). These are "passive" insofar as they set up a structure, but do not ensure the performance measures are used to affect decisions.

Source: Dorotinsky 2003a.

---

agencies ... But ... the benefits of disclosure in the long run make it worthwhile ... Greater disclosure can also increase the pressure for more systematic follow-up of recommendations, while motivating those involved in evaluations to produce a better product, since they know their report will be made public, rather than being buried on a shelf somewhere" (OECD 2001, p. 26).

Governments and organizations can use a wide array of strategies for sharing information with internal and external stakeholders. These strategies also involve a number of different media that can be used to share the performance information.

Empower the Media

The media can be an important partner in disseminating the findings generated by results-based M&E systems. For example, the media

"Performance information can make a dramatic contribution to improving government performance if it is effectively communicated to stakeholders, including citizens."

(Wye 2002, p. 53)

often report on whether governments or organizations have actually delivered on promised projects, programs, policies, and services. The media have also been instrumental in exposing corruption and calling for good or better governance in many countries.

Enact "Freedom of Information" Legislation

Freedom of information is another powerful tool that can be used to share information with concerned stakeholders. For example, the government of Romania enacted freedom of information legislation recently with the stipulation that, except for information that could impair the country's ability to protect and defend itself, anyone who asks for information about how well the government is performing will receive it (World Bank 2001d).

Institute E-Government

E-government is increasingly being used as a tool by governments around the world, and has become a particular priority among OECD countries. E-government involves the use of information technology to provide better accessibility, outreach, information, and services. It represents a new electronic environment in which stakeholders can interact directly with the government, obtain information from the government, and even transact business online. Developing countries are moving in this direction, too. The government of Jordan, for example, is beginning its e-government initiative with the introduction of electronic procurement and accounting.

Put Information on Internal and External Internet Sites

The use of internal (agency or government) and external Web sites that include published performance findings is yet another effective way of sharing information. Many agencies are also developing searchable databases for M&E findings.

Publish Annual Budget Reports

There is no more important way to communicate how taxpayer money is being spent than to publish the budget. Citizens will have the opportunity to "compare" the quality and level of services being provided by the government, and the priority of that service or program in the expenditure plan.

Engage Civil Society and Citizen Groups

Engaging civil society and citizens groups also involves the inclusion of " . . . accountability, advocacy and action-oriented audiences and . . . agree[ment] on the information (content and form) they need" (IFAD 2002, p. 6-6).

Strengthen Parliamentary Oversight

Strengthening parliamentary oversight is another important way to share and disseminate information. Many parliaments have active budget or public accounts committees in lower or upper chambers. There are also other agencies that provide parliaments with oversight, for example, the U.S. General Accounting Office (GAO), the audit and evaluation office of the Congress, or the National Audit Office for the Parliament in the U.K. The GAO and similar government organizations and agencies also perform an investigative function for the parliaments they serve. Parliaments in various countries—both developed and developing—are starting to ask for performance information as part of their oversight function (see box 9.8). They are looking to see that budgets are used effectively; thus, more governments are considering moving toward programmatic budgeting.

Strengthen the Office of the Auditor General

Many countries are also finding the Office of the Auditor General to be a key partner in determining whether governments are functioning effectively. Interestingly, as audit agencies demand more information about how well the public sector is performing and how projects, programs, and policies are actually being implemented, we are starting to see better implementation.

In Canada, the Treasury Board produced a "Guide for the Development of Results-Based Management and Accountability Frame-

---

Box 9.8

Canadian Government Performance Reports to Parliament

"Each year since 1997 the government has tabled two sets of departmental reports in Parliament. In the spring, departments and agencies produce their Reports on Plans and Priorities for the coming fiscal year. In the fall they provide parliamentarians with their Departmental Performance reports indicating achievements attained over the previous fiscal year." An annual report, "Canada's Performance," is produced for the Parliament. It contains 19 societal indicators grouped into four main themes: economic opportunities and innovation in Canada; the health of Canadians; the Canadian environment; and the strength and safety of Canadian communities. Parliamentarians have emphasized the need for such indicators of results findings to be relevant, temporal, available, comparable, and understandable.

Source: President of the Treasury Board of Canada 2002, pp. 2–3.

works." It is " . . . intended to serve as a blueprint for managers to help them focus on measuring and reporting on outcomes throughout the life cycle of a policy, program or initiative" (Treasury Board Secretariat of Canada 2001, p. 1).

Share and Compare Results Findings with Development Partners

Sharing and comparing results findings with development partners is also beneficial on a number of levels. " . . . [L]earning from evaluative knowledge becomes wider than simply organizational learning and also encompasses development learning. It helps to test systematically the validity, relevance and progress of the development hypotheses" (UNDP 2002, p. 76). Since the introduction of National Poverty Reduction Strategies and similar broadly based strategies and policies, the need for information sharing among development partners—especially bilateral and multilateral aid agencies—has increased.
"These and other joint initiatives are premised on the assumption that coordinated agency action will be more effective than individual efforts. Yet mechanisms for exchanging evaluation lessons between [aid] agencies are still weak, and practical hurdles continue to get in the way of more frequent joint evaluations—which, when they do occur, are generally seen as a very good way of sharing lessons and methodologies" (OECD 2001, p. 31). More could also be done with respect to sharing performance findings with donor recipient countries. All key stakeholders—particularly recipient countries—need to be part of the M&E process from start to finish.

There are many uses for performance findings. We looked at two successful examples involving crime information and a government organization with a mature, functioning M&E system. We also examined the many benefits of using findings, including continuous feedback, and organizational and institutional learning and knowledge. We acknowledged and examined the obstacles and incentives—many of them political—to using findings, and looked at some potential strategies for sharing information among internal and external stakeholders.

We turn now in the next chapter to the final step of our model on sustaining the results-based M&E system within your organization.

Chapter 10

Step 10: Sustaining the M&E System within the Organization

Figure 10.1

In the final step of our model, we turn to sustaining results-based M&E systems. An M&E system should be regarded as a long-term effort, as opposed to an episodic effort for a short period or for the duration of a specific project, program, or policy. Sustaining such systems within governments or organizations recognizes the long-term process involved in ensuring utility (for without utility, there is no logic for having such a system). Specifically, we will examine: (a) six critical components of sustaining results-based M&E systems; (b) the importance of incentives and disincentives in sustaining M&E systems; (c) possible hurdles in sustaining a results-based M&E system; (d) validating and evaluating M&E systems and information; and (e) M&E stimulating positive cultural change in governments and organizations.

Six Critical Components of Sustaining Results-Based M&E Systems

We will examine six critical components involved in building the sustainability of M&E systems. Each of these dimensions needs continuous attention and care.

Demand

If demand is episodic or haphazard, results-based M&E systems are not going to be used and sustained. Structured requirements for reporting results, including legislation, regulations, and international development requirements (HIPC and EU accession, for example), can help lead to sustained, consistent demand for such systems. Governments, civil society, and donors are increasingly requiring the results that M&E systems can best track, monitor, and measure.

In many cases, demand can also be stimulated when the strategic goals of the government are translated into results-based M&E systems, such as through National Poverty Reduction Strategies and other initiatives. These are not simply activity-driven initiatives; rather, they try to answer the "so what" question. What are the consequences of policy and program efforts to reduce poverty and address the most vulnerable groups?

Clear Roles and Responsibilities

Clear roles and responsibilities and formal organizational and political lines of authority must be established. The organization and people who will be in charge of collecting, analyzing, and reporting performance information must be clearly defined. Guidance is necessary. For example, a Ministry of Finance may be responsible for administering National Poverty Reduction Strategies or initiatives, and will need to issue directions to the sector or line ministries to collect and report on data relevant to tracking the various outcomes specified in the strategy.

Internal political coordination is key. A system should be built that links the central planning and finance ministries to the line and sector ministries. These bridges linking ministries are important, as is the need for horizontal communication to keep all concerned parties informed. If there are organizational problems, these should be dealt with sooner rather than later.

It is also important to build a continuous system of data collection and analysis that goes beyond the national government to other lev-

Sustainability and use of M&E systems are interdependent. Systems that are not used will not be sustainable. The issue of use has to be addressed first. It is the prerequisite to system sustainability.

els of government. <u>Data collection, analysis, and reporting should</u> be aligned throughout the various levels of government. For example, in the health or education sectors, focusing at the local and regional levels will be important because some of the requirements to meet national goals are going to take place there. Data analysis and reporting at these levels will then feed into the larger national data base in determining progress toward the desired outcomes.

Finally, M&E systems should be built in such a way that there is a demand for results information at every level that data are collected and analyzed. There is no level of the system that is a mere "pass through" of information. Pass-through parts of the system create tremendous vulnerability, and can lead to breakdowns in M&E systems. If people are not involved, if there is no ownership, then people in the "pass-through" levels will begin to lose interest and the result will be poor data collection and reporting.

Trustworthy and Credible Information

The M&E system must be able to produce results information that brings both good and bad news. Performance information should be transparent and made available to all key stakeholders. If debate of issues is not backed up by trustworthy and credible information, only personal opinions and presumptions are left.

It should also be noted that the producers of results information need protection from political reprisals. If bad news brings career problems to the messengers, fear will permeate the system and the reliability of the information produced will be compromised. A quick way to undermine an M&E system is to punish those who deliver bad news.

Information produced by the M&E system should be <u>transparent</u> and subject to independent verification. If data on government performance are held too close, or there are gatekeepers who prevent the release of such information, the system will again be faulty. As a further check on the system, it would be advisable to have a periodic independent review by the national audit office, parliament, or a group of academics to ensure that the data being generated by the system are accurate and reliable, and to build confidence among managers who could use the data.

Accountability

No part of the government should be exempt from accountability to stakeholders. Civil society organizations and NGOs (such as Transparency International) can play a key role in encouraging transparency and accountability, and can even help with collecting data. For example, NGOs in Bangladesh help to collect local educational data because the capacity to collect and report on such data is very weak within the government. The media, private sector, and parliament also have roles to ensure that the information produced is timely, accurate, available, and addresses government performance. It is also important not to reward failure. Accountability means that problems should be acknowledged and addressed.

Capacity

Sound technical skills in data collection and analysis are necessary for the system's sustainability. Managerial skills in strategic goal setting and organizational development are also needed. Data collection and retrieval systems must be up and running—and modernized. Governments will need to commit continuing financial resources to the upkeep and management of results-based M&E systems. Institutional experience and memory are also helpful in the long-term sustainability of these systems.

Incentives

Incentives need to be introduced to encourage use of performance information. This means that success needs to be acknowledged and rewarded, problems need to be addressed, messengers must not be punished, organizational learning is valued, and budget savings are shared. Corrupt or ineffective systems cannot be counted on to produce quality information and analysis.

Examples of the ways that governments have sought to incorporate and sustain results-based environments are provided in boxes 10.1 and 10.2, the U.K. Citizen's Charters and the U.S. Government Performance Results Act (GPRA), respectively, incorporate the critical sustainability components. The Citizen's Charter is relevant to the sustainability of M&E in that it establishes an ongoing government–citizen contract outlining responsibilities and performance expectations. The U.S. GPRA also legally institutionalizes M&E within government agencies, making such systems sustainable in the longer term.

Developing countries are also working toward creation of evaluation capacity, institutionalization of evaluation, and use of results findings within government—in short, sustainable M&E systems. Table 10.1 provides a comparative illustration of such efforts in Colombia, China, and Indonesia.

> **Box 10.1**
> Citizen's Charters in the United Kingdom
>
> In the U.K., there are contracts signed between the government and citizen groups, called "Citizen's Charters," that specify that the government will be accountable to the public for a certain level of performance.
>
> The Citizen's Charter, launched in 1991, aims to improve public services and make the sevices more responsive to users. There are now 40 main charters that cover key public services and set out the standards of service people can expect to receive. There are also over 10,000 local charters covering local service providers, such as schools, police forces, and fire services.
>
> In addition, Charter Quality Networks were relaunched as a network of managers from public services to exchange ideas on the charter program, customer service, and quality issues and to share best practice. There are now 22 Quality Networks around the U.K., involving over 1,500 people.
>
> As part of the Better Government initiative, the Charter Unit has set up a People's Panel of around 5,000 people across the U.K. The panel is being used to consult members of the public on their attitudes toward public services and generate ideas about how services can be improved. In addition to the Cabinet Office, other departments, agencies, and public bodies use the panel for research and consultation.
>
> Source: U.K. Cabinet Office.

The Importance of Incentives and Disincentives in Sustaining M&E Systems

Sustaining M&E systems also involves using appropriate incentives to keep managers and stakeholders on track and motivated. "Putting in place incentives for M&E means offering stimuli that encourage . . . M&E officers and primary stakeholders to perceive the usefulness of M&E, not as a bureaucratic task, but as an opportunity to discuss problems openly, reflect critically and criticize constructively in order to learn what changes are needed to enhance impact" (IFAD 2002, Section 7 p. 4). There are a variety of organizational, financial, resource, political, technical assistance, and training incentives that can be used to sustain M&E systems. Likewise, managers need to remove disincentives to sustaining M&E systems. Boxes 10.3 and 10.4 contain checklists of the kinds of incentives and disincentives that should be considered.

Possible Problems in Sustaining Results-Based M&E Systems

There are a number of hurdles that may arise in sustaining M&E systems. Hatry (1999) brings to light a number of likely problems in implementing and sustaining M&E systems, as follow:

Box 10.2
U.S. Government Performance and Results Act of 1993

Performance measurement in the U.S. began first with local governments in the 1970s, spread to state governments, and eventually to the federal level with the enactment of the Government Performance and Results Act (GPRA) in 1993. The U.S. federal government adopted a performance measurement system later than other levels of American government, and actually later than some foreign governments.

"The purposes of the [U.S. Government Performance and Results] Act are to: (1) improve the confidence of the American people in the capability of the Federal Government, by systematically holding Federal agencies accountable for achieving program results; (2) initiate program performance reform with a series of pilot projects in setting program goals, measuring program performance against those goals, and reporting publicly on their progress; (3) improve Federal program effectiveness and public accountability by promoting a new focus on results, service quality, and customer satisfaction; (4) help Federal managers improve service delivery, by requiring that they plan for meeting program objectives and by providing them with information about program results and service quality; (5) improve congressional decision-making by providing more objective information on achieving statutory objectives, and on the relative effectiveness and efficacy of Federal programs and spending; and (6) improve internal management of the Federal Government" (U.S. Office of Management and Budget 1993).

A recent survey of 16 programs across 12 U.S. government agencies found that "[m]any federal programs have already made use of regularly collected outcome data to help them improve their programs . . . Federal managers have used outcome data in a variety of ways, [including] to trigger corrective action; identify and encourage 'best practices'; motivate [and recognize staff]; and plan and budget . . . " At the same time, the survey found some continuing obstacles—indeed obstacles that can affect any organization—to the use of outcome data: (a) lack of authority or interest to make changes; (b) limited understanding of use of outcome data; (c) outcome data problems (such as old data, nondisaggregated data, lack of specificity, need for intermediate data, and so forth); and (d) fear of "rocking the boat" (Hatry, Morley, Rossman, and Wholey 2003, pp. 11–13).

Most recently, GPRA has been extended to the integration of the performance and budget areas. Efforts are also being made across the government to group GPRA strategic and annual planning and reporting more closely.

"Overall GPRA is just 'good business.' Its requirements have provided government Departments with tools for very basic ways of conducting business in sensible ways: set performance goals and measure both long and short-term outcomes. Any organization seeking to provide improved quality of life, greater quantity of services, and enhanced overall quality of customer services must have a vision and a mission, set goals and objectives, and must measure results" (ChannahSorah 2003, pp. 5–6.)

Table 10.1

Evaluation Capacity Development and Institutionalization—Key Issues Addressed in Colombia, China, and Indonesia

Issue	Colombia	China	Indonesia
Anchoring the evaluation regime	Constitution mandates the Executive to take the lead.	State Council draft resolution calls on the Central Executive Agencies to take lead.	Responsibility rests with the Executive through a Ministerial decree.
Positioning the evaluation function	Centralized in the National Planning Departmentt (NPD). Key line agencies provide inputs.	Decentralized in key central agencies.	Centralized in the National Development Planning Agency (BAPPENAS). Line agencies provide inputs.
Evaluation coverage	Public policy and major public sector programs.	Public sector projects.	Development policies, plans, programs, and projects.
Linking evaluation with other public sector functions	NPD plays a key role in policy and strategy formulation and budget allocation and monitoring.	No formal links have been established. State Planning Commission involved in public resources allocation and monitoring.	BAPPENAS to link evaluation to the annual budget allocation process.
Using evaluation in decisionmaking	Monitoring and evaluation information to flow to line agency heads and the NPD.	Monitoring and evaluation to inform central agency management.	Monitoring and evaluation information to flow through through line agency management to BAPPENAS.
Professionalizing the evaluation function	Evaluation is a trans-discipline cutting across specific professional skills.	Evaluation is seen primarily as applied socioeconomic analysis.	Evaluation is not seen as a separate profession, but a complementary discipline.
Resources for evaluation	Evaluation to be main-streamed in agencies' budgets.	Evaluation mainstreamed in central agencies' budgets.	Evaluation mainstreamed in agencies' budgets.

Note: BAPPENAS = Badan Perencanaan Pembangunan Nasional; NPD = National Planning Department.
Source: Guerrero 1999, p. 180.

Box 10.3

Checklist for Staff Incentives That Encourage Learning-Oriented, Participatory M&E

Are the following incentives in place?

- Clarity of M&E responsibility
- Financial and other physical rewards: appropriate salaries and other rewards
- Activity support: support, such as financial and other resources, for carrying out project, program, or policy activities
- Personnel and partner strategy: hiring staff who have an open attitude to learning, and signing on partners who are willing to try out more participatory forms of M&E
- Project, program, or policy culture: compliments and encouragement for those who ask questions and innovate, giving relatively high status to M&E among staff
- Performance appraisal processes: equal focus on staff capacity to learn and innovate, rather than just if they have reached their quantitative targets
- Showing the use of M&E data: making the data explicit and interesting by displaying them
- Feedback: telling data collectors, information providers, and others involved in the process how their data were used (analyzed), and what it contributed to the project.

Source: IFAD 2002.

Box 10.4

Checklist for Staff Disincentives That Hinder Learning-Oriented, Participatory M&E

Have the following disincentives been removed from project, program, or policy?

- Using the M&E unit as the place to park demoted or unqualified staff
- Not making clear how data will be or were used
- Chastising those who innovate within their project boundaries or those who make mistakes
- Focusing performance appraisals only on activities undertaken (outputs)
- Frequent rotation of staff to different posts
- Staff feeling isolated or helpless in terms of their contribution being recognized toward achieving the project goal (the "line of sight" issue)
- Unconstructive attitudes toward what constitutes participation or toward the primary stakeholder groups.

Source: IFAD 2002.

- Personnel training needs
- Overall system cost and feasibility
- Changes in legislative and agency priorities
- Maintaining indicator stability over time
- Documentation of the outcome measurement process (who will do what)
- Fear and resistance from program managers
- Participation by other levels of government and the private sector
- Aggregation of outcomes across projects, programs, or sites
- Community-wide versus program-specific outcomes
- Legislative support
- Politics.

Some of the most critical issues in implementing and sustaining M&E systems are the challenges in the human resource area. These challenges are perhaps not so different from all public sector human resource matters, but there are unique dimensions that have to be addressed. First, there are issues in recruiting and holding talented staff who can build and manage a new information system. Can they be found and, if so, can they be hired? Second is the issue of what staff will risk venturing into a new government initiative—or stated differently, what is the caliber of those who leave their present positions for positions in a new M&E unit? Third is the matter of whether the first cohort of those hired are change agents. Building an M&E system is a politically charged change process. Do those being hired understand this and are they ready to manage a change process? Fourth, can continuous training be provided for all personnel at all levels? New methodologies, technologies, and procedures are inevitable and need to be shared with staff. Can that training be provided? Furthermore, given staff turnover, how soon and how adequately can new staff be trained to quickly increase their productivity and contributions to the unit?

The M&E system will have to respond and adapt to changes in legislative and organizational priorities. In spite of these larger political and environmental changes, maintaining indicator stability over time is important. One wants to be able to compare similar issues and trends over a given period of time.

Validating and Evaluating M&E Systems and Information

Continued upgrading and improvement is important in sustaining results-based M&E systems. M&E systems themselves should be evaluated periodically, using internal or external evaluators. "Evaluators can assist in validating performance data and improving performance measurement systems. Evaluations of performance measurement systems should focus both on the technical quality of the measurement system and on the extent to which performance information is used in managing to achieve performance goals and in providing accountability to key stakeholders and the public" (Wholey 2001, p. 345). Evaluators can also verify and confirm the results of M&E systems.

M&E: Stimulating Positive Cultural Change in Governments and Organizations

M&E systems are essentially political challenges, and to a lesser extent, technical ones. Creating, implementing, and sustaining results-based M&E systems can help to bring about major cultural changes in the way governments and organizations operate. M&E systems can bring about positive cultural changes that lead to improved performance, enhanced accountability and transparency, and learning and knowledge (see box 10.5).

Good results-based M&E systems must be used to be sustainable. Six components are necessary in sustaining these systems: demand, incentives, clear roles and responsibilities, trustworthy and credible information, accountability, and capacity. Sustainable M&E systems do exist in many OECD countries, and some developing countries are on their way toward building and sustaining such systems as well. Above all, results-based M&E systems are powerful public management tools that facilitate positive cultural and political changes in governments and organizations to demonstrate results, accountability, and transparency. They also facilitate knowledge and learning. And, they are doable!

Last Reminders

- The demand for capacity building never ends. The only way an organization can coast is downhill.
- Keep champions on your side and help them.
- Establish the understanding with the Ministry of Finance and the parliament that an M&E system needs sustained resources.

Box 10.5

An Evaluation Culture and Collaborative Partnerships Help Build Agency Capacity

A recent study examined the development of an evaluation culture in five different U.S. government agencies: the Administration for Children and Families, the Coast Guard, the Department of Housing and Urban Development, the National Highway Traffic Safety Administration, and the National Science Foundation. The five agencies used various strategies to develop and improve evaluation. Agency evaluation culture, an institutional commitment to learning from evaluation, was developed to support policy debates and demands for accountability.

The study found that key elements of evaluation capacity were an evaluation culture, data quality, analytic experience, and collaborative partnerships. Agencies demonstrated an evaluation culture through regularly evaluating how well programs were working. Managers valued and used this information to test out new initiatives or assess progress toward agency goals. Agencies emphasized access to data that were credible, reliable, and consistent across jurisdictions to ensure that evaluation findings were trustworthy. Agencies also needed access to analytic experience and research expertise. Finally, agencies formed collaborations with program partners and others to leverage resources and expertise to obtain performance information.

Source: U.S. GAO 2003.

- Look for every opportunity to link results information to budget and resource allocation decisions.
- Begin with pilot efforts to demonstrate effective results-based monitoring. Begin with an enclave strategy (that is, islands of innovation) as opposed to a whole-of-government approach.
- Monitor both implementation progress and results achievements.
- Complement performance monitoring with evaluations to ensure better understanding of public sector results.

Chapter 11
Making Results-Based M&E Work for You and Your Organization

Why Results-Based M&E?

Results-based M&E has become a global phenomenon as national and international stakeholders in the development process have sought increased accountability, transparency, and results from governments and organizations. Multilateral development institutions, donor governments, parliaments, the private sector, NGOs, citizens' groups, and civil society are all voicing their interest in and concern for tangible results. Political and financial support for governments and their programs are becoming increasingly linked with a government's ability to implement good policies, demonstrate effectiveness in the use of resources, and deliver real results.

The MDGs, the HIPC initiative, IDA funding, WTO membership, and EU accession are examples of just some of the international initiatives and forces for change in the direction of results-based M&E. Internally, governments are facing the challenges of deregulation, commercialization, and privatization, as well as fluctuating budgets and resources.

For these reasons, governments and organizations are turning to results-based M&E in the hope that this public management tool can help them devise appropriate policies, manage financial and other resources, and fulfill their mandates and promises to internal and external stakeholders.

Results-based M&E moves beyond the traditional input–output-focused M&E, and, when used effectively, helps policymakers and decisionmakers focus on and analyze *outcomes* and *impacts*. After all, inputs and outputs tell little about the effectiveness of a given policy, program, or project. While traditional M&E remains an important part of the chain of results-based M&E, it is the outcomes and impacts that are of most interest and import to governments and their stakeholders.

Building and sustaining results-based M&E systems is admittedly not an easy task. It requires continuous commitment, champions, time, effort, and resources. There may be many organizational and technical challenges to overcome in building these systems. Political challenges are usually the most difficult. And it may take several attempts before the system can be tailored to suit a given governmental or organizational policy, program, or project. But it is doable. And it is certainly worthwhile in light of the increasingly common demands for and conditions attached to demonstrating good performance.

Good M&E systems also build knowledge capital by enabling governments and organizations to develop a knowledge base of the types of policies, programs, and projects that are successful—and more generally, what works, what does not, and why. Results-based M&E systems also help promote greater transparency and accountability, and may have beneficial spill-over effects in other parts of a government or organization. In short, there is tremendous power in measuring performance.

Many of the OECD countries have had 20 or more years of experience in M&E, and are at varying stages of progress with regard to results-based M&E systems. The OECD countries—like their developing country counterparts—created evaluation cultures and M&E systems in response to varying degrees of internal and external pressures. Furthermore, developed countries have chosen a variety of starting points for implementing results-based M&E systems, including whole-of-government, enclave, and mixed approaches.

Recent OECD survey results found that most OECD member countries now include performance information in their budgets.

With respect to results considerations, about half of the countries have taken into account the distinction between outputs and outcomes. Much remains to be done though, such as linking performance targets to expenditures, and using performance information to determine budgetary allocations. Thus, in many OECD countries, results-based M&E is still a work in progress.

The lessons learned from the OECD countries' experiences are useful and applicable to developing countries as they now face the challenges of creating their own M&E systems and cultures. OECD countries with democratic political systems, strong empirical traditions, civil servants trained in the social sciences, and high levels of expenditure on education, health, and social welfare have been among the most successful in adopting results-based M&E systems. In fact, building such systems is first and foremost a political activity with technical dimensions rather than vice versa. The OECD experience demonstrates that creating results-based M&E systems requires continuous effort to achieve comprehensive coverage across governmental management and budgetary systems.

Developing countries face a variety of unique challenges as they try to answer the "so what" question: What are the results and impacts of government actions and interventions? These countries may encounter such obstacles as lack of demand for and ownership of M&E systems, weak institutional capacity, lack of bureaucratic cooperation and coordination, lack of highly placed champions, weak or nonexistent legal and regulatory frameworks, a traditional M&E culture, lack of workforce capacity, political and administrative cultures not conducive to M&E implementation, and so forth. Despite these obstacles, many developing countries have made impressive progress in developing results-based M&E systems. The challenges are difficult, but good government is essential for achieving economic, social, and human development. Developing countries deserve good government no less than others.

Finally, given the increasing number of internal and external partnerships that are being formed to accomplish development goals, a new need has emerged for M&E systems that encompasses these broader partnership efforts. International coordination of results is the next stage in the evolutionary process of extending results-based M&E.

How to Create Results-Based M&E Systems

The ten-step model presented here can help governments and organizations create, develop, and sustain results-based M&E systems. This model may be used for policies, programs, and projects. Though visually it appears as a linear process, in reality it is not. One will inevitably move back and forth along the steps, or work on several steps simultaneously.

The model has some unique features, including Step 1, conducting a readiness assessment. This assessment—often missed or omitted—is a diagnostic tool that determines whether governments are actually ready and able to move forward in building, using, and sustaining M&E systems. The three main parts of the readiness assessment include an examination of incentives or demands for designing and building a results-based M&E system, roles and responsibilities and existing structures for assessing performance of the government, and capacity building requirements. More specifically, the readiness assessment looks at eight key areas, including the following: what or who is encouraging the need for M&E systems; motivations of champions; ownership and beneficiaries of systems; how the system will support better resource allocation and achievement of goals; dealing with negative or detrimental information generated by M&E; existing capacity to support M&E systems; and links between the M&E system and project, program, sector, and national goals.

A variety of lessons learned have already been generated by readiness assessments conducted in developing countries. For example, Bangladesh had few of the necessary requirements to begin building M&E systems. Assessments in Egypt and Romania, however, yielded vital information about likely entry points for beginning work on M&E. Highly placed political champions and strong, sustained political leadership were found to be key ingredients in the M&E mix. Other findings are that ministries may be at different stages in the ability to conduct M&E. It may be possible to move forward with M&E by working with pockets of innovation within government. Communication and coordination within and between government agencies and departments and among donors are also important. Developing countries may currently lack the institutional, human, and technical capacity to design, implement, and use results-based M&E systems; however, this is not an insurmountable obstacle. Training and technical assistance can be provided to remedy these difficulties. But no amount of training and technical assistance can substitute for indigenous political will. Often the political challenges are more difficult to overcome than the technical ones.

Choosing outcomes to monitor and evaluate is the second step. All governments must set goals, regardless of whether they have the capacity to conduct M&E. Outcomes will show which road to take. Building the M&E system is essentially a deductive process in which inputs, activities, outputs, and outcomes are all derived from the setting of longer term strategic goals. Likewise, setting outcomes is the first building block for developing a performance framework. Indicators, baselines, and targets will all flow from the outcomes.

Building M&E systems is a participatory political process, and key internal and external stakeholders should be consulted during the various steps of the model—including the readiness assessment, the setting of outcomes, establishment of indicators, and so on. Critical stakeholders and their main concerns will need to be identified. Existing problems need to be reformulated into a set of positive outcomes. Outcome statements need disaggregation, and each statement should contain only one goal. (This becomes important when developing indicators and targets). Agreeing on strategic priorities and outcomes will then help drive resource allocation.

Key performance indicators (Step 3) can only be set after agreeing upon and setting common goals. As with the case of outcomes, the interests of multiple stakeholders should be taken into account when selecting indicators. Indicators are the quantitative or qualitative variables that provide a simple and reliable means to measure achievement of goals. As stressed throughout the model, indicators should be developed for all levels of the results-based M&E system, meaning that indicators will be needed to monitor progress with respect to inputs, activities, outputs, outcomes, and impacts continually. Progress needs to be monitored at all levels of the system to provide feedback on areas of success, as well as areas where improvements may be needed.

Good performance indicators should be clear, relevant, economic, adequate, and monitorable ("CREAM"). Every indicator also needs it own separate M&E system, so caution should be exercised in setting too many indicators. Proxy and predesigned indicators may be adopted with full recognition of the pros and cons of using them.

Constructing good indicators often takes more than one try; arriving at the final set of indicators will take time. Piloting of indicators is essential. Indicators should be well thought through. And they should not be changed very often—this can lead to chaos in the overall data collection system. It should also be remembered that performance indicators can be used to provide continuous feedback, and can provide a wealth of performance information. Many developing countries are making progress in the performance indicator selection process.

Baselines, Step 4, are derived from outcomes and indicators. A performance baseline is basically information—qualitative or quantitative—that provides data at the beginning of, or just prior to, the monitoring period. It is used as a starting point from which to monitor future performance. Or, stated somewhat differently, baselines are the first measurements of the indicators. The challenge is to obtain adequate baseline information on each of the performance indicators for each outcome.

Eight key questions were outlined with respect to building baseline information: sources of data, data collection methods, who collects data, how often data are collected, cost and difficulty to collect data, who analyzes data, who reports data, and who uses data. Sources are who or what provide data—not the method of collecting data. Data sources may be primary or secondary.

There are a variety of data collection methods along the continuum from informal and less structured to more structured and formal methods. Data collection methods include conversation with concerned individuals, community interviews, reviews of official records, key informant interviews and participant observation, focus group interviews, direct observations, questionnaires, one time surveys, panel surveys, census, and field experiments. Data collection strategies necessarily involve some tradeoffs with respect to cost, precision, credibility, and timeliness.

Establishing baseline data on indicators is crucial in determining current conditions and in measuring future performance. Subsequent measurements from the baseline will provide important directional or trend data, and can help decisionmakers determine whether they are on track with respect to their goals.

Selecting results targets is Step 5. Targets are the interim steps on the way to a longer-term outcome. Again, a deductive reasoning process is involved, in which targets are based on outcomes, indicators, and baselines. Selecting targets should also entail a consultative, political, participatory process with key stakeholders. Targets can be determined by adding desired levels of improvement to baseline indicator levels (assuming a finite and expected level of inputs and activities). Targets should be feasible given all of the resource (input) considerations. Each indicator is expected to have only one target over a specified time frame.

Target setting is the final step in building the performance framework. The performance framework in turn becomes the basis for planning—with attendant implications for budgeting, resource allocation, staffing, and so forth. Performance frameworks have broad applicability and can be usefully employed as a format for National Poverty Reduction Strategies, project plans, programs, and policies.

Monitoring for results, Step 6, entails both implementation monitoring (means and strategies) and results monitoring. The key principles of building a monitoring system include recognizing the performance information needs at the policy, program, and project levels; the need for performance information to move both horizontally and vertically in the organization; identifying the demand for performance information at each level; and identifying the responsibilities at each level.

The major criteria for collecting quality performance data are the reliability, validity, and timeliness of the data. Every monitoring system needs ownership, management, maintenance, and credibility. Monitoring for results also calls for data collection and analysis of performance data. There will be quality assurance challenges in building monitoring systems. These are to be expected, so it is important to pretest data collection instruments and procedures.

Building the monitoring system framework means that each outcome will require an indicator, baseline, target, data collection strategy, data analysis, reporting plan, and identified users.

Achieving results through partnership is essential. Means and strategies will need to be set by multiple partners. One must look beyond one's own organizational unit when considering available inputs. Partnerships may be created elsewhere in one's own organization, or even with other organizations inside or outside of government.

Step 7 involves using evaluation information to support a results-based M&E system. Monitoring and evaluation are complementary, and both are needed in these systems. Evaluation information can be used for a variety of purposes: making resource allocation decisions; rethinking causality of problems; identifying emerging problems; supporting decisionmaking in selecting among competing alternatives;

supporting public sector reform; and so on. Evaluation information can also be relevant at all phases of a given policy, program, or project cycle.

The timing of evaluations is another consideration. Evaluative information is essential when: (a) regular measurements of key indicators suggest a sharp divergence between planned and actual performance; (b) performance indicators consistently suggest weak or no results from an initiative; (c) resource allocations are being made across policies, programs, or projects; and (d) similar projects, programs, or policies are reporting divergent evidence of outcomes.

There are seven different types of evaluation: performance logic chain, pre-implementation assessment, rapid appraisal, case study, meta-evaluation, impact evaluation, and process implementation. Each is appropriate to specific kinds of evaluation questions. Quality evaluations can be characterized by impartiality, usefulness, stakeholder involvement, value for money, feedback and dissemination, and technical adequacy.

Reporting findings, Step 8, is a critical step in the process. Continuous performance data and findings should be used to help improve policies, programs, and projects. In analyzing and reporting data, the more data measurements there are, the more certain one can be of trends, directions, and results. There is an implicit tradeoff between measurement frequency and measurement precision. Cost and capacity also come into play.

Performance data should be reported in comparison to earlier data and to the baseline. Also, to measure and compare against expected results, one must be able to compare present and past circumstances. Monitoring data are not causality data. They do not tell why an event occurred. It is also important to take into account the target audience when reporting findings.

Using findings, Step 9, will better inform the decisionmaking process. There are a wide range of uses of performance findings. For example, performance-based budgets budget to outputs, but also help decisionmakers manage to outcomes. Another noteworthy phenomenon is that if performance information is asked for, improved performance will occur. Using continuous findings can also help to generate knowledge and learning within governments and organizations. Building a credible knowledge management system is another key component of using findings.

There are a variety of strategies that can be used to share information. A good communication strategy is essential for disseminating and sharing information with key stakeholders. Sharing information with stakeholders helps to bring them into the business of government and can help to generate trust. This is, after all, one of the purposes of building a results-based M&E system.

Finally, Step 10 deals with sustaining the M&E system. We suggested there are six critical components to doing so: demand, clear roles and responsibilities, incentives, trustworthy and credible information, accountability, and capacity. We also examined the incentives and disincentives that may come into play in sustaining M&E systems. And we also know that problems will occur in implementing and sustaining the systems.

Summing Up

Results-based M&E systems are a powerful public management tool that can be used by governments and organizations to demonstrate accountability, transparency, and results. They can help to build and foster political and financial support and harmony for common policies, programs, and projects. And they can help the government build a solid knowledge base.

Importantly, results-based M&E systems can also bring about major political and cultural changes in the way governments and organizations operate—leading to improved performance, enhanced accountability and transparency, learning, and knowledge.

Results-based M&E systems should be considered a work in progress. Continuous attention, resources, and political commitment are needed to ensure the viability and sustainability of these systems. Building the cultural shift necessary to move an organization toward a results orientation takes time, commitment, and political will. In the absence of the efforts to undertake this transformation, the only way an organization can coast is downhill!

Building and sustaining a results-based M&E system takes time and effort. No system is perfect, and there are many different approaches, but the journey is worth the effort, and the rewards can be many.

Annexes I–VI

Assessing Performance-Based Monitoring and Evaluation Capacity:
An Assessment Survey for Countries, Development Institutions, and Their Partners

Introduction

Countries across the globe are facing pressures to reform the policies and practices of their public sectors. It is vital that an effective and efficient public sector contribute to sustainable development, economic growth, and the well-being of its citizens. Focusing on the performance of the government thus becomes an important factor in being able to achieve the desired goals of growth and economic and social development.

As governments begin to address these challenges, they will want to document their results so as to provide credible and trustworthy information both to their citizens and for their own management use. A results-based monitoring and evaluation (M&E) system is an important tool that will allow governments to acquire this evidence.

The Survey

This assessment survey is a diagnostic tool that focuses on the current capacity of a government to design and build a results-based M&E system. The intent is to learn what capacity and infrastructure now exist and what new capacity and infrastructure have to be built. The survey is divided into three sections: Incentives; Roles and Responsibilities; and Capacity Building.

The survey has been created as a tool to assist individual governments, the donor community, and their multiple development partners also involved in public sector reform to systematically address the prerequisites (present or not) for such an M&E system. With such information, the government, the donors, and partners can then address the challenges of what training, what organizational capacity building, and what sequencing of efforts will be needed to design and construct the necessary infrastructure to produce, collect, analyze, and report relevant performance information. In short, it provides the basis for an action plan to move forward within the country. Furthermore, this survey can help ensure that strategic goals are clearly framed, that targets and baseline data are understood as critical, and that the construction of relevant indicators needs to be identified in the context of building the M&E system.

The information is to be gathered from key informants (government officials, members of civil society, NGOs, and so forth) in the country. It is advised that the survey be administered in person by someone familiar with M&E capacity building as there are a number of open-ended questions where follow up and clarification questions will be useful. The survey consists of 40 questions and it is estimated (from the pilot) that it will take about 65 minutes to complete.

Background Information:
Name of Respondent:_____
Position:_____
Organization:_____
Years in Current Position: _____
Years in Current Organization:_____
Date of Interview: _____
Interview Conducted
By:_____

Part I: The Incentives For Designing and Building a Performance-Based M&E System

1. How would you describe the process of setting priority goals and objectives in the central ministries? In the sector or line ministries?

2. Can you identify any organizations that regularly ask for information on how well the government is performing?
   - Ministry of Finance
   - Ministry of Planning
   - Prime Minister's Office
   - President's Office
   - Individual Sector or Line Ministries
   - Parliament
   - Supreme (National) Audit Organization
   - Donors
   - Private Sector
   - Media
   - NGOs
   - Citizens

3. Does the Ministry of Finance or Ministry of Planning require any type of performance-based information on government projects, programs, and policies be provided by the sector ministries and other agencies in submitting their annual budget proposals?
   - Information on activities or outputs (expected from projects and programs)
   - Information on outcomes or results (longer-term goals)
   - Information from evaluations or other formal reviews
   - Expenditure data on priority goals for the government

4. Do any sector ministries or other agencies have requirements for reporting how well projects and programs are performing within their own organization? If so, which ones and what are the requirements?

5. Are there senior officials who advocate collecting and using information on government performance, for example, the Minister of Finance or Minister of Planning, the Minister of Health, or Advisors to the President?

6. Are there senior officials that would resist requests for producing this kind of performance-based information? Reasons for the resistance?

7. Do any sector or line ministries undertake or commission evaluations or formal reviews of the performance of projects, programs, or policies in their ministry? If so, which ones and what types of reviews?
   - formal evaluations
   - client satisfaction surveys
   - performance audits
   - performance-based budget reviews
   - other

8. Are there formal requests from the parliament for information on the performance of the government to be supplied by the Ministry of Finance or Ministry of Planning or any of the sector ministries?
   - for budget hearings
   - for parliament deliberations on the performance of government programs
   - for crafting of legislation

9. Can you cite evidence of use by the parliament of the performance information from the government:
   - for hearings
   - for oversight of government performance
   - for the drafting of legislation

10. Does the parliament have a "Public Accounts Committee" or a "Public Expenditure/Budget Committee?" If so, what are the functions of these committees? Do they use performance information as part of their activities?

11. Has civil society (media, NGOs, private sector, and so forth) requested information on

government performance from the government? If so, please describe.

12. Has civil society published or broadcasted any information on government performance? If so, please describe.

13. How easy (or not) has it been for members of civil society to obtain information related to the performance of the government?

14. Are NGOs or others in civil society collecting data for their own use or as external monitors on how well the government is performing? If so, please describe.

15. Does any "freedom of information" legislation now exist? If not, is any such legislation planned?

16. What information do the donors request of the government on how well their individually sponsored projects and programs are performing?

17. Do the donors also ask for any other performance-based information from the government? If so, please describe.

18. How would you describe the audit function for the national government? Is there an independent audit organization in the government and what is its function? Do individual ministries each have an internal audit function and what is its role?

19. Are there any sector ministries that you would suggest represent a good model for using performance-based information to manage the activities and programs?

20. Are there any public sector reforms (with or without donor support) that are taking place in the national government that include efforts to strengthen systems to collect and manage information related to government performance?

21. How would you assess the government's I-PRSP and full PRSP (as well as CDF, if relevant) documents in terms of their inclu-

sion of a system to track and report on the PRSP goals?

22. Can you describe the status of the government's efforts to implement an M&E system within their PRSP (and CDF, if relevant) initiatives?

Part II: Roles and Responsibilities for Assessing Performance of the Government

23. Are the regional and local levels of government collecting information on their performance to support budget expenditure decisions or to enhance their program management?

24. Are there any evident links between the Ministry of Finance and Ministry of Planning fiscal year budget allocations and sector or line ministry performance?

25. Are there any formal roles or responsibilities for civil society in the national government's planning processes?

26. Are there any formal roles or responsibilities for civil society in the government's procedures for fiscal year budget allocation decisions?

27. Is there any evident role for development assistance or donor agencies in the national planning process and setting of strategic goals? And in the national fiscal year budget allocation decisions?

28. How would you describe the fiscal year budget monitoring that the Ministry of Finance or Ministry of Planning do of the sector or line ministries—none, light, medium, heavy? Can you give some examples to support your choice?

29. Is there any evidence that donor reporting requirements either conflict with one another or impose duplication for the government in meeting these requirements?

30. What kind of financial expenditure data are collected—and by whom—on the costs and

outputs of the functions and activities of the national government?

31. Can you describe what financial expenditure data are collected—and by whom—on the costs and outputs of the functions and activities of regional or local governments?

32. How available are expenditure data to persons and organizations outside the government? To civil society, to the media, to NGOs, to others?

33. Who in the government is responsible for the collection of socioeconomic and poverty data for the country? With whom are these data shared?

34. What are the roles and responsibilities of the national statistics office?
   - In what areas are statistics collected?
   - At what levels in the country (city, regional, national)?
   - To whom are the statistical data provided?
   - What information is or is not made public?
   - What organizations assist in collecting statistical information?
   - What special surveys are conducted, for example, Household Income and Expenditure Survey (HIES), HIV/AIDS, and others?

35. What are the roles and responsibilities of the National Audit Office?
   - What is its authority to audit central and sector or line ministries?
   - Does it have authority at regional and local levels of government?
   - To whom are findings reported?
   - Are these findings made public?
   - Does the National Audit Office have any oversight on the quality of information produced in the government?

36. Are there any organizational units in the national government that have evaluation expertise and undertake evaluations?

37. What data systems do the planning units within the central and sector or line ministries have available to them?
   - budget data
   - output data
   - outcome or impact data
   - performance audits
   - financial audits
   - project and program completion reports
   - donor data systems
   - other

Part III: Capacity Building Requirements for a Performance-based M&E System

38. How would you assess the skills of civil servants in the national government in each of the following six areas:
   - project and program management
   - data analysis
   - policy analysis
   - setting project and program goals
   - budget management
   - performance auditing

39. Are you aware of any technical assistance, capacity building, or training in M&E now underway or done in the past two years for any level of government (national, regional, or local)? Please describe who provided this help. Has it been related to:
   - the CDF or PRSP process
   - strengthening of budget systems
   - strengthening of the public sector administration
   - government decentralization
   - civil service reform
   - individual central or line ministry reform?

40. Are you aware of any institutes, research centers, private organizations, or universities in the country that have some capacity to provide technical assistance and training for civil servants and others in performance-based M&E?

Readiness Assessment
Toward Results-Based Monitoring and Evaluation in Egypt

A World Bank Diagnostic Mission
June 1–9, 2001
Cairo, Egypt

Contents

Executive Summary

Background. In September 2000, the Board of Directors of the World Bank approved a program to strengthen results-based monitoring and evaluation in the operations of the Bank and its borrowers. Both borrowers and the Bank need good information on performance to allocate resources wisely, design and implement projects and programs effectively and evaluate the effects of their activities on the achievement of development goals.

For the World Bank, this program, called the Monitoring and Evaluation Improvement Program, is particularly important at a time when the Bank is shifting toward more programmatic lending and encouraging greater transparency and accountability for results on the part of its borrowers. Investments within the country-led Comprehensive Development Framework and Poverty Reduction Strategy Papers depend upon tracking results (or the outcomes of government), rather than traditional monitoring and evaluation approaches, which typically track inputs and processes. Results-based monitoring and evaluation focus management on performance and on progress towards these desired development outcomes. Thus, this program also supports the Bank's strategy of encouraging countries to monitor progress on international development goals.

The Government of Egypt, through the Minister of Finance, has expressed a desire to participate in the program. The Minister is eager to reform the budget to achieve a greater focus on improving the government's performance both in efficiency and effectiveness measures. The Minister and others in the Government of Egypt understand that a new focus on results is both necessary and consistent with the many efforts underway to reform public management systems the world over.

Methodology. For those countries participating in the Monitoring and Evaluation Improvement Program, the first action undertaken by the World Bank is to conduct a short diagnostic study in order to evaluate the status of results-based monitoring and evaluation in that country and to identify opportunities for strengthening performance-based efforts both underway and planned. The World Bank, (through its Operational Policy and Country Services Organization) conducted a diagnostic mission to Egypt on June 1-9, 2001 (see Annex A).

The diagnostic team met with many key government officials, academics, donors and others outside the government and reviewed a variety of reports and documents to learn how a shift to results based monitoring and evaluation could strengthen effective public management in Egypt (see Annex B). The team looked for organizations and parts of organizations that are beginning to move toward results-based monitoring and evaluation in order to achieve development goals. The team mapped monitoring and evaluation efforts currently underway and did an assessment of research and data collection capacity inside and outside the government. With an eye to finding opportunities for strengthening monitoring and evaluation, the team looked for evidence of performance-based budgeting and for innovation in these areas. At the request of H.E. the Minister of Finance, the team sought to identify practical steps to encourage the development of a "climate of performance" in the Egyptian government.

The team's considerations included:

- What is driving the need for results-based monitoring and evaluation systems in the Egypt (incentives/demands)?
- Where in the government does accountability for effective (and efficient) delivery of programs lie?
- Is there a codified (through statute or mandate) strategy or organization in the government for tracking development goals?
- Where does capacity lie with the requisite skills for designing and using results-based monitoring and evaluation systems in the pilot country? How has this capacity (or lack-

thereof) contributed to the use of monitoring and evaluation in the country context?

Areas Recommended for Moving Forward

First, Establish cross-ministerial leadership group to promote performance and results-based monitoring and evaluation. A leadership team of ministers who are committed to change in their own organizations could accelerate the adoption of results-based monitoring and evaluation and introduction of a more results-based budget process. Such a group, under the leadership of the Minister of Finance, could play several key roles, for example: developing an overall strategy to guide the effort; providing guidance and an evaluation framework for pilot activity in individual ministries and other organizations; and developing a plan to expand pilot activity and share best practices and lessons across ministries. This group should determine whether mechanisms that other countries have used to give impetus and mandates to reform efforts—such as presidential decrees, amendments to budget laws, and legislation—should be pursued in the Egyptian context.

Second, Support the initiative of the National Council for Women to monitor and evaluate the implementation of gender-related initiatives in the 2002-2006 plan. Under the patronage of the First Lady, the Council has worked very effectively with the Ministry of Planning and line ministries as they have developed their plans. We believe that the next step of monitoring and evaluating implementation presents a particular opportunity to be a catalyst for change across several ministries. Because the Council includes a broad range of actors from inside and outside government, including academics, the private sector, non-governmental organizations, the media, and concerned ministries, it can help promote consensus about measurement issues and transparency in reporting on results.

Third, Build capacity to support reform. No country has succeeded with a significant reform effort without a dedicated, well-organized team to support it. A core team could support the ministerial group and the pilots so as to minimize bureaucratic red tape and expedite innovation and learning; identify lessons learned; and determine ways to mainstream these lessons into the government. The team could draw on the career staff of several ministries and upon the significant resources in the Egyptian academic and non-governmental community.

Fourth, Modernize statistical policy. Despite the manifest capacity of the Egyptian statistical system, there is evidence that it lags behind both in the quality of statistics produced and the attention given to the needs of its clients. Egypt should review its statistical law with a view to separating the responsibilities of the Central Agency for Public Mobilization and Statistics (CAPMAS) for military mobilization from its role as an independent statistical agency. Many countries employ a national statistical commission or similar coordinating body to set policies and standards for the production and dissemination of official statistics. Egypt should adopt a similar strategy for coordinating data policies and standards. Such a commission should include in its membership both representatives of the agencies charged with producing statistics and senior statisticians drawn from universities and the private sector.

Fifth, Increase client focus. The value of statistics lies not in their production, but in their use. It should be the goal of all producers of statis-

tics to encourage their widespread dissemination, within the government and to non-governmental users. To better understand the needs of their clients, agencies responsible for producing statistics could create advisory groups to represent users. Another useful function of such groups would be to encourage the exchange of information between data users, who may find solutions to common problems. Such advisory groups would meet regularly with the managers of statistical units in the agencies. At the highest level, an advisory group to CAPMAS or the proposed statistical commission would provide input on the needs of all users of Egyptian statistical information.

Sixth, Participate in the IMF Special Data Dissemination System. As Egypt prepares to enter international capital markets, it will become more important for it to produce credible statistics. An important step in this direction would be subscription to the Special Data Dissemination Standard. (See the IMF disseminations standard bulletin board: http://dsbb.imf.org.) The SDDS requires countries to adopt international standards for reporting on major economic and financial statistics and to maintain a current listing of its policies and standards. Working toward SDDS participation would provide a powerful driver for modernizing Egypt's statistical system.

Finally, Donor support. There is an important role for donors to play in supporting Egypt's shift to results-based monitoring and evaluation with training and technical assistance. In doing so, donors can draw both on in-country expertise in universities and think tanks as well as the substantial international experience in results-based approaches.

Background

In September 2000, the Board of Directors of the World Bank approved a program to strengthen results-based monitoring and evaluation in the operations of the Bank and its borrowers. Both borrowers and the Bank need good information on performance to allocate resources wisely, design and implement projects and programs effectively and evaluate the effects of their activities on the achievement of development goals.

For the World Bank, this program, called the Monitoring and Evaluation Improvement Program, is particularly important at a time when the Bank is shifting toward more programmatic lending and encouraging greater transparency and accountability for results on the part of its borrowers. Investments within the country-led Comprehensive Development Framework and Poverty Reduction Strategy Papers depend upon tracking results (or the outcomes of government), rather than traditional monitoring and evaluation approaches, which typically track inputs and processes. Results-based monitoring and evaluation focus management on performance and on progress towards these desired development outcomes. Thus, this program also supports the Bank's strategy of encouraging countries to monitor progress on the international development goals.

The Government of Egypt, through the Minister of Finance, has expressed a desire to participate in the program. The Minister is eager to reform the budget to achieve a greater focus on improving the government's performance both in efficiency and effectiveness measures. The Minister and others in the Government of Egypt understand that a new focus on results is both necessary and consistent with the many efforts underway to reform public management systems the world over.

The International Experience

For the past two decades, governments in developed countries and, more recently, developing countries have been "in search of results." According to a recent OECD review," Improved performance of the public sector is a central factor in maintaining welfare of individuals and the competitiveness of the economy. Performance management is the key aspect of public sector reforms of many OECD Member countries."

The strategies used to achieve greater performance vary across countries, however, there appears to be a number of similar elements that contribute to a successful shift to a results-based culture. Among these elements are:
- A clear mandate for making such a shift;
- The presence of strong leadership, usually through a strong champion or champions at the most senior level of government;
- The use of reliable information for policy and management decisions;
- Economic pressures and other incentives for change (often, a concerned citizenry or the need to reduce the cost of burdensome civil service payrolls);
- Clear links to budget and other resource allocation decisions;
- Involvement of civil society as an important partner with government; and
- Pockets of innovation that can serve as beginning practices or pilot programs.

There appears to be no one right way to introduce performance management into the many institutions and policy-making activities of government. Often, depending on the presence (or absence) of the elements listed above, governments try one or more of the following strategies: 1) comprehensive or whole-of-government approach, 2) sector specific, or 3) customer focused.

In the comprehensive approach, a number of countries have introduced strategic plans, performance indicators, and annual performance plans over a period of years and integrated then into annual budget documents (Australia, United States). Other approaches include putting program performance indicators in the annual financial reports that can be audited (Finland, Sweden, United States) or using performance agreements between ministers and heads of government agencies (New Zealand, United Kingdom). Argentina and Romania are also piloting performance-based budgeting strategies. Here, performance indicators for government programs are linked to allocated budget envelopes; reported in budget annexes at the start of each budgeted year; and audited at year's end. And some countries, such as Malaysia, have embraced the total quality management approach, focusing on process reengineering and achieving strict quality standards.

While most of the OECD countries have adopted a whole-of-government approach to introduce performance management, many countries, like the United States, began with performance pilots. By first piloting in a few programs and sectors, governments hoped to create favorable conditions for public sector learning and experimentation before " mainstreaming" the effort. Other countries find that moving forward in those sectors where a clear reform effort is underway (for example, the health sector in Bangladesh, Ghana and the Kyrgyz Republic) allows innovative efforts to move forward, regardless of whether commitments have been made by the president or prime minister to im-

plement a more comprehensive strategy. Still other countries have found it useful to focus on the customers or beneficiaries of government services or on one client group, such as women/girls or children. This strategy includes developing key performance indicators within line ministries with a specific focus on improving those government programs to support a particular group of citizens. This strategy can also help to move forward a national agenda in a program area, rather than waiting for the entire government to embrace performance management.

Other strategies used by governments to introduce performance management include:

- Selection of free-standing authorities, granting them greater flexibility to use resources and hold their leaders responsible for results. Examples: Next Steps Agencies, Performance Based Organizations.
- Encouragement and recognition of pilot activities within many organizations that can lead the way and be replicated in other places. Example: Reinvention Laboratories.
- Introduction of total quality management: this model, developed by industry to improve manufacturing processes has been applied in a few countries to public sector reform, generally after the reform process is well underway. The focus of quality management on customer requirements is relevant to reform efforts at all stages. Example: Malaysia.

No strategy can simply be mapped from one country or situation to another. Furthermore, in practice, the strategy that is used by a given country at a particular point in time may be a combination of one or more approaches like these. Furthermore, reform efforts are multi-year affairs and strategies inevitably evolve over time.

Methodology

For those countries participating in the Monitoring and Evaluation Improvement Program, the first action undertaken by the World Bank is to conduct a short diagnostic study in order to evaluate the status of results-based monitoring and evaluation in that country and to identify opportunities for strengthening performance-based efforts both underway and planned. The World Bank, (through its Operational Policy and Country Services Organization - OPCS) conducted a diagnostic mission to Egypt on June 1–9, 2001 (see Terms of Reference for this mission in Annex A).

The team looked for organizations and parts of organizations that are beginning to move toward results-based monitoring and evaluation in order to achieve development goals. The team mapped monitoring and evaluation efforts currently underway and did an assessment of research and data collection capacity inside and outside the government. With an eye to finding opportunities for strengthening monitoring and evaluation, the team looked for evidence of performance-based budgeting and for innovation in these areas. At the request of H.E. the Minister of Finance, the team sought to identify practical steps to encourage the development of a "climate of performance" in the Egyptian government.

The team's considerations included:

- What is driving the need for results-based monitoring and evaluation systems in the Egypt (incentives/demands)?
- Where in the government does accountability for effective (and efficient) delivery of programs lie?
- Is there a codified (through statute or mandate) strategy or organization in the government for tracking development goals?

- Where does capacity lie with the requisite skills for designing and using results-based monitoring and evaluation systems in the pilot country? How has this capacity (or lack-there-of) contributed to the use of monitoring and evaluation in the country context?

Summary of Findings

The team found significant interest in moving toward a "climate of performance." This was described in various ways in our interviews, but the interviewees seemed to have in common a desire to use good information to allocate resources, assess progress, and achieve development goals in the most effective and efficient way. Outlined below are the major findings from the diagnostic assessment. In each section the team will present both opportunities noted and potential obstacles for shifting the focus of government in Egypt to achieving results.

Leadership

Successful efforts to shift the focus of government to results have enjoyed high levels of sustained leadership. Successful reforms have generally been led from the executive branch – from the Cabinet Office (United Kingdom), the Treasury (New Zealand), the Vice President (United States), or the Chief Minister (Andhra Pradesh, India).

In Egypt, the team noted the interest expressed in shifting to a climate of performance on the part of many senior government officials, including the Prime Minister and the Cabinet. The President himself has called for better information to support economic decision-making. The First Lady chairs the National Council for Women, which is developing a system to monitor and evaluate efforts across many ministries to enhance the status and condition of women in Egypt.

The Minister of Finance is playing a key leadership role. He has a strong desire to reform the Egyptian budget to better support performance. In meetings with the diagnostic team, he underscored the importance he places on giving increased attention to improving the management of public expenditures, noting that "I want to be able to tell Egyptian taxpayers that the government is spending their money efficiently and effectively."

For an effort to be successful, it is also important that the line ministries—who are responsible for resource expenditures and overseeing the implementation of specific programs—be fully engaged. The team found significant interest in monitoring and evaluating for results on the part of several line ministers. The Minister of Electricity, who led reform efforts at the International Atomic Energy Agency before assuming his current responsibilities, recommended that a group of ministers concerned with improving the management of critical infrastructure and public utilities take on a leadership role.

A recent review of the Egyptian civil service underscores the importance of the leadership of such ministers in a few countries, "The most important point is the interest and commitment shown by the head of the organization—the minister or the senior-most bureaucrat in the organization . . . the ministers of Egypt enjoy considerable degrees of freedom and influence in their respective ministries to introduce changes in organization and management of the personnel. 'Hands-on-management' concept is really practiced by strong executives in Egyptian government"[1]

Finally, in many countries, the legislative arm of government has also played an important leadership role, by enacting a reform framework (New Zealand), key legislation (such as the Government Performance and Results Act in the United States), allowing flexibilities and incentives, or conducting studies, audits or hearings on government performance. This aspect was beyond the scope of the team's exploration at this time; it may be useful to address the role of the Egyptian legislature, the People's Assembly, the Shura Council and the Central Audit Organization, which reports to them, in the future.

Incentives or Key Drivers

In most countries that have moved to a results-based system, there has usually been a clear driver for reform. For some, entry into the European Union provides an incentive for change. In countries seeking debt relief, change has been driven by a requirement to develop a Poverty Reduction Strategy Paper, which includes a well-constructed performance-based monitoring and evaluation framework of indicators and performance measures. For some developed and developing countries, significant deficits have brought cuts in government spending and forced a greater focus on government efficiency and effective allocation of resources. For others, public dissatisfaction with the cost and performance of government has become a political issue, resulting in political commitments that have driven change.

The team did not find any single compelling driver of change in Egypt. During the second half of the 1990s, economic growth has been robust. Although the deficit reached up to 3 percent of GDP in 1998 and there are other qualitative weaknesses in economic performance, economic drivers are not sufficient to create a compelling need for change. Rather than a single driver, however, the people we interviewed suggested a variety of reasons that are driving different actors in the public sector to give greater consideration to performance:

- *Egyptian-European Partnership Agreement.* The Prime Minister has recently stressed the importance of completing plans to modernize the State in conjunction with the signing of the Egyptian-European Partnership Agreement. This agreement is also the reason for the urgency of an industrial modernization program to prepare Egyptian industries to compete with foreign products;
- *Presidential decree corporatizing economic authorities.* The economic authorities such as the Rail Road Authority , the Cairo Water Authority and the Electricity Authority currently receive LE 3 billion in annual subsidies and more than LE 280 billion in cumulative investments. The government aims to improve the performance of these authorities and move them towards a privatization strategy; and
- *Donor interest.* Several donors have an explicit interest in enhanced performance of the public sector and are providing related training, technology and technical support (see below). The World Bank has identified the creation of a more results-based budget process as one of its priorities.

Mandates or Clear Authorities

Countries that have embarked on a significant program to shift to a results focus have not only had a reason to change, they have generally established a formal mandate to do so. This has taken a variety of forms, for example legislation, presidential or prime ministerial decrees, or executive orders. In some cases, countries have found that sufficient authority exists but that existing mandates have not been fully implemented.

In Egypt, there are a number of individual organizations or groups with specific mandates.

For example, Presidential Decree No. 90 established the National Council for Women in February 2000 and directs the Council to "follow up on and evaluate the implementation of public policy on women's issues" in addition to advising on policy and other responsibilities. This council, chaired by the First Lady is composed of thirty members from government, academia, media and other organizations. It is now working with the Ministry of Planning and the line ministries as they are preparing Egypt's next five-year plan to assure that the issues that most affect women are reflected in that document. The Council intends to put in place a system to monitor and evaluate the implementation of the plan to fulfill the mandate specified in the Presidential Decree.

The Information and Decision Support Center of the Egyptian Cabinet has the mandate to establish and operate information centers in all of the governorates of Egypt to support decision-making. An additional example is the Central Audit Organization (CAO) with a long-standing legal mandate to conduct audits of performance as well as financial auditing. In this case, however, the people we spoke with reported that CAO is almost exclusively focused on financial issues.

In summary, the team did not identify any over-arching mandate in Egypt that would guide a substantial shift to results-based monitoring and evaluation. Moreover, the team did not identify existing legislation or decrees that provide the framework and authority for broad change.

A Well-Defined Strategy

A key criterion for a successful shift towards results requires the development of a well-communicated and executable strategy. This strategy should be directed by senior government leadership and embody a clear mandate for informed decision-making and a focus on achieving desired results of government. Supporting the strategy should be an implementation plan that includes clear goals, direction and timelines.

Recognizing that a shift to a performance orientation will require a significant multi-year effort, Egypt's Minister of Finance has begun to define an approach with several aspects. He wants to draw on external examples of reform and recently supported the visit of a team of government officials to Malaysia to look at its experience. He has identified a few activities underway that could become pilot tests for performance budgeting. He recognizes the importance of using good data for monitoring and evaluating the effort. This is an excellent starting point for developing an effective strategy.

The next critical element is to develop a broader strategy for change that is both effective and bold, yet practical and feasible. Such a strategy should provide a framework for various ongoing efforts to shift to a results-based system for the use of public expenditures as well as serve to stimulate and guide additional initiatives. There is no single answer for what constitutes the best strategy. Rather the leadership team should develop a strategy that reflects the constraints and opportunities in Egypt at this time and start the process of change.

In developing its strategy, Egypt may wish to consider a number of lessons from international experience while building on its own considerable experience and expertise. First and foremost, a successful strategy will need to be clear about its objectives. It must be simple and easy to communicate. It should engage and inspire government employees to help bring about change as it will not be possible to increase the efficiency and effectiveness of the Egyptian government while ignoring the millions of civil servants who do the work and interact with citizens. A successful strategy should be responsive to the real needs of citizens as they interact with their government. And it should include frequent monitoring and adjustment to keep it on track. A successful strategy should support the leaders of change—giving them sufficient training and coaching, allowing them to take risks and be recognized for successes. Finally, of course, a successful strategy is one that is turned into actions, brings about real changes in the performance of government, and increases the efficient and effective use of resources

Pockets of Innovation

The team found a number of pockets of innovation in performance measurement in Egypt showing that it is feasible to shift to a results-based approach in the Egyptian context and providing useful starting points for a broader effort. Several ministries have ongoing pilot activities or centers of excellence that include a greater emphasis on results. The team heard about initiatives in the Ministry of Electricity and Energy and in the Petroleum Authority as well as the Broadcasting Authority. The team met extensively with the Minister of Health and Population, to discuss his strategy for collecting real-time health statistics to support better health policy-making.

The Ministry of Finance itself has identified several pilot activities that are introducing new approaches to management. For example, the National Center for Education Research and Development has introduced a number of innovations in a program to reduce educational disparities and enhance quality of education. With support from the European Union, the World Bank and the Government of Egypt, the Center is working with fifteen governorates, mapping areas with the greatest need and consulting local communities on their priorities. The Ministry of Finance is also adopting a results focus in its Debt Management Unit and in the Sales Tax Unit where it is seeking to introduce a program of total quality management.

One of the most innovative approaches we saw was the assessment system of the Social Fund for Development, an Egyptian government organization that administers funds from some seventeen donors for development projects. To help guide their allocation of resources, they have developed a Community Needs Assessment application, which includes a set of composite indicators for health status, education, infrastructure and housing conditions, and other basic needs. Each index combines information on service levels and the impact on peoples' well being. The resulting indexes, disaggregated to the district level, will be combined with information on population size and restrictions imposed by donors, to allocate Social Fund resources. The allocation system is currently undergoing sensitivity testing before being deployed.

The Cabinet's Information and Decision Support Center is providing technical support for decision-making to Egypt's Cabinet and to its governors and district officials through a national network of information centers. The Center has integrated national databases and is now making them available to local government officials via CD-ROMs and to the public via the Internet. The Center also produces monthly economic bulletins and an annual statistical report on the nation and on each governorate. It assists local government entities to produce annual statistical reports and to develop and maintain local websites. The Center has launched one of Egypt's first e-government projects that will allow citizens to do government transactions online and at kiosks.

At the same time, we found that these efforts to shift to results-based management remain fragmented and disconnected (further discussion of this issue is found below). There is little incentive or opportunity to share information or lessons across organizational boundaries.

Information Driving Decision-Making

During the team's visit to the National Center for Educational Research and Development, we saw a clear example of a key decision-maker using information to make policy. During the meeting with the team, the Minister of Education called to ask the Center's director for the results of a review of international practice on the frequency of student testing. He had asked her to carry out the review as input to his consideration of changes to Egypt's practice of annual testing. This real-time example of a senior policy-maker seeking out good information to support decisions is the hallmark of a modern results-based monitoring and evaluation system.

Through interviews we learned of other innovative applications of research and statistical indicators for improving the quality of decision-making in the Egyptian government. Many of the International Development Goals and indicators to measure the goals are incorporated in data sets used by Egyptian agencies to monitor their programs (see Annex C). For example, the Ministry of Health routinely tracks a set of performance indicators to monitor the success of its overall program. However, according to our interviews, such examples of using research and statistical information as inputs to decision-making are still the exception rather than the rule. One particularly pessimistic review of the research environment in Egypt noted, "The research outputs are not usually considered by the policymakers, no matter how relevant the research topics to the problems that the country is facing, or how sound the analyses and conclusions reached. In Egypt, the design and application of policies are neither supported nor guided by serious research."[2]

Research Capacity. *Egypt has significant research and statistical capacity and well-trained researchers in both public and private institutions, which are a significant resource for decision-makers seeking to shift to a greater focus on results. One of the private centers, Egypt's Economic Research Forum, is the regional hub for the World Bank-sponsored Global Development Network. It is being considered as a candidate to become an International Center of Excellence. These Centers will be part of the "Evaluation Partnership Program for Monitoring and Evaluation Capacity Development" that is in place between the Policy and Operations Evaluation Department of the Ministry of Foreign Affairs (Government of the Netherlands) and the World Bank's Operations Evaluation Department.*

The Social Research Center at American University of Cairo has developed a program of training courses for evaluators and its director is leading the monitoring and evaluation effort with the National Council for Women. In addition, the Public Administration Research and Consultation Center at Cairo University has a program of research and training on public administration including recent programs on leadership for the top management of Egypt's Electricity Authority, training on decision support for Egypt's People's Assembly and Shura Coun-

cil and a program for journalists on covering the public budget.

Statistical System. Egypt's statistical system has a long history, and has grown into a large and multifaceted system, capable of carrying out complex studies on a large scale. The value of high-quality statistical information is recognized inside and outside the government. The expansion of information communication technology throughout Egypt has increased the capacity of the statistical system and resulted in innovative efforts to use statistics for planning, monitoring, evaluating, and decision support. As Egypt moves to implement performance-based management techniques, one of its strengths is its statistical system. At the same time, there are weaknesses in the system that must be addressed if Egypt is to move forward rapidly and with confidence in the quality of its official statistics.

Sources of Official Statistics. The principle sources of official statistics in Egypt are the Central Agency for Public Mobilization and Statistics (CAPMAS), the Ministry of Planning, the line ministries (including Economy, Finance, Health, and Education), and the Central Bank. In addition numerous studies that have produced specialized databases have been carried out by academic research centers and non-governmental organizations, often in collaboration with government agencies. CAPMAS has two roles in the statistical system: it collects and disseminates statistics and it is the authorizing agency for all statistical research carried out in Egypt. In the latter capacity, CAPMAS reviews all proposed survey instruments; it may require changes to or deletion of items on the instrument; and it receives a copy of all data collected through authorized instruments. In addition, CAPMAS' role as the agency for public mobilization has disposed it to a very restrictive view of what statistics may be published, viewing many official statistics as having military value. Likewise it has been very sensitive to the types of questions asked by private researchers. However, in the past five years, we were told, CAPMAS has adopted a more liberal standard for what data can be disseminated and routinely authorizes questionnaires.

Expansion of Statistical Activities. Although Egypt appears to have a highly centralized statistical system, we learned during our mission that many agencies are developing their own data systems, which in some cases go far beyond the traditional collection of administrative statistics. For example, because the Ministry of Health and Population regards health as a comprehensive concept involving both physical and social well being, it is developing a program for collection of health and social statistics at the household level. This complements its management information system which, when complete, will integrate health records from over 4500 primary care units into a national database. Others are proceeding to develop new statistical measures, which are not available from CAPMAS or other sources. The Ministry of the Economy, for example, has begun work on production indexes and a set of "leading indicators" for the economy. The expansion of statistical activities beyond the traditional collection and reporting systems raises new challenges for maintaining standards and ensuring comparability across different data sets.

Quality of Statistics. During our interviews, we heard many concerns raised about the reliability of statistics in Egypt. Some of these concerns were based on well-documented inadequacies: the fiscal statistics from the Ministry of Finance are not complete (because of numerous extra budgetary items) and are slow in closing; national account statistics (now produced by the Ministry of Planning with input from CAPMAS) are not compiled to current standards, are not complete, and have been arbitrarily revised. In both cases, technical assistance projects supported by donors are underway and should result in substantial improvements. In other cases, the doubts concerned the appropriate definitions of and methodologies for calculating poverty, illiteracy, and unemployment rates. The lack of faith in the quality of statistics has a corrosive effect on public dialogue: debates over how to address the serious issues of development devolve into conflicting claims about the accuracy of the statistics.

The Role of CAPMAS. Concerns were also raised about the role of CAPMAS. Academic researchers and others outside the government felt that its role as the authorizing agency for survey research exerts a deadening influence on independent studies. CAPMAS' capacities, especially for executing surveys, is widely recognized, but it is not viewed as an innovator or a source of leadership in advancing statistics in Egypt. Despite the liberalization of dissemination rules, CAPMAS appears to see its principal role to be the regulation, rather than the creation, of information. Despite its leading role as the national statistical office of Egypt, CAPMAS does not participate in international statistical forums, such as the United Nations Statistical Commission, nor has it expressed interest in joining the IMF's General Data Dissemination System or working toward the Special Data Dissemination Standard.

Measuring Organizational Performance. What the team did not find was any systematic collection and use of data to measures client satisfaction. While these are not development "results," they are important measures of organizational performance. Experience has shown the importance of a balanced scorecard of results that includes these aspects alongside the major societal and financial outcomes that are expected.

Links to Resource Decisions

The budget is a key instrument in any country for making choices about priorities and implementing governmental policy. Recently, as an OECD official noted, "There has been a quiet revolution in the methods and philosophies of budgeting that began in a few developed countries in the 1980s, and it is being felt around the world. Most countries have embarked on some sort of reform to budgeting aimed at improvements in macroeconomic stability, improved prioritization of expenditure and more effective policy implementation."

Egypt's budget process does not currently lend itself to prioritizing expenditures or effectively assuring implementation of policy. Focused on finances and other inputs, neither the budget process nor its format facilitate linking funds with their intended result. In addition, the budget approval process used by the People's Assembly, the controls exercised by the Ministry of Finance and the oversight of the Central Auditing Organization are focused on financial aspects without regard to their relation to outcomes.

The World Bank has identified the budget as a priority area for reform in Egypt, noting that "despite robust economic growth, social outcomes—especially in health and education—have not improved at a commensurate rate . . . The first step to ensuring that the nation's resources are better spent in these areas is by taking steps to improve the results orientation of the budget, especially the recurrent budget."[3] The current budget structure and process is not conducive to a performance orientation. The *Egypt Social and Structural Review* identifies several issues that suggest the magnitude of the challenge that will be required to move to a budget process that is focused on performance:

- *Prioritization of Expenditures.* The current budget process does not include common approaches to encouraging prioritization such as providing budget ceilings or envelopes to encourage line ministries to prioritize budget requests. In addition, ad hoc budget negotiations and revisions during the year further undermine the implementation of budget priorities established by the Cabinet and the People's Assembly.

- *Incentives for Efficient Service Delivery.* The budget process does not reward efficient service delivery either in budget negotiations or through incentives such as sharing of savings or allowing greater flexibility in how resources may be used.

- *Transparency.* Information about the Egyptian budget is restricted to a high degree. The budget approved by the People's Assembly is not made public; sections of budget documents are made available on a "need to know" basis, basic financial statistics are not published or published in a very aggregated form and audit reports are narrowly disseminated and do not include information on the effectiveness and efficiency of expenditures.

- *Comprehensiveness.* Responsibility for the preparation and execution of the Egyptian budget is divided between the Ministries of Finance and Plan (see table). This makes responsible fiscal policy and realistic planning difficult since investment projects can have a large impact on overall budget levels and make it difficult to project recurrent cost requirements.

Government of Egypt: Budget Categories

Ministry of Finance		Ministry of Plan	
Chapter 1	Chapter 2	Chapter 3	Chapter 4
Wages & salaries (including allowances)	Materials & supplies	Investment expenditures	Debt service payments

Implementing a Workable Strategy

There is strong interest on the part of several ministers in coming together to shape an effort to strengthen the use of results-based monitoring and evaluation in the government. They may consider forming a leadership team that:

- Defines objectives and develops a strategic vision;
- Provides a timeframe and evaluation framework for pilots and other activitiesl
- Measures progress; and
- Recognizes and supports progress.

It will be important to support the leadership team with a dedicated, well-organized group to assure that the vision gets turned into action. The roles that such a group might play include developing an action plan, assuring that there is adequate training and support is in place, measuring progress, identifying successful efforts and sharing lessons learned across organizational boundaries. The group should include committed, energetic individuals, with no other job to attend to. The group should have a well-communicated and clear authority from the minister, prime minister, or president.

In developing such a team, it is probably desirable to draw upon more than one ministry and to assign people to a cross-ministry team for time-limited assignments. The National Council for Women developed a very interesting "virtual team" – bringing together people responsible for writing the national plan in all of the ministries. The small core group at the Council held workshops for these cross-ministerial groups to orient them to the Council's concerns and has subsequently worked with them as they wrote their individual ministry's plans.

The Minister of Finance expressed strong interest in training activities to support this initiative. There are few specific courses that are focused on performance budgeting and results-based monitoring and evaluation. The World Bank, through its OPCS and OED units, has developed a course on Developing and Building Performance-Based-Monitoring and Evaluation Systems for Government Officials. There is also the International Program for Development Evaluation Training to be held in Ottawa, Canada in July (the launching of this program is July, 2001). There are also substantial resources both in Egypt and internationally that could be drawn upon for training. As examples, the Institute of National Planning has a course on performance budgeting that was developed for the Cairo Water Authority; the Social Research Center has a training program on monitoring and evaluation that could be built upon; and the Public Administration Research and Consultation Center at Cairo University has developed several relevant training programs.

Donor Sponsored Activities

During the diagnostic mission, the team met with USAID, the largest single donor in Egypt. While USAID does not have any specific plans to provide additional technical assistance in the area of performance-based monitoring and evaluation, USAID's extensive experience in this area is a significant resource and USAID expressed an interest in working more closely with the World Bank in this area.

There are a number of donors providing technical assistance to the Egyptian Government who can further Egypt's shift to a results-based focus. A few ongoing activities that are supported by donors are listed below:

Illustrative Current Technical Assistant Activities

- The Data Access and Transmission Activity (DATA) Project is assisting the Government of Egypt to develop and maintain national accounts compliant with the 1993 System of National Accounts. This project, funded by USAID, is upgrading the information technology systems in the Ministry of Planning and providing technical assistance to strengthen Egypt's collection, tabulation, and dissemination of key economic data.
- Egypt's Industrial Modernization Programme is assisting Egypt's industrial sector to prepare for trade liberalization. Funded by the European Union, the Government of Egypt and the private sector, the project is providing technical assistance to small and medium enterprises and to the sector overall. Currently a Danish team is reviewing Egypt's national system for quality.
- A USAID-funded activity has installed a computer network in Egypt's Parliament to facili-

tate access to information in the legislative process. According to project documents, there has been an increased demand by members of the Peoples' Assembly for better information, especially from government agencies, and for quantitative information on topics under debate.
- The IMF has been providing short-term technical assistance to help the authorities in addressing the shortcomings in the national database, mainly in the areas of national accounts, balance of payments, monetary, fiscal, and prices statistics. Long-term assistance had been provided in the past in areas of balance of payments and external debt.
- UNDP is providing support and technical assistance both to the Information and Decision Support Center and to the Ministry of Finance.

Moving to Results-Based Monitoring and Evaluation: Recommendations

Shifting a public sector institution to focus on performance, much less an entire government, requires a major, multi-year effort with strong leadership and commitment to change. Even governments that embarked on this course more than a decade ago are still evolving. International experience has also shown that sometimes the biggest pay off is from some of the early, relatively straightforward steps on a much longer journey to a culture of performance that effectively links resources and results. The Government of Egypt is at the beginning of this journey. We believe the following steps will advance it.

- *Establish a cross-ministerial leadership group to promote performance and results-based monitoring and evaluation.* A leadership team of ministers who are committed to change in their own organizations could accelerate the adoption of results-based monitoring and evaluation and introduction of a more results-based budget process. Under the leadership of the Minister of Finance, such a group could play several key roles, for example: developing an overall strategy to guide the effort; providing guidance and an evaluation framework for pilot activity in individual ministries and other organizations; and developing a plan to expand pilot activity and share best practices and lessons across ministries. This group should determine whether mechanisms that other countries have used to give impetus and mandates to reform efforts—such as presidential decrees, amendments to budget laws, and legislation—should be pursued in the Egyptian context.

- *Support the initiative of the National Council for Women* to monitor and evaluate the implementation of gender-related initiatives in the 2002-2006 plan. Under the patronage of the First Lady, the Council has worked very effectively with the Ministry of Planning and line ministries as they have developed their plans. We believe that the next step of monitoring and evaluating implementation presents a particular opportunity to be a catalyst for change across several ministries. Because the Council includes a broad range of actors from inside and outside government, including academics, the private sector, non-governmental organizations, the media, and concerned ministries, it can help promote consensus about measurement issues and transparency in reporting on results.

- *Build capacity to support reform.* No country has succeeded with a significant reform effort without a dedicated, well-organized team to support it. A core team could support the ministerial group and the pilots so as to minimize bureaucratic red tape and expedite innovation and learning; identify lessons learned and ways to mainstream these lessons into the government. The team could draw on the career staff of several ministries and upon the significant resources in the Egyptian academic and non-governmental community.

- *Modernize statistical policy.* Despite the manifest capacity of the Egyptian statistical system, there is evidence that it lags behind both in the quality of statistics produced and the attention given to the needs of its clients. Egypt should review its statistical law with a view to separating the responsibilities of CAPMAS for military mobilization from its role as an independent statistical agency. Many countries employ a national statistical commission or similar coordinating body to set policies and standards for the production and dissemination of official statistics. Egypt should adopt a similar strategy for coordinating data policies and standards. Such a commission should include in its membership both representatives of the agencies charged with producing statistics and senior statisticians drawn from universities and the private sector.

- *Increase client focus.* The value of statistics comes not in their production, but in their use. It should be the goal of all producers of statistics to encourage their widespread dissemination, within the government and to non-governmental users. To better understand the needs of their clients, agencies responsible for producing statistics could create advisory groups to represent users. Another useful function of such groups would be to encourage the exchange of information between data users, who may find solutions to common problems. Such advisory groups would meet regularly with the managers of statistical units in the agencies. At the highest level, an advisory group to CAPMAS or the proposed statistical commission would provide input on the needs of all users of Egyptian statistical information.

- *Participate in the IMF Special Data Dissemination System.* As Egypt prepares to enter international capital markets, it will become more important for it to produce credible statistics. An important step in this direction would be subscription to the Special Data Dissemination Standard (see the IMF disseminations standard bulletin board: http://dsbb.imf.org). The SDDS requires countries to adopt international standards for reporting on major economic and financial statistics and to maintain a current listing of its policies and standards. Working toward SDDS participation would provide a powerful driver for modernizing Egypt's statistical system.
- *Encourage donor support.* There is an important role for donors to play in supporting Egypt's shift to results-based monitoring and evaluation with training and technical assistance. In doing so, donors can draw on in-country expertise in universities and think tanks as well as the substantial international experience in results-based approaches.

Near-Term Activities to be Supported by the World Bank

1. Provide technical support to the Minister of Finance in im plementing his vision to shift the budget process to one that focuses on results.

Organize and coordinate a workshop or consulting session aimed to directly support a newly chartered inter-ministerial Group. The main theme of this workshop will be performance-based budgeting, drawing on international experiences and resulting in the creation of a vision and action plan for Egypt. Approach: interactive. Duration: Two days. In the first day, World Bank experts will share their practical views based on hands-on international experiences. H.E. the Minister of Finance will introduce and discuss the vision, strategy and action plan for Egypt in the second day. The timing of this activity is expected to be early fall, 2001.

Suport the National Council for Women as it prepares to develop a monitoring and evaluation framework for measure the implementation of the gender-related objetives established in all relevant ministries as part of the 2002–2006 national plan expected to be finalized in October 2001.

The National Council for women has specifically requested technical assistance in the area of designing and building a results-based monitoring and evaluation system to track the results of gender-related programs im plemented across a number of line ministries. This support may include advice, consultation and training and should be linked to the upcoming World Bank–sponsored gender assessment.

The World Bank should begin communicating immediately with the Council and its technical advisors as to the timing and specifics of holding a consultation session in Cairo for key members of the Council during early fall 2001. Curriculum for a possible trianing course will be developed in conjunction with the American University in Cairo, and other research centers with expertise in this area. The Secretary General of the National Council for Women should be a member of the inter-ministerial council discussed above.

2. Improve Egypt's statistical capacity.

The goal of subscribing to the IMF Special Data Dissemination Standard (SDDS) and assigning responsibility to the appropriate agency should be announced. Subscription to the SDDS will help Egypt in its plans to offer sovereign bonds on the international capital markets. Although final acceptance of Egypt's metadata in the SDDS may have to wait on completion of ongoing work on its fiscal and national accounts, the plan to subscribe, including a proposed date, should be set as soon as possible.

Annexes

Annex A.   Terms of Reference
Annex B.   Interviews Conducted
Annex C.   Egypt and the International
                Development Goals
Annex D.   Endnotes, References, and
                Resources

Annex A

Terms of Reference
Performance-Based M&E Diagnostic Mission
Egypt June 2–6, 2001

Background

Egypt is included among eight country pilots that have been selected to participate in a Bank-wide program approved by the Board of Directors in September. This Program, the M&E Improvement Program, has as its main goal to help both Bank and Borrower officials to better track the results of development by strengthening their use of performance-based monitoring and evaluation (M&E) systems. These systems (now well-understood to support good public management) can help government officials identify and set realistic goals and outcomes for public sector programs. Two key requirements of a usable performance-based M&E system are 1) the inclusion of performance indicators that will be regularly monitored to assess progress in meeting development goals, and 2) a valid and verifiable system for data collection and reporting on those indicators.

During the upcoming mission to Egypt, the mission team will meet with a number of officials in the Government, and in donor and other stakeholder organizations to learn how performance-based M&E systems could support effective public management. The Team will begin to map M&E efforts currently underway and assess where existing capacity in data collection and reporting lies inside and outside the government. The Team will also assess where potential opportunities for designing and building performance-based M&E systems and where potential barriers for being successful in this effort may exist.

Meetings to be Held with Key Officials

Among those whose views will be important to understand will be officials from the following organizations:

Ministry of Finance	- Minister of Finance - Individuals involved in budget formulation - (If the proposed Fiscal Policy Decision Support Unit has been created, then the Team would like to meet with the head of this unit) - Individuals involved in the corporatization of the 62 public economic authorities
Ministry of Planning	- Individuals who prepare and oversee the investment budget - Head of the Statistical Office
Prime Minister's Office	Individuals who are directly responsible for setting sector priorities and overall economic development planning
Central Accounting Office (CAO)	Head of this office or senior officials in charge of ex post review of budget accounts
Ministry of Health and Population;	- Head of Administrative Reform Units
Ministry of Agriculture and Ministry of Education	- Head of Administrative data and reporting systems
Ministry of Health and Population	Head of unit that is responsible for outsourcing non-essential services
Health Insurance Organization	Director or lead individual
Agriculture Research Center	Official
National Center for Educational Research	Head Official
National Statistical Office (or that office responsible for conducting household surveys)	Head
Donors	One meeting with key donors, such as USAID, UNDP and others with a large presence in the country.

Below is a partial list of questions that might be asked of these officials:
1) What is driving the need for results-based monitoring and evaluation systems in the Egypt ? (incentives/demands)

2) Where in the government does accountability for effective (and efficient) delivery of programs lie?
3) Is there a codified (through statute or mandate) strategy or organization in the

government for tracking development goals?

4) Where does capacity lie with the requisite skills for designing and using results-based monitoring and evaluation systems in the pilot country? How has this capacity (or lack thereof) contributed to the use of M&E in country?

Expected Outputs from the Mission

At the end of this mission, we hope to have identified at least one or more champions within the government with interest in designing a performance-based M&E system to support sector/program goals monitoring. Second, we hope to form partnerships with other key donors with similar interest in helping Egypt build capacity in the area of performance management for national and sector-wide programs. Finally, we plan to develop an action plan and set of recommendations that can be incorporated into a program aimed to strengthen the government or key stakeholder's use of performance-based monitoring and evaluation.

Annex B

Interviews Conducted

Economic Research Forum
*Information and Decision Support Center of
    the Egyptian Cabinet*
International Monetary Fund
Ministry of Electricity & Energy
Ministry of Education
Ministry of Finance
Ministry of Health
Ministry of Industry and Technology
Ministry of International Cooperation
Ministry of Planning

CAPMAS
Institute for National Planning
National Council for Women
*Public Administration Research Center,
    Cairo University*
Social Fund for Development
Social Research Center
United Nations Development Programme
*United States Agency for International
    Development*

Annex C

Egypt and the International Development Goals

Seven goals for international development have been identified from the agreements and resolutions of the world conferences organized by the United Nations in the first half of the 1990s. These goals are:

1. Reduce the proportion of people living in extreme poverty by half between 1990 and 2015;

2. Enroll all children in primary school by 2015;

3. Make progress towards gender equality and empowering women by eliminating gender disparities in primary and secondary education by 2005;

4. Reduce infant and child mortality rates by two-thirds between 1990 and 2015;

5. Reduce maternal mortality ratios by three-quarters between 1990 and 2015;

6. Provide access for all who need reproductive health services by 2015, and

7. Implement national strategies for sustainable development by 2005 so as to reverse the loss of environmental resources by 2015.

Many of these goals and indicators to measure the goals are incrporated in data sets used by Egyptian agencies to monitor their programs.

A new household expenditure survey, from which poverty rates can be calculated, will be released shortly. How to measure poverty and the proper definition of the national povrety line is much debated. The 1996 Human Development Report for Egypt reported on five poverty lines: a food-based poverty line, a lower and an upper income poverty line, and a lower and an upper expenditure poverty line.

Enrollment levels in primary and secondary school are widely reported and Egypt is working toward a goal of universal enrollment in basic (through grade 8) education. However, only gross enrollments (including out-of-age stu-

dents) appear in the CAPMAS Statistical Yearbook or in the Human Development Report of Egypt. Statistics on girls' enrollments are widely reported, as are the proportion of women on school and university faculties. Literacy rates are also closely watched and reported on. Many official and semi-official publications cite improvement of the status of women as a primary social goal.

Among the health indicators, life expectancy at birth, infant and child mortality rates, and maternal mortality ratios are all reported. CAPMAS has recently completed a new set of maternal mortality estimates. In its health status index, the Social Fund for Development uses the infant mortality rate, the under-five mortality rate, and the maternal mortality ratio as its measures of human well-being. The Ministry of Health has an extensive program of reproductive health care through its primary health care units, which record fertility information and contraceptive prevalence in their service populations. They also collect information on water supply.

All of this is evidence that Egypt is actively engaged in monitoring progress along the same dimensions of human well-being as the International Development Goals and has need of high quality data to do so.

Annex D

Notes, References, and Resources

Notes

1. Valsan, E.H. The Egyptian Civil Service and the Continuing Challenge of Reform. In *Research in Public Administration*. Volume 5: 223-226, 1999.

2. Korayerm, Karima. "The Research Environment in Egypt," in *Research for Development in the Middle East and North Africa*. IDRC, www.idrc.ca/books/focus/930/15koraye.html.

3. *Egypt Social and Structural Review*, draft, The World Bank, 2001.

References

Egypt: Human Development Report, Institute of National Planning, 1998, 2000.

El Saiedi, H.E. Dr. Ali, *Restructuring of the Power*

Sector and Enhancement of Private Opportunities, Presentation to the American Chamber of Commerce in Egypt, October 2000.

Healthy Egyptians 2010, Ministry of Health and Population

Korayerm, Karima. "The Research Environment in Egypt," in *Research for Development in the Middle East and North Africa.* IDRC, www.idrc.ca/books/focus/930/15koraye.html.

Public Debt Management Program, Arab Republic of Egypt, Ministry of Finance, Presentation to the Euromoney Conference, Emerging Arab Economies: Breaking New Ground in the Global Markets, September 2000.

The National Council for Women. Pamphlet, n.d. See also http://ncw.gov.eg

Towards a More Result Oriented Budget Process, in Egypt: Public Expenditure Review of the Social Sectors, World Bank, Social and Economic Development Group, Middle East and North Africa Region, January 1999.

Valsan, E.H. The Egyptian Civil Service and the Continuing Challenge of Reform. In *Research in Public Administration.* Volume 5: 223-226, 1999

www.IDSC.gov.eg (web site of the Information and Decision Support Center of the Egyptian Cabinet)

http://www.oecd.org/puma (web site of OECD's Programme on Public Management and Governance)

Millennium Development Goals (MDGS)
List of Goals and Targets

Goal 1: Eradicate extreme poverty and hunger

Target 1: Halve, between 1990 and 2015, the proportion of people whose income is less than one dollar a day

Indicators

1. Proportion of population below $1 per day
2. Poverty gap ratio [incidence x depth of poverty]
3. Share of poorest quintile in national consumption

Target 2: Halve, between 1990 and 2015, the proportion of people who suffer from hunger

4. Prevalence of underweight children (under-five years of age)
5. Proportion of population below minimum level of dietary energy consumption

Goal 2: Achieve universal primary education

Target 3: Ensure that, by 2015, children everywhere, boys and girls alike, will be able to complete a full course of primary schooling

Indicators

6. Net enrolment ratio in primary education
7. Proportion of pupils starting grade 1 who reach grade 5
8. Literacy rate of 15-24 year olds

Goal 3: Promote gender equality and empower women

Target 4: Eliminate gender disparity in primary and secondary education preferably by 2005 and to all levels of education no later than 2015

Indicators

9. Ratio of girls to boys in primary, secondary and tertiary education
10. Ratio of literate females to males of 15–24 year olds
11. Share of women in wage employment in the non-agricultural sector
12. Proportion of seats held by women in national parliament

Goal 4: Reduce child mortality

Target 5: Reduce by two-thirds, between 1990 and 2015, the under-five mortality rate

Indicators

13. Under-five mortality rate
14. Infant mortality rate
15. Proportion of 1 year old children immunised against measles

Goal 5: Improve maternal health

Target 6: Reduce by three-quarters, between 1990 and 2015, the maternal mortality ratio

Indicators

16. Maternal mortality ratio
17. Proportion of births attended by skilled health personnel

Goal 6: Combat HIV/AIDS, malaria and other diseases

Target 7: Have halted by 2015, and begun to reverse, the spread of HIV/AIDS

Indicators

18. HIV prevalence among 15–24 year old pregnant women
19. Contraceptive prevalence rate
20. Number of children orphaned by HIV/AIDS

Target 8: Have halted by 2015, and begun to reverse, the incidence of malaria and other major diseases

21. Prevalence and death rates associated with malaria
22. Proportion of population in malaria risk areas using effective malaria prevention and treatment measures
23. Prevalence and death rates associated with tuberculosis
24. Proportion of TB cases detected and cured under DOTS (Directly Observed Treatment Short Course)

Goal 7: Ensure environmental sustainability

Target 9: Integrate the principles of sustainable development into country policies and programmes and reverse the loss of environmental resources

Indicators

25. Proportion of land area covered by forest
26. Land area protected to maintain biological diversity
27. GDP per unit of energy use (as proxy for energy efficiency)
28. Carbon dioxide emissions (per capita)
[Plus two figures of global atmospheric pollution: ozone depletion and the accumulation of global warming gases]

Target 10: Halve, by 2015, the proportion of people without sustainable access to safe drinking water

29. Proportion of population with sustainable access to an improved water source

Target 11: By 2020, to have achieved a significant improvement in the lives of at least 100 million slum dwellers

30. Proportion of people with access to improved sanitation
31. Proportion of people with access to secure tenure
[Urban/rural disaggregation of several of the above indicators may be relevant for monitoring improvement in the lives of slum dwellers]

Goal 8: Develop a Global Partnership for Development

Target 12: Develop further an open, rule-based, predictable, non-discriminatory trading and financial system
Includes a commitment to good governance, development, and poverty reduction—both nationally and internationally

Target 13: Address the Special Needs of the Least Developed Countries
Includes: tariff and quota free access for LDC exports; enhanced programme of debt relief for HIPC and cancellation of official bilateral debt; and more generous ODA for countries committed to poverty reduction

Target 14: Address the Special Needs of land-locked countries and small island developing states
(through Barbados Programme and 22nd General Assembly provisions)

Target 15: Deal comprehensively with the debt problems of developing countries through national and international measures in order to make debt sustainable in the long term

Indicators

Some of the indicators listed below will be monitored separately for the Least Developed Countries (LDCs), Africa, landlocked countries and small island developing states.

Official Development Assistance
32. Net ODA as percentage of DAC donors' GNI (targets of 0.7% in total and 0.15% for LDCs)

33. Proportion of ODA to basic social services (basic education, primary health care, nutrition, safe water and sanitation)
34. Proportion of ODA that is untied
35. Proportion of ODA for environment in small island developing states
36. Proportion of ODA for transport sector in land-locked countries

Market Access
37. Proportion of exports (by value and excluding arms) admitted free of duties and quotas

38. Average tariffs and quotas on agricultural products and textiles and clothing
39. Domestic and export agricultural subsidies in OECD countries
40. Proportion of ODA provided to help build trade capacity

Debt Sustainability
41. Proportion of official bilateral HIPC debt cancelled
42. Debt service as a percentage of exports of goods and services
43. Proportion of ODA provided as debt relief
44. Number of countries reaching HIPC decision and completion points

Goal 8: (continued)

Target 16: In cooperation with developing countries, develop and implement strategies for decent and productive work for youth

Target 17: In cooperation with pharmaceutical companies, provide access to affordable, essential drugs in developing countries

Target 18: In cooperation with the private sector, make available the benefits of new technologies, especially information and communications

Indicators

45. Unemployment rate of 15–24 year-olds

46. Proportion of population with access to affordable essential drugs on a sustainable basis

47. Telephone lines per 1,000 people
48. Personal computers per 1,000 people

National Evaluation Policy for Sri Lanka

Sri Lanka Evaluation Association (SLEva) jointly with the Ministry of
Policy Development and Implementation

December 2003
National Evaluation Policy of the
Government of Sri Lanka

Preamble

The Government of Sri Lanka fully recognises the growing international consensus that evaluation is an essential aspect of good governance to improve development effectiveness, transparency, accountability and informed decision making. The term 'evaluation' in this document is referred in the development context and the definition of the Development Assistance Committee (DAC)/ OECD of "the systematic and objective assessment of an on-going or completed project, programme or policy, its design, implementation and results with the aim to determine the relevance and fulfilment of objectives, development efficiency, effectiveness, impact and sustainability" is used. An evaluation should provide information that is credible and useful, enabling the incorporation of lessons learned into the decision making process. Systematic evaluation of projects, programmes, institutions and policies is vital to improve *performance accountability, lesson learning and policy refinement* in the public sector[1]. Evaluation is also a tool for public sector reforms. The ultimate success of evaluation depends on how well planners and decision makers **use** *evaluation findings and lessons learned to improve policy formulation and planning*. Therefore it is necessary to establish strong *links between on the one hand evaluation, and on the other, policy formulation, reforms, planning and budgeting*. The

adoption of a national policy on evaluation would provide guidance and direction on the use of evaluation and its role in national development.

The current situation and the need for a National Evaluation Policy

Globally, public sector performance has been an issue among citizens. Taxpayers have challenged governments to *demonstrate value for money* in the provision of public service. The relevance of institutions and their mandates have been questioned in a world of rapid change. Similarly with regard to projects and programmes, the *increasing share of problem projects and unsatisfactory performance of completed projects* emphasise the need for systematic evaluation. Available evidence highlights that significant proportions of development programmes have failed to fully achieve their envisaged development objectives. For example in Sri Lanka, it is reported that only 44% of the Asian Development Bank funded post-evaluated projects, have been successful in terms of their contribution to the social and economic development[2]. It has been widely accepted that timely evaluations and the use of reliable evaluative knowledge help governments to *improve policy and project designs, increase returns from investments and speed up the implementation* of on-going projects.

The government is conscious and mindful of the fact that, at present, high proportion of monitoring and evaluation resources are devoted to *monitoring the inputs and physical and financial implementation* of large projects and little attention is devoted to assessing the results, *sustain-*

ability, *delivery of services, the quality, distribu-*
tion of benefits of projects among various socioeconomic groups or geographical regions. Monitoring and Evaluation System in the past tend to
be more *implementation biased,* data rich, information poor and *disbanded with termination* of
projects. Evaluations in many cases are *donor
driven.* Misperceptions of evaluations as policing
or fault-finding exercises and lack of local demand are other problems that inhibit the practice
of evaluations. In addition the mechanism to incorporate evaluation findings into new project designs needs to the strengthened. These issues need
to be addressed immediately.

The need to achieve results from public development interventions has become extremely important with resource constraints and persistent
development disparities resulting from ineffectiveness and inherent weaknesses of programmes.
This pressure to demonstrate results has led to the
introduction of Results-Based Monitoring and
Evaluation (RBME) system in the government
machinery. The need for planned and systematic
evaluation at all levels of government is therefore
timely. This becomes even more crucial in Sri
Lanka, at the present time when there is enor-
mous potential to move into a period of rapid development—including the reconstruction of the
war affected and adjacent areas—following the
onset of the peace process, as well as the major
*economic reform programme under the "Regain-
ing Sri Lanka" initiative.*

The formal adoption of a national evaluation
policy and its implementation would set up an enabling
environment to continuously track progress, review performance and *fine tune policies* in order to realize the
vision and aspiration of private sector led economic development. Furthermore creation of a
suitable policy environment for evaluations complements the tools package necessary for systematic development monitoring and linking per-

formance monitoring and evaluation to policy
through the reinvigorated National Operations
Room (NOR)[3] of the Ministry of Policy Development and Implementation (MPDI). Accessibly
of the development information to the policy
makers and general public is essential to ensure a
"functional National Operations Room"

National Evaluation Policy

Objectives of the National Evaluation Policy

The National Evaluation Policy is intended to
achieve the following objectives.

a. Promote the correct understanding of evaluation and create an evaluation culture among
the public sector managers to use evaluations
to *'manage for results'.*
c. Promote the practice of evaluation through
catalysing the generation of necessary *human
and institutional capacities, tools and methodologies.*
d. Enable *Learning of lessons* from past experiences to identify the policies, programmes,
projects and delivery systems most likely to
succeed and factors most likely to contribute to
that success.
e. *To contribute to improve the design of development policies* and programmes through effective integration of evaluation findings into
the policy formulation, reforms, planning and
budgeting process.
f. To enhance or promote *accountability, transparency and good governance.*

Fundamental Principles of National Evaluation Policy

The national evaluation policy is based on the following fundamental principles.

• Evaluations are *practical assessments* serving
practical ends, neither scientific research stud-

ies undertaken for advancement of knowledge nor acts of policing.

- Evaluation should be seen primarily as an instrument of *accountability and lessons learning*. Independence is of utmost importance for objectivity and credibility of evaluation. However, participation needs to be built-in for lessons learning purposes. Depending on the needs and circumstances, management should justify the selection of external, internal or joint evaluations. All public sector institutions should be encouraged to use evaluations as instruments to account for the results as well as lesson learning.

- All types of evaluations—Ex-post, impact and mid-term evaluations—that serve different purposes and, are conducted at different phases of the project cycle, need to be encouraged. Preference should be given to on-going and mid term evaluations. In order to have a wider perspective of development, the government accords special attention to the *evaluation of sectors, institutions, policies and thematic areas*.

- The evaluation findings and lessons should be *linked to the policy formulation, reforms, planning and budgeting process*. The government should learn from evaluation findings and communicate and share evaluation information with other stakeholders. Findings of evaluations of development policies and programmes should be readily available to public and media. Specific website(s) may be maintained for this purpose.

- Evaluations should be made *mandatory* under certain circumstances and adequate provision should be made *up-front*. The policy, programme or project proponents should ensure *evaluability. Concerns for evaluation should be built-in at the time of planning and design of programmes and policies. Subjects to be evaluated should be selected on the basis of their potential learning content and development relevance. (See selection criteria below)*

- Use of performance indicators and logical framework based approaches should be made mandatory for all policy, programme or project preparation initiatives, thereby making it possible to subsequently evaluate them meaningfully.

- *The civil society organizations (CSOs), private sector and academics* should be encouraged to undertake evaluations preferably in partnership with relevant public institutions.

- The national and sub-national level execution authorities are responsible to ensure that *discipline of evaluations is sufficiently deployed* within their major cost centres.

It is emphasised that all public sector institutions embed evaluation into their development management practices.

Operationalization

Selection Criteria for Evaluation

It may not be advisable to evaluate all development programmes for both practical and financial reasons. The authorities responsible for the execution of a given programme or project should initiate action for undertaking evaluation of major projects, programmes and policies. In this regard all Sectoral Ministries should develop their own evaluation plan. Further, the Economic Policy Committee and/or NOR and/or National Level Monitoring Committees should identify areas for evaluation on a rolling biennial plan. When selecting projects and programmes for evaluation on their own, the Sectoral Ministries may form a team comprising of the following;

1. Representative of the Monitoring and Progress Review Division (MPDI) of the MPDI or NOR.
2. When foreign funded projects are to be se-

lected, representatives of the Department of External Resources and funding agency.

3. Representatives of the Department of National Planning and Department of National Budget.
4. Representatives of the academia and/or civil society organizations such as Sri Lanka Evaluation Association (SLEvA).

This committee should screen and select suitable projects for evaluations. This will enable the MPRD/ MPDI to maintain track of the current evaluation studies. The following criteria should be used by the selection committee when selecting projects or programmes for evaluation.

1. *Policy relevance* e.g. poverty reduction,
2. National importance and the *scale of funding*
3. The innovative value and replicability of project or programme. In this context some 'small' projects could also be evaluated.
4. Public interest and problem nature

Evaluations should not only cover problem areas but also draw lessons on success stories. With the change in the role of government as a facilitator and the need to finance and execute public investments by private sector, it is necessary to encourage private sector to undertake independent evaluations of their own activities - specially investments of a public nature. These evaluations should be carried out through the representation bodies such as Chambers. Such evaluations are necessary to demonstrate private sector's contribution to the national development and to increase public accountability and transparency. It is also necessary for the evaluation to focus its attention to policies connected with private sector rather than purely projects.

Implementation of National Evaluation Policy

Implementation of the National Evaluation Policy is the responsibility of all Ministries and Agen-cies involved in national development work. The MPDI shall provide necessary assistance and guidelines, training and refresher courses regularly to implement the national evaluation policy more effectively. The Central Performance Evaluation Unit (CPEU) of the MPDI will serve as a focal point for implementing the National Evaluation Policy. The secretaries of the line ministries should be responsible for the development of an evaluation plan in their respective sectors or areas.

Each Sectoral Ministry when initiating independent evaluations within their own areas of responsibility, should in consultation with MPDI, develop evaluation plans and terms-of-reference. Ministries may obtain the services of public sector, private sector, universities, CSOs and individual professional evaluators to undertake such studies. The respective sectoral Ministry in consultation with the CPEU of the MPDI and other relevant stakeholders should develop the terms of reference (TOR) for such evaluations. The Central Evaluation Unit on the other hand is responsible for more comprehensive and strategically important evaluation of a thematic nature.

MPDI in close collaboration with professional evaluation associations develop and promote evaluation culture, standards, guidelines, methodologies, best practices, monitor and develop evaluation capacity, sensitise policymakers, and facilitate the dissemination of evaluation findings.

The evaluations initiated by the Sectoral Ministries would tend to be more of leaning exercises while those conducted by the Central Evaluation Unit of the MPDI would tend to be more accountability and policy influence oriented. Some form of compromise and balance is needed between accountability and lessons learning.

Dissemination of Evaluation Findings

Each sector that undertakes an evaluation should also develop a dissemination strategy for sharing lessons internally and as well as externally. All Sectoral Ministries should forward reports of evaluations to the CPEU of the MPDI (especially electronically). This will enable evaluation findings to be synthesized and linked to the Evaluation Information System (EIS) of the NOR of the MPDI and Economic Policy Committee (EPC) to ensure integration of evaluation findings into the policy, planning, budgeting and reform processes. Evaluation information should be made accessible to the parliament, national audits and general public. The Sectoral Ministries should after the completion of the evaluation dissemination workshop, prepare a *plan of action*, which should identify the specific follow-up action with well defined time scales and responsibilities. Copies of such plan of action and the progress should be submitted to the MPDI. MPDI and the Line Ministries are responsible to ensure the implementation of the plan of action and ensure that evaluation funding, lessons and follow-up actions are integrated into the development planning and management framework.

The project proponents and the national planning authorities should ensure the incorporation of evaluation findings in the formulation of new projects and programmes. For this purpose the evaluation findings and lessons should be presented in a brief, reader friendly summary. The project submission formats and related procedures should be suitably modified to internalise evaluation findings into the planning, budgeting, public expenditure review, and policy formulation process. In this regard a close collaboration should be established among, evaluation, planning, budgeting, audit, finance, public expenditure and policy review functions of the government.

Guidelines, Methodologies, Standards and Ethics

Both on-going as well as ex-post evaluations should examine the relevance, efficiency, effectiveness, impact and sustainability of policy or programme initiatives. Evaluation methodology should look into the *financial, economic, social (including conflict sensitivity), environmental, gender, institutional and sustainability* aspects. The use of *financial and economic cost benefit analysis* to assess the value for money, need to be encouraged. Moreover, the evaluation methodology should integrate *social and environment* concerns. *Beneficiary assessment* should form an integral part of evaluating social programmes. Due consideration should be given to the political and policy environment. Concerns for evaluation should be integrated at the time of planning and formulation of the project. Use of programme theory, logic model or *Logical Framework Analysis* (LFA) with well-defined performance indicators at the time of project preparation is mandatory for projects which are over US $ 10 million. Projects less that US $ 10 million should also be encouraged to use such approaches whenever possible with baseline and benchmark indicators. The CPEU with SLEvA and other professional CSOs are encouraged to proactively participate in the preparation of major projects by reviewing and confirming the performance indicators, both baseline and targets. As evaluations are practical investigations and not scientific research studies, simple, cost effective and less time consuming *participatory rapid appraisal methodologies* may be used preferentially.

It is also necessary to develop *local evaluation methodologies, guidelines, standards, ethics and practices* in par with accepted international standards. Evaluation methodology, knowledge and expertise should be developed to take into account the specific needs of sectors. The MPDI in collaboration with the Sri Lanka Evaluation Association and other CSOs should undertake this task.

Capacity Building and Partnerships

The availability of adequately skilled competent human resources in evaluation is essential. Government recognises the need to build a *professional cadre of evaluators* and accords high priority for capacity building efforts. The Universities and public sector training institutions should be encouraged to run *evaluation modules* as part of their normal programmes. The government would also encourage joint evaluations and regional networking to share knowledge on evaluation techniques and methodologies. Joint evaluations while ensuring independence would also help to establish local ownership and in-house capacity building in evaluation. By end 2005, it is envisaged that all major evaluations should have significant national ownership. Local participation should be ensured in planning, designing, implementation and dissemination of evaluation to enhance local ownership.

Sectoral ministries should strengthen the capacity for performance evaluation, ex-post evaluation and impact evaluations in their area of responsibility. The MPDI must provide central direction for evaluation and should (a) upgrade the CPEU as a centre of excellence to provide leadership, guidance and support to the practice of evaluation; (b) use evaluation findings where appropriate in decision making; (c) set standards, ethics and best practices and (d) monitor the evaluation capacity in the public sector.

The CPEU of MPDI jointly with professional civil society evaluation organizations will assist sectoral Ministries to build evaluation capacity, develop standards, methodologies and upgrade capacity of their staff. As part of the efforts to *build local evaluation consultancy industry,* the Sectoral Ministries, may *outsource evaluation work* to private sector and civil society organizations (CSOs). Government will encourage such *collaboration and partnership* with NGOs and CSOs to introduce participatory evaluations in the public sector.

Many donor funded post evaluations have been conducted by donors themselves without much in-country participation. Such unilateral approach, though helps to ensure *objectivity* of evaluation, does not assist in the development of in-country capacities nor does it help to linking the evaluation to overall planning process. Government should encourage donors to strengthen in-country evaluation capacity. Moreover, all evaluation missions on foreign funded projects and independent evaluations should have links with the CPEU to ensure central coordination on evaluation. A documentation centre should be in place at CPEU to access all the evaluation reports.

Consultants and Contracting

The Sectoral Ministries shall select qualified, competent and experienced professional firms or individuals whenever possible locally. The government is committed to *promote domestic capacity* in evaluation. Joint ventures between domestic evaluation professionals and foreign consultants should also be encouraged to transfer knowledge and skills on evaluation methodologies, techniques and practices.

Financing Evaluation

It is necessary to have *sufficient financial resources* for conducting evaluations of an acceptable quality. Ministries and Provincial Councils should make necessary provision in the annual budget estimates for the conduct of evaluations. In addition to the financial support under the consolidated funds of the government, it is also necessary to have *built-in-funds* under foreign aided projects for the conduct of evaluations. It is necessary for the government to provide regular funding for post-evaluations, which cannot be generally built into the foreign funded projects. Similarly financing arrangements should be made for institutional, policy and thematic evaluations. There should be a separate special vote under the MPDI and other line ministries for such purposes.

Oversight

The MPDI will *monitor* the implementation of this policy to ensure its success in meeting the intended objectives. Secretary, MPDI in close consultation with the professional CSOs such as SLEvA, Chamber of Commerce, Organization of Professional Association, will monitor the implementation of the policy every year. A consultative and oversight modality, which would, inter alia, reflect the creation of the evaluation culture in the public sector would be developed for this purpose by the MPDI in consultation with the stakeholders.

Notes

1. Utility of evaluations applies also to other sectors. This document however is focused on national policy for the public sector. It may be applied in other sectors as desired.
2. Country synthesis report on evaluation of the Asian Development Bank, 1999. The performance of projects funded by other donor agencies is not known to be any better.
3. National Operations Room (NOR) which will be the focal point to collect, analyse and present economic and development information policy makers and monitor and evaluate national and subnational development work and investments.

Andhra Pradesh (India) Performance Accountability Act 2003
(Draft Act) (APPAC Act of 2003)

Preamble

An Act to enhance accountability, manage Information Systems, evaluate performance of individuals, Departments and Institutions in the State of Andhra Pradesh and for all matters connected there with or incidental thereto.

The State of Andhra Pradesh is poised for Good Governance with efficient management of all resources and moving towards being a Swarnandhrapradesh.

Where the scientific and systematic development of the state can be best possible through efficient management of Information Systems emanating from Gross root level. Such development seeks for a need based evaluation of the performance of Individuals, Departments and Institutions.

And where the individuals, Departments and Institutions shall be accountable for their performance with incentives and dis-incentives.

Such a system of accountability and evaluation shall establish SMART Governance (Simple, Moral, Accountable, Responsive and Transparent).

Contents

Chapter 1

1. An Act

To provide for the establishment of strategic planning and performance measurement in the State Government and for other purposes.

Be it enacted by the State Legislative Assembly of the Government of Andhra Pradesh (GOAP).

2. Short Title

This Act may be cited as "The Andhra Pradesh Performance Accountability Act 2003".

It shall extend to the whole of the State of Andhra Pradesh including

  a) All Departments under the State Government;
  b) All Semi Government bodies, Local bodies, Co-operative Institutions etc., under the control of the Government;
  c) All Public Sector Institutions under the control of the Government; and
  d) All Organizations or Institutions or individuals receiving any form of grant or assistance or aid, whether monetary or otherwise from the Government or public funds.

(1) It shall come into force on such date, as the Government may, by notification in the Andhra Pradesh Gazette.

Chapter 2
Findings and Purposes

1. Findings
The Government finds that:

(a) Lack of efficiency in State-run programs undermines the confidence of people and reduces Government's ability to address adequately issues of public interest;

(b) Functionaries in the Government are disadvantaged in their efforts to improve the program efficiency and effectiveness, due to inadequate information flow; and

(c) Policy making and financial decisions are seriously handicapped by insufficient articulation to programme goals and objectives, performance and results.

2. Purposes
Purposes of this Act: are to:

(a) Improve confidence of the people, in the capability of the State Government by systematically holding the Government Departments, Institutions and individuals accountable for achieving program results;

(b) Initiate a series of performance reforms by setting up program goals, measuring performance against those goals, and reporting publicly on their progress;

(c) Improve Government effectiveness and public accountability by focusing on results, service quality, and customer satisfaction;

(d) Motivate Government functionaries to improve service by orienting them for planning to achieve objectives by providing them with information about service quality and results;

(e) Improve decision making at various levels by providing more objective information on achieving goals, improving effectiveness and efficiency of Government programs and spending; and

(f) Improve the internal management of the State Government.

Chapter 3
History of Administrative Reforms in AP

The State of Andhra Pradesh has been a pioneer in initiating Administrative Reforms for improving the performance of State run Programs

1. K. B. Lal Ananthraman & Sriramulu Committee on Administrative Reforms (1976)

2. M. K. Rustomji & Associates on Administrative Reforms (February 1986)

3. Action Plan for Administrative Reforms (June 1986)

4. Committee on Administrative Reorganization—S.R. Ramamurthy, G.R. Nair and K.V. Natarajan (April 1990)

5. Staff Review Committee—B.C. Gangopadhyaya & J.M. Girglani (April 1994)

6. Cabinet Sub-Committee on Administrative Reforms—headed by Sri Devender Goud (January 1997);

7. Three officers Committee on
   a) Reorganisation of Secretariat Departments (M.V.P.C. Sastry);
   b) Reorganisation of Commissionarates and Heads of Departments (N.S. Hariharan);
   c) Delegation of powers to District collectors etc (B. Danam)

8. Special five-member Committee in each department headed by the Secretary concerned (December 1997);

9. Task Force on Good Governance—headed by Sri Madhav Godbole (January 2000)
10. Cabinet Sub-Committee on Administrative Reforms headed by Sri Vidyadher Rao (2000)
11. Strategy paper on Governance and Public Management (January 2002)

Chapter 4
Performance Accountability System (PAS)

Performance Accountability System shall be established in each Department or Institution comprising of a comprehensive framework of Performance Management Activities including:
1. Strategic Planning
2. Information Flow
3. Performance Measurement
4. Performance Monitoring and Evaluation
5. Performance Budgeting

Chapter 5
Strategic Planning

1. Strategic Planning

Every Government Department or Institution shall draw up a strategic plan which shall be in congruence with the Vision of the State Government.

1) It shall focus on (a) the baseline, (b) Identify benchmarks (c) spell out objectives and strategies;
2) The strategic plan shall cover a period of one year from the fiscal year in which it will be submitted, and shall be updated and revised;
3) While developing a strategic plan, the Government shall be consulted and the views and suggestions of those potentially affected by or interested in such a plan may also be taken.

4) At the beginning of each Financial Year, the heads of the departments shall prepare a plan for the year in consultation with the Secretary and the concerned Minister. This plan shall be submitted to the Minister to be in turn presented in the assembly.
5) The functions and activities of the strategic plan shall be inherently Government functions and they shall be performed only by the Government functionaries.

2. Contents of a Plan

The strategic plan shall contain
1) A comprehensive mission statement covering the major functions and operations of the department to enhance policy making capability in Government and to improve the performance of the key parts of the public service which contribute significantly to the social and economic development of the state;
2) A Vision statement indicating the direction in which the Department intends to move and what are the major achievements that it aims at;
3) General goals and objectives, including outcome-related goals and objectives for major functions of the department
4) A description of how the goals and objectives are to be achieved (Action Plan), including a description of the operational processes, skills and technology and the human, capital, information and other resources required to meet those goals and objectives
5) A description of how the performance goals included in the plan shall be related to the departmental goals
6) A description of various levels of accountability, i.e.; the measurable goals

7) An identification of those key factors external to the agency and beyond the control that could significantly affect the achievement of the general goals and objectives and

8) Comprehensive description of the evaluation tools used in assessing or revising the objectives and formulation of compatible goals

Chapter 6
Information Flow

1. Classification of Information
   (1) All information called for, from any source shall be either coded, verbal, textual, numerical, audio-visual, alpha-numerical, graded or percentages or any other kind as prescribed and shall be in the prescribed formats, specific to each level, in each Department or Institution.
   (2) The information shall be classified as Ordinary, Urgent, and Top Priority and shall be designated as X, XX, XXX in the formats and confidential information shall be designated as 'Confidential'.

2. Information centers
   (1) There shall be three main levels of information centers i.e. (a) State level, (b) District / Unit level and (c) Mandal / Sub-unit level for each Department or Institution.
   (2) Each Department or Institution shall identify and designate the three levels as specified in subsection (1) for communicating the information from lower to higher level and shall be notified in the Gazette.
   (1) There shall be one nodal officer (by designation) at each level, who shall be the head of the office of that unit and shall be personally accountable for collection, compilation,

analysis, documentation, retrieval, preservation and communication of information, assisted by his subordinate officers and staff.

3. Explanation
   (a) In case, where any Department or Institution has no District level office within the total jurisdiction of the District or forms a part of the District or spreads over two or more Districts, it shall be identified as the unit office.
   Example: A circle office in an Engineering Department shall be the unit office for the purpose of this clause.
   (b) In case, where any Department or Institution has no Mandal level office within the total jurisdiction of the Mandal or forms a part of the Mandal or spreads over two or more Mandals, it shall be identified as sub-unit office.
   Example: A division office in an Engineering Department shall be the sub-unit office for the purpose this clause.
   (4) All the individuals working in the area of operation at each information centre shall personally be accountable for assisting the nodal Officer at that particular level for submission of systematic and periodic information to the next higher level.

4. Mode of Communication
   (1) The mode of communication of information from one level to another level shall be predetermined with approved process either through verbal, personal, telephonic, telegraphic, wireless, postal, electronic or any other prescribed media of data communication systems.
   (2) It may be with one or more modes as given in sub-clause (1) and shall be specified in the prescribed formats.

5. Formats

(1) The collection, compilation, analysis, documentation, preservation and communication of any kind of information shall be in the prescribed formats, specific to each Department or Institution and shall be approved by the Apex Committee as prescribed in the Section ......

(2) Each format shall be coded with nine digit code covering Department code (three digits) Information classification code (three digits) and individual format number (three digits). Explanation:

(a) For the purpose of Management of Information Systems, each Department or Institution shall be given a specific code number in three digits (example: 036)

(b) Information classification code shall be specific to each Department or Institution and shall be in three digits (example 027)

(c) The format number shall be the serial number of the format under each Information classification code in three digits (example: 054)

(3) The formats shall be designed to extract the right information suitable for analysis and amenable for computerization.

(4) It shall specify periodicity, the designation of officer (to authenticate the information), mode of communication etc., along with necessary instructions thereon for collection, compilation, analysis, documentation and communication of information.

(5) The formats specified under this section shall be periodically reviewed and updated and such updated formats shall have the codes with suffix alphabets in succession for each updation.
(Example: 036 027 054 A)

6. Periodicity of Information flow

(1) The periodicity of flow of information from one level to another level may be online, hourly, daily, weekly, fortnightly, monthly, quarterly, and half yearly or yearly as prescribed in the individual formats.

(2) All other correspondence in which any information is called for from the subordinate offices, other than those called through the approved formats as specified in subsection (1) shall contain invariably the date and time of receipt of information and the mode of communication through which the information shall be sent to the such higher office and vice-versa.

7. Power to obtain information

(1) The Apex Committee as specified in Section ...... in each Department may, with a view to achieve the objectives of the Act shall call for any information from individuals and all unit and sub-unit offices in their jurisdiction, in the prescribed formats.

(2) The Apex Committees shall also have the power to call for any other information related from other Departments or Institutions and it may be at the Apex committee level.

(3) The Government shall have the power to call for any information from any Department or Institution and also from any of the citizens in the state in connection with the services rendered through different Departments and agencies of the Government.

Chapter 7
Performance Measurement and Documentation

1. Performance measurement
Performance measurement shall connect the strategic plans to results and shall be a continuous process of

1) Performance Achievement through a set of Indicators i.e. achievement of monthly and cumulative physical and financial targets—indicators, functionaries, institutions & territorial jurisdiction;
2) Progress of important projects (physical and financial)
3) Achievement of process targets in relation to benchmarks and best practices at all levels of Government
4) Collating Information i.e. the information received at each information centre shall be abstracted and such abstracted information shall flow from lower information centre to the next higher centre in the prescribed formats in the given time schedule.
5) Introduction of an Online Performance Tracking System
6) Measurement of Results
7) Identifying Success/Failure

Explanation:
The Mandal / Sub-unit shall abstract the information at their level and send to the information Center at the District / Unit in one or more modes as specified in the formats; and so on.

The analysis of information shall be either manual or through computer or any other means as specified in the formats.

The information officer at each information center shall be personally accountable for the analysis and shall authenticate the abstracts before sending them to the next higher information center.

2. Documentation
   (1) All information collected, analyzed shall be documented through paper or electronic or any other prescribed media before the next information is received in the periodicity at the information center.
   (2) There shall be a documentation officer designated for the purpose under the control of each nodal officer who shall be personally accountable for documentation, preservation and retrieval of the information and shall take all measures for the safety, security of all records and for retrieval of information at any given time, whenever called for.
   (3) The procedure for documentation shall be as prescribed.
3. Research and Analysis Wing (RAW)
   (1) There shall be one Research and Analysis Wing (RAW) at the state level information center in each Department or Institution to analyze historic and current data received from various information centers and other sources.
   (2) It shall be headed by one of the senior officers of the Department or Institution with complementary staff and shall be under the control of the Secretary of the Department concerned.
   (3) It shall periodically analyze the information to draw out the trends for policy making by the Government in each Department on its objectives, as prescribed.
   (4) Subject specialists may be associated with the Departmental officers and staff in the Research and Analysis Wing.
   (5) The procedures and the functions of the Research and Analysis Wing shall be as prescribed.

Chapter 8
Monitoring and Evaluation

1. Evaluation
   (1) Evaluation of performance shall be on each individual working in the jurisdiction of

three level centers i.e. (a) state level centre (b) District/Unit level (c) Mandal/Sub-unit level a nd in each Department or Institution in the State.

(2) Performance indicators shall be evolved for each level as specified in Section (1) pertaining to their jurisdiction in the prescribed formats approved by the Apex Committee in each Department or Institution and may be periodically revised by the Government, as per necessity.

2. Evaluation parameters

(1) The parameters for evaluation of individuals, Departments or Institutions shall be, as approved by the concerned Apex Committees or the Government, as the case may be.

(2) The parameters shall include indicating the performance of individuals, Departments or Institutions for revenue recovery, economy in expenditure, usefulness in expenditure, skills in planning, time management, achievement of goals, quickness of disposals, Administrative skills, monitoring and inspection, or such other parameters as prescribed.

(3) All parameters shall be scalable or quantifiable with time, money, work wise etc., and shall be specified for individuals, Departments or Institutions in a scientific manner.

(4) There shall be four grades for evaluation of the performance for each individual Department or Institution (Example: A, B, C, and D) as approved by the Government

3. Evaluation Authority

(1) The following officers shall review the performance of individuals working in their jurisdiction with the prescribed indicators. Mandal / Sub. Unit level — Officer In charge of Mandal/Sub Unit District / Unit level — District Collector/ Unit Officer

State Level — Secretary or Head of the Department

(2) The Chief Minister or the Chief Secretary of the State shall review performance of all Departments or Institutions at Government level assisted by one or more Secretaries designated for the purpose.

(3) The Authority to review the performance of all other Organizations or Institutions or individuals receiving any form of grant or assistance or aid, whether monitory or otherwise from Government or Public funds shall be as prescribed.

4. Review Meetings

(1) The Officer In charge at Mandal / Sub-unit shall review the performance in his jurisdiction in the prescribed formats, once in a month (i.e.) 1st day in every month.

(2) The District Collector or the Unit Officer of concerned Department or Institution shall review the performance in his jurisdiction in the prescribed formats, once in a month (i.e.,) on 5th of every month.

(3) The Secretary or the Head of the Department as the case may be, shall review the performance of the Department or Departments or Institutions as the case may be in the prescribed formats, once in a month (i.e.) on 10th of every month.

(4) The Chief Minister or the Chief Secretary shall review the performance of all the Departments in the 2nd week of every quarter (i.e.) during the month of January, April, July and October every year.

(5) Special review meetings for any purpose shall be conducted at any level, mentioned under this section, in addition to the regular review meetings, as per the Government Orders from time to time.

(6) The procedure for review meetings and the accountability for the individuals shall be as prescribed.

Chapter 9

Incentives and Disincentives

1. Incentives
   1) Incentives for individuals, Departments or Institutions for their high performing may instituted as a special recognition and it shall be as specified.
   2) The Apex Committee shall be the Authority for awarding such incentives to individuals in their jurisdiction, as per the norms of the Government.
   3) The Government shall be the Authority for awarding such incentives to the Department or Institutions.

2. Disincentives
   (1) In the case of non-performance, disciplinary action shall be initiated by competent authorities by way of penalties as prescribed under CCA Rules for the following, under this Act.
       a) Non submission of information
       b) Consistent delay in submissions of information
       c) Submission of false information
       d) Inaccurate analysis
       e) Breach of official duty in connection with the Accountability fixed under this Act and Rules.
       f) Failure of performance as prescribed
       g) Financial irregularities
       h) Misuse of Stores or Tools and Plant.
       i) Failure to convene review meetings, follow-up actions, Inspections monitoring etc.,
       j) Failure for documentation and preservation of records.

3. Appellate Authority

The appellate authority on the orders of the Apex Committee or the Government as the case may be under this Act shall be the High Court of Andhra Pradesh.

Chapter 10

Apex Committees

1. Formation of Apex Committee
   (1) There shall be one Apex Committee for each Department or Institution headed by the Minister in charge of the Department or Institution as Chairman and the Secretary or Head of the Department concerned as the Vice-Chairman.
   (2) The Apex committee shall be a nine member committee including the Chairman and Vice-Chairman along with seven other members (by designation) drawn from different activities like Administration, Accounts, Technical etc., in that Department or Institution.
   (3) The Apex Committee may co-opt experts, up to a maximum of six members or invite any guest members for suggestions.
   (4) The Apex committee shall be for a period of three years and any casual vacancy shall be filled in by the Apex Committee by co-opting members
   (5) The function of the Apex Committee shall be as prescribed and shall be the Authority for implementation of the Act in their Jurisdiction of the Department or Institution.

2. Meetings
   (1) The Apex Committee in each Department or Institution shall meet compulsorily on 10th day of every quarter i.e. during January, April, July and October every year.
   (2) The meeting shall be chaired by the Chair-

man for every meeting or by the Vice-Chairman in the absence of the Chairman.

(3) The Chairman at his discretion may specially convene the Apex Committee meeting during other times, as per the need.

(4) One of the Apex Committee members shall act as convenor for organizing the meetings who shall be nominated by the Chairman.

(5) The convenor shall be personally responsible for convening the Quarterly meetings and special meetings on the dates specified and shall document all minutes of the meeting and the action taken reports.

(6) The convenor shall initiate all actions necessary for implementation of the minutes of the meeting and shall also bring all matters in respect of the actions taken and to be taken on the minutes of the meeting to the notice of the Apex Committee for further action every time.

Chapter 11

Annual Performance Reports

1. Performance books
   (1) There shall be a performance book for every individual which shall be maintained by the officer in charge and handed over to his successor at the time of change in incumbency at all the three levels.

   (2) It shall contain self appraisal of the controlling officer as well as the appraisal of the subordinates on set goals and achievements for each month.

   (3) It shall be reviewed by the Departmental promotion committees or officers at the time of promotion to next higher cadre and it shall be an open book, not confidential.

2. Department manuals and Function manuals
   (1) There shall be a Department manual for every Department or Institution for its smooth working to achieve its objectives.

   (2) There shall also be a Function manual for each type of job with detailed procedures and accountability at different levels in each Department or Institution.

   (4) All the individuals working in the Department or Institution shall be governed by the Department manual and Function manual.

3. Job charts
   (1) There shall be a job chart for every post, specific to its situation in each Department or Institution and the individuals working in that post shall be accountable for his performance as per the job chart.

   (4) Separate job charts shall be prepared for the same post in different environments specific to its situation.
   Explanation:
   An individual though holds the same post, may work in different environments which requires some specific jobs to be performed
   Example: An engineer in the construction unit, survey unit, water management unit, designs unit will have different jobs to perform and so shall have different job charts specific to his situation.

   (5) The preparation of job charts, scope and fixation of responsibilities shall be as prescribed.

4. Check lists
   (1) There shall be prescribed checklists for every transaction requiring sanctions or approvals, either technical, monitory or administrative in every Department or Institution.

   (2) The check lists shall be a combined checklist for submission, processing and sanction/ approval levels and shall be duly authenticated by the individuals at various

levels and they shall be accountable at their level.

5. Year book

(1) Every information center shall, for the purpose of efficient discharge of its functions under this Act, and guide that centre for subsequent year of operation shall document in typed script or in any other mode as prescribed regarding:

(a) Budgetary details;

(b) All sanctions and approvals;

(c) Full details of receipts and expenditure;

(d) Incumbency of officers and staff;

(e) Details of all activities in its jurisdiction; and

(f) Other information as prescribed from time to time.

(2) The documentation officers concerned shall be personally responsible for preparation of this year book by 1st May every year.

(3) The modalities for preparation of the year book, distribution, preservation etc., shall be as prescribed.

Chapter 12
Human Resources Development

1. Training Institutes

1) There shall be a nodal training Institute at the State level for Human Resources Development, for officers and staff and District training centers under its control.

2) The nodal training Institute shall monitor and coordinate the activities of all other training Institutes in various Departments, as prescribed.

3) There shall be a central training Budget to be operated by the nodal training Institute

for distribution among various Departments, as a percentage on budget estimates, as prescribed from time to time.

4) The nodal training Institute shall develop a strategic plan for all the training Institutes based on the training needs assessment for officers and staff in various Departments and Institutions.

2. Trainings

1) The Trainings for officers and staff may be imparted for Administrative skills, Technical skills, Management skills, and other skills as prescribed, for improving the efficiency and effectiveness for achieving the program objectives of the state.

2) The Trainings may be of the following categories and may be imparted during the tenure of the office.

(a) Orientation Trainings;

(b) In-service Trainings;

(c) Special Trainings; and

(d) Other Trainings as prescribed.

3) The training components, duration, number of trainings, selection of participants and other modalities required for organizing the training programs shall be, as prescribed.

3. Feed back analysis

The effectiveness of the training shall be monitored and accountability fixed on the trainees based on the feed back analysis from trainees during and after training.

Chapter 13
SMART Governance

Government of Andhra Pradesh is working towards a SMART Government

S: Simplifying Government: To enable Government to improve quality of service to the customer and increase his value for money through simplifying procedures.

M: Moral Government: To develop an effective HRM Plan by embedding new structures and approaches to HRM

A: Accountable Government: To improve the quality and timelines of delivery of services and to develop a flexible result-focused performance culture across the public service through systems which effectively monitor and measure performance.

R: Responsive Citizen Focused Government: To ensure people have a strong voice in the governance of the state, through participatory mechanisms into planning and monitoring of service delivery, enhancing decentralization and ensuring inclusiveness of the poor and disadvantaged

T: Transparency in Government: To improve planning, resource allocation, monitoring, management and accounting systems and access to information so that accountability is clear, spending is transparent and public expenditure is more effectively controlled.

Chapter 14

Miscellaneous

1. Power to remove difficulties
    (1) If any difficult arises in giving effect to the provisions of this Act, the Government as the occasion may require, by order published in the Andhra Pradesh Gazette, do any thing which appears to them necessary for removing the difficulty.
    (2) All orders made under this section shall as soon as may be, after they are made, be placed on the table of the legislative Assembly of the state and shall be subject to such modifications by way of amendments or repeal as the Legislative Assembly may make either in the same session or next session.

2. Power to make Rules.
    (1) The State Government may, by notification in the official Gazette, make rules to carry out the purpose of this Act.
    (2) Every Rule under the Act shall immediately after it is made, be laid before the Legislative Assembly of the State, if it is in session and if it is not in session in the session immediately following for a total period of fourteen days which may be comprised in one session or in two successive sessions, and if, before the expiration of the session in which it is so laid or the session immediately following, the Legislative Assembly agrees in making, any modification in the rule or in the annulment of the rule, the rule shall, from the date on which the modification or annulment is notified, have effect only in such modified form or shall stand annulled as the case may be, so however, that any such modification or annulment shall be without prejudice to the validity of anything previously done under that rule.

3. Protection of Actions done in good faith
No penalty shall be levied against an individual, Department or Institution to discharge any function under this Act, for any loss or damage caused or likely to be caused by any action which is in good faith done or intended to be done in pursuance of this Act or under the Rules made thereunder.

Some Definitions
In this Act, unless the context otherwise requires,
    1. **'Government'** means the State Government

2. **'Department'** means any State Government Department under the Control of Government of Andhra Pradesh.

3. **'Institution'** means an Institution established under law by the State or any other Institution which receives any form of grant or assistance or aid, either monetary or otherwise from the Government.

4. **'Individual'** means an individual working in the Department or Public Institution and receiving salary or any form of remuneration or assistance from the Government or public funds.

5. **'Incentives'** means all kinds of incentives either monetary, commendatory, promotions, awards etc., given for the rated performance of individuals, Departments or Institutions based on the approved reports of the Statutory Committees instituted for the purpose.

6. **'Disincentives'** means all kinds of disincentives either monitory, condemnatory, de-promotions, penalties etc., given for the rated performance of individuals, Departments or Institutions based on the approved reports of Statutory Committees instituted for the purpose.

7. **'Information'** means information either coded, verbal, textual, numerical, alphanumeric, audio-visual, graded, percentages, etc., generated or to be generated by individuals, Departments and Institutions (both basic data and analyzed data) in performance of duties.

8. **'Information Systems'** means the approved system of collection, compilation, analysis, documentation; retrieval and communication of the information from Gross root level to Apex level, as prescribed.

9. **'Performance'** means all kinds of scalable performance in respect of achieving the objectives for the set goals, either monetary, service, or other wise as prescribed.

10. **'Notification'** means notification published in the Andhra Pradesh Gazette and the word notified shall be construed accordingly.

Glossary
OECD Glossary of Key Terms in Evaluation and Results-Based Management (2002)

Accountability: Obligation to demonstrate that work has been conducted in compliance with agreed rules and standards or to report fairly and accurately on performance results vis-à-vis mandated roles and/or plans. This may require a careful, even legally defensible, demonstration that the work is consistent with the contract terms.

Note: Accountability in development may refer to the obligations of partners to act according to clearly defined responsibilities, roles and performance expectations, often with respect to the prudent use of resources. For evaluators, it connotes the responsibility to provide accurate, fair and credible monitoring reports and performance assessments. For public sector managers and policy-makers, accountability is to taxpayers/citizens.

Activity: Actions taken or work performed through which inputs, such as funds, technical assistance and other types of resources are mobilized to produce specific outputs.

Related term: development intervention.

Analytical tools: Methods used to process and interpret information during an evaluation.

Appraisal: An overall assessment of the relevance, feasibility and potential sustainability of a development intervention prior to a decision of funding.

Note: In development agencies, banks, etc., the purpose of appraisal is to enable decision-makers to decide whether the activity represents an appropriate use of corporate resources.

Related term: ex-ante evaluation.

Assumptions: Hypotheses about factors or risks which could affect the progress or success of a development intervention.

Note: Assumptions can also be understood as hypothesized conditions that bear on the validity of the evaluation itself, e.g., about the characteristics of the population when designing a sampling procedure for a survey. Assumptions are made explicit in theory-based evaluations where evaluation tracks systematically the anticipated results chain.

Attribution: The ascription of a causal link between observed (or expected to be observed) changes and a specific intervention.

Note: Attribution refers to that which is to be credited for the observed changes or results achieved. It represents the extent to which observed development effects can be attributed to a specific intervention or to the performance of one or more partner taking account of other interventions, (anticipated or unanticipated) confounding factors, or external shocks.

Audit: An independent, objective assurance activity designed to add value and improve an organization's operations. It helps an organization accomplish its objectives by bringing a systematic, disciplined approach to assess and improve the effectiveness of risk management, control and governance processes.

Note: a distinction is made between regularity (financial) auditing, which focuses on compliance with the applicable statutes and regulations; and performance auditing, which is concerned with relevance, economy, efficiency and effectiveness. Internal auditing provides an assessment of internal controls undertaken by a unit reporting to management while external auditing is conducted by an independent organization.

Base-line study: An analysis describing the situation prior to a development intervention, against which progress can be assessed or comparisons made.

Benchmark: Reference point or standard against which performance or achievements can be assessed.

Note: A benchmark refers to the performance that has been achieved in the recent past by other comparable organizations, or what can be reasonably inferred to have been achieved in the circumstances.

Beneficiaries: The individuals, groups, or organizations, whether targeted or not, that benefit, directly or indirectly, from the development intervention.

Related terms: reach, target groups.

Cluster evaluation: An evaluation of a set of related activities, projects and/or programs.

Conclusions: Conclusions point out the factors of success and failure of the evaluated intervention, with special attention paid to the intended and unintended results and impacts, and more generally to any other strength or weakness. A conclusion draws on data collec-

tion and analyses undertaken, through a transparent chain of arguments.

Counterfactual: The situation or condition which hypothetically may prevail for individuals, organizations, or groups where there is no development intervention.

Country Program Evaluation/ Country Assistance Evaluation: Evaluation of one or more donor's or agency's portfolio of development interventions, and the assistance strategy behind them, in a partner country.

Data collection tools: Methodologies used to identify information sources and collect information during an evaluation.

Note: Examples are informal and formal surveys, direct and participatory observation, community interviews, focus groups, expert opinion, case studies, literature search.

Development intervention: An instrument for partner (donor and non-donor) support aimed to promote development.

Note: Examples are policy advice, projects and programs.

Development objective: Intended impact contributing to physical, financial, institutional, social, environmental, or other benefits to a society, community, or group of people via one or more development interventions.

Economy: Absence of waste for a given output.

Note: An activity is economical when the costs of the scarce resources used approximate the minimum needed to achieve planned objectives.

Effect: Intended or unintended change due directly or indirectly to an intervention.

Related terms: results, outcome.

Effectiveness: The extent to which the development intervention's objectives were achieved, or are expected to be achieved, taking into account their relative importance.

Note: Also used as an aggregate measure of (or judgment about) the merit or worth of an activity, i.e., the extent to which an intervention has attained, or is expected to attain, its major relevant objectives efficiently in a sustainable fashion and with a positive institutional development impact.

Related term: efficacy.

Efficiency: A measure of how economically resources/inputs (funds, expertise, time, etc.) are converted to results.

Evaluability: Extent to which an activity or program can be evaluated in a reliable and credible fashion.

Note: Evaluability assessment calls for the early review of a proposed activity in order to ascertain whether its objectives are adequately defined and its results verifiable.

Evaluation: The systematic and objective assessment of an on-going or completed project, program or policy, its design, implementation and results. The aim is to determine the relevance and fulfillment of objectives, development efficiency, effectiveness, impact and sustainability. An evaluation should provide information that is credible and useful, enabling the incorporation of lessons learned into the decision-making process of both recipients and donors.

Evaluation also refers to the process of determining the worth or significance of an activity, policy or program. An assessment, as systematic and objective as possible, of a planned, on-going, or completed development intervention.

Note: Evaluation in some instances involves the definition of appropriate standards, the examination of performance against those standards, an assessment of actual and expected results and the identification of relevant lessons.

Related term: review.

Ex-ante evaluation: An evaluation that is performed before implementation of a development intervention.

Related terms: appraisal, quality at entry.

Ex-post evaluation: Evaluation of a development intervention after it has been completed.

Note: It may be undertaken directly after or long after completion. The intention is to identify the factors of success or failure, to assess the sustainability of results and impacts, and to draw conclusions that may inform other interventions.

External evaluation: The evaluation of a development intervention conducted by entities and/or individuals outside the donor and implementing organizations.

Feedback: The transmission of findings generated through the evaluation process to parties for whom it is relevant and useful so as to facilitate learning. This may involve the collection and dissemination of findings, conclusions, recommendations and lessons from experience.

Finding: A finding uses evidence from one or more evaluations to allow for a factual statement.

Formative evaluation: Evaluation intended to improve performance, most often conducted during the implementation phase of projects or programs.

Note: Formative evaluations may also be conducted for other reasons such as compliance, legal requirements or as part of a larger evaluation initiative.

Related term: process evaluation.

Goal: The higher-order objective to which a development intervention is intended to contribute.

Related term: development objective.

Impacts: Positive and negative, primary and secondary, long-term effects produced by a development intervention, directly or indirectly, intended or unintended.

Independent evaluation: An evaluation carried out by entities and persons free of the control of those responsible for design and implementation of the development intervention.

Note: The credibility of an evaluation depends in part on how independently it has been carried out. Independence implies freedom from political influence and organizational pressure. It is characterized by full access to information and by full autonomy in carrying out investigations and reporting findings.

Indicator: Quantitative or qualitative factor or variable that provides a simple and reliable means to measure achievement, to reflect the changes connected to an intervention, or to help assess the performance of a development actor.

Inputs: The financial, human, and material resources used for the development intervention.

Institutional Development Impact: The extent to which an intervention improves or weakens the ability of a country or region to make more efficient, equitable, and sustain-

able use of its human, financial, and natural resources, for example through: (a) better definition, stability, transparency, enforceability and predictability of institutional arrangements and/or (b) better alignment of the mission and capacity of an organization with its mandate, which derives from these institutional arrangements. Such impacts can include intended and unintended effects of an action.

Internal evaluation: Evaluation of a development intervention conducted by a unit and/or individuals reporting to the management of the donor, partner, or implementing organization.

Related term: self-evaluation.

Joint evaluation: An evaluation to which different donor agencies and/or partners participate.

Note: There are various degrees of "jointness" depending on the extent to which individual partners cooperate in the evaluation process, merge their evaluation resources and combine their evaluation reporting. Joint evaluations can help overcome attribution problems in assessing the effectiveness of programs and strategies, the complementarity of efforts supported by different partners, the quality of aid coordination, etc.

Lessons learned: Generalizations based on evaluation experiences with projects, programs, or policies that abstract from the specific circumstances to broader situations. Frequently, lessons highlight strengths or weaknesses in preparation, design, and implementation that affect performance, outcome, and impact.

Logical framework (Logframe): Management tool used to improve the design of interventions, most often at the project level. It involves identifying strategic elements (inputs, outputs, outcomes, impact) and their causal relationships, indicators, and the assumptions or risks that may influence success and failure. It thus facilitates planning, execution and evaluation of a development intervention.

Related term: results-based management.

Meta-evaluation: The term is used for evaluations designed to aggregate findings from a series of evaluations. It can also be used to denote the evaluation of an evaluation to judge its quality and/or assess the performance of the evaluators.

Mid-term evaluation: Evaluation performed toward the middle of the period of implementation of the intervention.

Related term: formative evaluation.

Monitoring: A continuing function that uses systematic collection of data on specified indicators to provide management and the main stakeholders of an ongoing development intervention with indications of the extent of progress and achievement of objectives and progress in the use of allocated funds.

Related term: performance monitoring, indicator.

Outcome: The likely or achieved short-term and medium-term effects of an intervention's outputs.

Related terms: result, outputs, impacts, effect.

Outputs: The products, capital goods and services that result from a development intervention; may also include changes resulting from the intervention which are relevant to the achievement of outcomes.

Participatory evaluation: Evaluation method in which representatives of agencies and stakeholders (including beneficiaries) work together in designing, carrying out and interpreting an evaluation.

Partners: The individuals and/or organizations that collaborate to achieve mutually agreed upon objectives.

Note: The concept of partnership connotes shared goals, common responsibility for outcomes, distinct accountabilities and reciprocal obligations. Partners may include governments, civil society, non-governmental organizations, universities, professional and business associations, multilateral organizations, private companies, etc.

Performance: The degree to which a development intervention or a development partner operates according to specific criteria/standards/guidelines or achieves results in accordance with stated goals or plans.

Performance indicator: A variable that allows the verification of changes in the development intervention or shows results relative to what was planned.

Related terms: performance monitoring, performance measurement.

Performance measurement: A system for assessing performance of development interventions against stated goals.

Related terms: performance monitoring, indicator.

Performance monitoring: A continuous process of collecting and analyzing data to compare how well a project, program, or policy is being implemented against expected results.

Process evaluation: An evaluation of the internal dynamics of implementing organizations, their policy instruments, their service delivery mechanisms, their management practices, and the linkages among these.

Related term: formative evaluation.

Program evaluation: Evaluation of a set of interventions, marshaled to attain specific global, regional, country, or sector development objectives.

Note: a development program is a time bound intervention involving multiple activities that may cut across sectors, themes and/or geographic areas.

Related term: Country program/strategy evaluation.

Project evaluation: Evaluation of an individual development intervention designed to achieve specific objectives within specified resources and implementation schedules, often within the framework of a broader program.

Note: Cost benefit analysis is a major instrument of project evaluation for projects with measurable benefits. When benefits cannot be quantified, cost-effectiveness is a suitable approach.

Project or program objective: The intended physical, financial, institutional, social, environmental, or other development results to which a project or program is expected to contribute.

Purpose: The publicly stated objectives of the development program or project.

Quality assurance: Quality assurance encompasses any activity that is concerned with assessing and improving the merit or the worth of a development intervention or its compliance with given standards.

Note: examples of quality assurance activities include appraisal, RBM, reviews during implementation, evaluations, etc. Quality assurance may also refer to the assessment of the quality of a portfolio and its development effectiveness.

Results-Based Management (RBM): A management strategy focusing on performance and achievement of outputs, outcomes and impacts.

Related term: logical framework.

Review: An assessment of the performance of an intervention, periodically or on an ad hoc basis.

Note: Frequently "evaluation" is used for a more comprehensive and/or more in-depth assessment than "review." Reviews tend to emphasize operational aspects. Sometimes the terms "review" and "evaluation" are used as synonyms.

Related term: evaluation.

Risk analysis: An analysis or an assessment of factors (called assumptions in the logframe) that affect or are likely to affect the successful achievement of an intervention's objectives. A detailed examination of the potential unwanted and negative consequences to human life, health, property, or the environment posed by development interventions; a systematic process to provide information regarding such undesirable consequences; the process of quantification of the probabilities and expected impacts for identified risks.

Sector program evaluation: Evaluation of a cluster of development interventions in a sector within one country or across countries, all of which contribute to the achievement of a specific development goal.

Note: a sector includes development activities commonly grouped together for the purpose of publication such as health, education, agriculture, transport, etc.

Self-evaluation: An evaluation by those who are entrusted with the design and delivery of a development intervention.

Stakeholders: Agencies, organizations, groups or individuals who have a direct or indirect interest in the development intervention or its evaluation.

Summative evaluation: A study conducted at the end of an intervention (or a phase of that intervention) to determine the extent to which anticipated outcomes were produced. Summative evaluation is intended to provide information about the worth of the program.
Related term: impact evaluation.

Sustainability: The continuation of benefits from a development intervention after major development assistance has been completed.
The probability of continued long-term benefits. The resilience to risk of the net benefit flows over time.

Target group: The specific individuals or organizations for whose benefit the development intervention is undertaken.

Terms of reference: Written document presenting the purpose and scope of the evaluation, the methods to be used, the standard against which performance is to be assessed or analyses are to be conducted, the resources and time allocated, and reporting requirements. Two other expressions sometimes used with the same meaning are "scope of work" and "evaluation mandate."

Thematic evaluation: Evaluation of a selection of development interventions, all of which address a specific development priority that cuts across countries, regions, and sectors.

Triangulation: The use of three or more theories, sources or types of information, or types of analysis to verify and substantiate an assessment.
Note: by combining multiple data sources, methods, analyses or theories, evaluators seek to overcome the bias that comes from single informants, single methods, single observer or single theory studies.

Validity: The extent to which the data collection strategies and instruments measure what they purport to measure.

Source: OECD 2002a.

Notes

1. A complete list of the MDGs—including targets and indicators—can be found in annex 3.
2. "Technical cooperation expenditures totaled US$14.3 billion in 1999, according to the Development Assistance Committee (DAC) of the OECD. This is a large amount, almost double the sum in 1969. If personnel and training in investment and other projects are included, the figure would be even larger, $24.6 billion (Baris et al., 2002)" (Fukuda-Parr, Lopes, and Malik 2002 pp. 3–4).
3. While we refer to the country as the unit of analysis here, we will immediately stress that the same concept of a readiness assessment could be applicable to a sector, a region, a program, or even an individual project. It is also applicable in civil society and the private sector.
4. A version of the readiness assessment for countries, individual ministries, and development organizations that wish to undertake a self-assessment is contained in annex 1, "Assessing Results-Based M&E Capacity: An Assessment for Countries, Development Institutions and Their Partners." See also "A Diagnostic Guide and Action Framework" (Mackay 1999). Some questions in the readiness assessment in this handbook are drawn from that earlier work.
5. There are other models for setting good performance indicators. For example, the UNDP uses another formula, the SMART principle; the characteristics of good indicators are S=specific, M=measurable, A=attainable, R=relevant, and T=trackable (Kahn 2001, p. 24).
6. Also see annex 6 for a complete glossary of key terms in evaluation and results-based management.

References

Binnendijk, Annette. 2000. "Results Based Management in the Development Cooperation Agencies: A Review of Experience." Paper prepared for OECD/DAC Working Party on Aid Evaluation. Paris. February 10–11. (Revised October 2000.)

Carroll, Lewis. 1865. *Alice's Adventures in Wonderland*. Reprint edition 2002. New York: Sea Star Books.

ChannahSorah, Vijaya Vinita. 2003. "Moving from Measuring Processes to Outcomes: Lessons Learned from GPRA in the United States." Presented at World Bank and Korea Development Institute joint conference on Performance Evaluation System and Guidelines with Application to Large-Scale Construction, R&D, and Job Training Investments. Seoul, South Korea. July 24–25.

Crawford, David. 2003. "With Help from Corporations, German Group Fights Corruption." *Wall Street Journal*, November 26.

The Daily Star. 2003. "Saidi Predicts Gains from Joining IMF Data System: Part of Good Governance." January 28.

Dorotinsky, William. 2003a. "Active and Passive Approaches to Use of Results Findings." World Bank. Personal communication with authors, December 5, 2003.

Dorotinsky, William. 2003b. Information on Monitoring for Results in Brazil. World Bank. Personal communication with authors, December 5, 2003.

Fukuda-Parr, Sakiko, Carlos Lopes, and Khalid Malik, eds. 2002. *Capacity for Development: New Solutions to Old Problems*. London: Earthscan Publications, Ltd.

Furubo, Jan-Eric, Ray C. Rist, and Rolf Sandahl, eds. 2002. *International Atlas of Evaluation*. New Brunswick, N.J.: Transaction Publishers.

Guerrero, R. Pablo. 1999. "Evaluation Capacity Development: Comparative Insights from Colombia, China, and Indonesia," in Richard Boyle and Donald Lemaire, eds., *Building Effective Evaluation Capacity: Lessons from Practice*. New Brunswick, N.J.: Transaction Publishers.

Hatry, Harry P. 1999. *Performance Measurement: Getting Results*. Washington, D.C.: The Urban Institute Press.

Hatry, Harry P., Elaine Morley, Shelli B. Rossman, Joseph P. Wholey. 2003. "How Federal Programs Use Outcome Information: Opportunities for Federal Managers." Washington, D.C.: IBM Endowment for The Business of Government.

Hauge, Arild. 2001. "Strengthening Capacity for Monitoring and Evaluation in Uganda: A Results Based Perspective." World Bank Operations Evaluation Dept. ECD Working Paper Series, Number 8. Washington, D.C.

IDA (International Development Association). 2002. "Measuring Outputs and Outcomes in IDA Countries." IDA 13. World Bank. Washington, D.C.

IFAD (International Fund for Agricultural Development). 2002. "A Guide for Project M&E: Managing for Impact in Rural Development." Rome: IFAD. Available at http://www.ifad.org/evaluation/guide/

IMF (International Monetary Fund). 2002. "What is the General Data Dissemination System (GDDS)?" Washington, D.C.: IMF.

———. 2003. "Financial Soundness Indicators." Washington, D.C.: IMF. Available at http://imf.org/external/np/sta/fsi/eng/fsi.htm

Khan, M. Adil. 2001. *A Guidebook on Results Based Monitoring and Evaluation: Key Concepts, Issues and Applications*. Monitoring and Progress Review Division, Ministry of Plan Implementation, Government of Sri Lanka. Colombo, Sri Lanka.

Kumar, Krishna, ed. 1993. *Rapid Appraisal Methods.* World Bank. Washington, D.C.

Kusek, J. Z. and R. C. Rist. 2001. "Building a Performance-Based Monitoring and Evaluation System: The Challenges Facing Developing Countries." *Evaluation Journal of Australasia.* 1(2): 14–23.

———. 2003. "Readiness Assessment: Toward Performance Monitoring and Evaluation in the Kyrgyz Republic." *Japanese Journal of Evaluation Studies.* 3(1): 17–31.

Lee, Yoon-Shik. 1999. In Richard Boyle and Donald Lemaire, eds. *Building Effective Evaluation Capacity: Lessons from Practice.* New Brunswick, N.J.: Transaction Publishers.

———. 2002. In Jan-Eric Furubo, Ray C. Rist, and Rolf Sandahl, eds. *International Atlas of Evaluation.* New Brunswick, N.J.: Transaction Publishers.

Leeuw, Frans L. 2003. "Evaluation of Development Agencies' Performance: The Role of Meta-Evaluations." Paper prepared for the Fifth Biennial World Bank Conference on Evaluation and Development. Washington, D.C. July 15–16.

Mackay, Keith. 1999. "Evaluation Capacity Development: A Diagnostic Guide and Action Framework." World Bank Operations Evaluation Department. ECD Working Paper Series, Number 6. Washington, D.C.

———. 2002. "The Australian Government: Success with a Central, Directive Approach," in Furubo, Rist, and Sandahl, eds., *International Atlas of Evaluation.* New Brunswick, N.J.: Transaction Publishers.

Marchant, Tim. 2000. Africa Region presentation. World Bank. Washington D.C.

NYC.gov. 2003. "New York City Continues to be the Nation's Safest Large City." http://www.nyc.gov/html/om/html/2003a/crime_falls.html

O'Connell, Paul E. 2001."Using Performance Data for Accountability: The New York City Police Department's CompStat Model of Police Management." PricewaterhouseCoopers Endowment for The Business of Government: Arlington, Va.

OECD (Organisation for Economic Co-operation and Development). 2001. "Evaluation Feedback for Effective Learning and Accountability." Paris: OECD/ DAC.

———. 2002a. "Glossary of Key Terms in Evaluation and Results-Based Management." Paris: OECD/ DAC.

———. 2002b. Public Management and Governance (PUMA). "Overview of Results-Focused Management and Budgeting in OECD Member Countries." Twenty-third Annual Meeting of OECD Senior Budget Officials. Washington, D.C. June 3–4.

Osborne, David and Ted Gaebler. 1992. *Reinventing Government.* Boston, Mass.: Addison-Wesley Publishing.

Picciotto, Robert. 2002. "Development Cooperation and Performance Evaluation: The Monterrey Challenge." World Bank working paper prepared for roundtable on "Better Measuring, Monitoring, and Managing for Development Results," sponsored by the Multilateral Development Banks in cooperation with the Development Assistance Committee of the Organisation for Economic Co-operation and Development. Washington, D.C., June 5–6.

President of the Treasury Board of Canada. 2002. "Canada's Performance 2002: Annual Report to Parliament." Ottawa, Canada.

Republique Française. 2001. Ministère de l'Economie des Finances et de l'Industrie. "Towards New Public Management. Newsletter on the Public Finance Reform." No. 1. September.

Schacter, Mark. 2000. "Sub-Saharan Africa: Lessons from Experience in Supporting Sound Governance." World Bank Operations Evaluation Department. ECD Working Paper Series, Number 7. Washington, D.C.

Schiavo-Campo, Salvatore. 1999. "'Performance' in the Public Sector." *Asian Journal of Political Science* 7(2): 75–87.

Sri Lanka Evaluation Association and the Ministry of Policy Development and Implementation. 2003. "National Evaluation Policy for Sri Lanka." Colombo, Sri Lanka.

Stiglitz, Joseph and Roumeen Islam. 2003. "Information is Capital." *Le Monde*. January 3.

TI (Transparency International). 1997. Available at http://www.transparency.org/

———. 2002. Available at http://www.transparency.org/

Treasury Board Secretariat of Canada. 2001. "Guide for the Development of Results-Based Management and Accountability Frameworks." Ottawa, Canada.

Tufte, Edward R. 2001. *The Visual Display of Quantitative Information*. Cheshire, Conn.: Graphics Press.

———. 2002. *Visual Explanations: Images and Quantities, Evidence and Narrative*. Cheshire, Conn.: Graphics Press.

U.K. Cabinet Office. n.d. Available at http://www.cabinet-office.gov.uk

United Nations. n.d. Available at http://www.un.org/millenniumgoals/

———. 2003. "Indicators for Monitoring the Millennium Development Goals." New York, N.Y.: United Nations. Available at http://www.developmentgoals.org/mdgun/MDG_metadata_08-01-03_UN.htm

UNDP (United Nations Development Programme). 2001. "Human Development Report." New York: Oxford University Press. Also available at http://www.undp.org/hdr2001/faqs.html##1

———. 2002. *Handbook on Monitoring and Evaluating for Results*. New York: UNDP Evaluation Office.

UNPF (United Nations Population Fund). 2002. "Monitoring and Evaluation Toolkit for Programme Managers." Office of Oversight and Evaluation. Available at http://www.unfpa.org/monitoring/toolkit.htm

U.S. Department of Labor. 2002. "Annual Performance Plan: Fiscal Year 2003." Washington, D.C.

U.S. General Accounting Office (GAO). 2002. "Highlights of a GAO Forum, Mergers and Transformation: Lessons Learned for a Department of Homeland Security and Other Federal Agencies." Washington, D.C.

———. 2003. "Program Evaluation: An Evaluation Culture and Collaborative Partnerships Help Build Agency Capacity." Washington, D.C.

U.S. Office of Management and Budget. 1993. "Government Performance Results Act of 1993." Washington, D.C.

United Way of America. 1996. "Outcome Measurement Resource Network." Available at http://national.unitedway.org/outcomes/resources/mpo/contents.cfm

Valadez, Joseph, and Michael Bamberger. 1994. *Monitoring and Evaluating Social Programs in Developing Countries: A Handbook for Policymakers, Managers, and Researchers*. Washington, D.C.: The World Bank.

Webb, E. J., D. T. Campbell, R. D. Schwartz, L. Sechrest, 1966. *Unobtrusive Measures: Nonreactive Research in the Social Sciences*. Chicago: Rand McNally.

Wholey, Joseph S. 2001. "Managing for Results: Roles for Evaluators in a New Management Era." *The American Journal of Evaluation*. 22(3): 343–347.

Wholey, Joseph S., Harry Hatry, and Kathryn Newcomer. 1994. *Handbook of Practical Program Evaluation*. San Francisco: Jossey-Bass Publishers.

World Bank. "Core Welfare Indicators Questionnaire." Washington, D.C. Available at http://www4.worldbank.org/afr/stats/pdf/cwiq.pdf

———. "Ghana Core Welfare Indicators." Washington, D.C. Available at http://www.worldbank.org/afr/stats/pdf/ghcoreinds.pdf

———. "Introducing the Core Welfare Indicators Questionnaire (CWIQ)." Washington, D.C. Available at http://www4.worldbank.org/afr/stats/pdf/cwiqloop.pdf

———. 1997. *World Development Report 1997: The State in a Changing World*. New York: Oxford University Press.

———. 2000. "Rural Development Indicators Handbook." 2nd Edition. Washington, D.C. Available at http://www-wds.worldbank.org/servlet/WDS_IBank_Servlet?pcont=details&eid=000094946_01061604041624

———. 2001a. International Program for Development Evaluation Training (IPDET).

http://www.worldbank.org/oed/ipdet/

———. 2001b. "Outcomes-Based Budgeting Systems: Experience from Developed and Developing Countries." Washington, D.C.

———. 2001c. "Readiness Assessment—Toward Results-Based Monitoring and Evaluation in Egypt." Washington, D.C.

———. 2001d. "Readiness Assessment—Toward Results-Based Monitoring and Evaluation in Romania." Washington, D.C.

———. 2001e. "Readiness Assessment—Toward Results-Based Monitoring and Evaluation in the Philippines." Washington, D.C.

———. 2002a. Albania country documents and reports. Washington, D.C. Available at http://lnweb18.worldbank.org/eca/albania.nsf

———. 2002b. "Heavily Indebted Poor Country Initiative (HIPC)." Washington, D.C. Available at http://www.worldbank.org/ug/hipc.htm

———. 2002c. "Readiness Assessment—Toward Results-Based Monitoring and Evaluation in Bangladesh." Washington, D.C.

———. 2002d. "Republic of Albania: Establishment of a Permanent System of Household Surveys for Poverty Monitoring and Policy Evaluation." Concept document. Washington, D.C.

———. 2003a. Operations Evaluation Department Web site: http://www.worldbank.org/oed/ecd/.

———. 2003b. Overview of Poverty Reduction Strategies. http://www.worldbank.org/poverty/strategies/overview.htm

———. 2003c. "Toward Country-Led Development: A Multi-Partner Evaluation of the CDF." *OED Precis,* Number 233. Washington, D.C.

Worthen, Blaine, James Sanders, and Jody Fitzpatrick. 1997. *Program Evaluation: Alternative Approaches and Practical Guidelines.* New York: Longman Publishers.

Wye, Chris. 2002. "Performance Management: A 'Start Where You Are, Use What You Have' Guide." Arlington, Va.: IBM Endowment for Business in Government. Managing for Results Series.

Useful Web Sites

E-Government in New Zealand: http://www.e-government.govt.nz/

Egyptian Museum, Cairo:
http://www.touregypt.net/egyptmuseum/egyptian_museum.htm

Monitoring and Evaluation Capacity Development:
http://www.worldbank.org/oed/ecd/

Monitoring and Evaluation News:
http://www.mande.co.uk/

OECD Development Assistance Committee Working Party on Aid Evaluation:
http://www.oecd.org/home/

OECD E-Government:
http://www.oecd.org/department/0,2688,en_2649_34131_1_1_1_1_1,00.html

OECD Public Management Program:
http://www1.oecd.org/puma/

Transparency International: http://www.transparency.org/

United Nations Online Network in Public Administration and Finance
http://www.unpan.org/

USAID Center for Development Information and Evaluation: http://www.usaid.gov/pubs/usaid_eval/

World Bank Operations Evaluation Department:
http://www.worldbank.org/oed/

www.worldbank.org/oed/ecd (M&E capacity building)

http://www.worldbank.org/oed/ipdet/

WWW Virtual Library: Evaluation, http://www.policy-evaluation.org/

Additional Reading

Introduction

Kettl, Donald F. 2002. *The Global Public Management Revolution: A Report on the Transformation of Governance.* Washington, D.C.: Brookings Institution.

Kusek, J. Z. and R. C. Rist. 2000. "Making M&E Matter—Get the Foundation Right." *Evaluation Insights.* 2(2):7–10.

———. 2002. "Building Results-Based Monitoring and Evaluation Systems: Assessing Developing Countries Readiness." *Zeitschrift für Evaluation.* (1): 151–158.

———. 2003. "Readiness Assessment: Toward Performance Monitoring and Evaluation in the Kyrgyz Republic." *Japanese Journal of Evaluation Studies.* 3(1): 17–31.

Mayne, John and Eduardo Zapico-Goni, eds. 1999. *Monitoring Performance in the Public Sector: Future Directions from International Experience.* New Brunswick, N.J.: Transaction Publishers.

Picciotto, Robert and Eduardo D. Wiesner, eds. 1998. *Evaluation and Development.* New Brunswick, N.J.: Transaction Publishers.

The World Bank. 1994. *Report of the Evaluation Capacity Task Force.* Washington, D.C.

Chapter 1

Boyle, Richard and Donald Lemaire, eds. 1999. *Building Effective Evaluation Capacity: Lessons from Practice.* New Brunswick, N.J.: Transaction Publishers.

Kusek, Jody Zall, and Ray C. Rist. 2000. "Making M&E Matter—Get the Foundation Right." *Evaluation Insights.* 2(2):7–10

———. 2001. "Building a Performance-Based M&E System: The Challenges Facing Developing Countries." *Evaluation Journal of Australasia.* 1(2):14–23.

———. 2002. "Building Results-Based Monitoring and Evaluation Systems: Assessing Developing Countries' Readiness." *Zeitschrift für Evaluation,* (1): 151–158.

———. 2003. "Readiness Assessment: Toward Performance Monitoring and Evaluation in the Kyrgyz Republic." *Japanese Journal of Evaluation Studies.* 3(1):17–31.

Chapter 2

International Fund for Agricultural Development (IFAD). 2002. "Managing for Impact in Rural Development: A Guide for Project M&E." Rome: IFAD. Available at http://www.ifad.org/evaluation/guide/

Khan, M. Adil. 2001. "A Guidebook on Results Based Monitoring and Evaluation: Key Concepts, Issues and Applications." Monitoring and Progress Review Division, Ministry of Plan Implementation, Government of Sri Lanka. Colombo, Sri Lanka.

International Development Association (IDA). 2002. "Measuring Outputs and Outcomes in IDA Countries." IDA 13. World Bank, Washington, D.C.

Chapter 3

Hatry, Harry P. 2001. "What Types of Performance Information Should be Tracked," in Dall W. Forsythe, ed., *Quicker, Better, Cheaper? Managing Performance in American Government.* Albany, N.Y.: Rockefeller Institute Press.

Kusek, J. Z. and Ray C. Rist. 2000. "Making M&E Matter—Get the Foundation Right." *Evaluation Insights* 2(2):7–10.

Mayne, John and Eduardo Zapico-Goni, eds. 1999. *Monitoring Performance in the Public Sector: Future Directions from International Experience.* New Brunswick, N.J.: Transaction Publishers.

Shand, David. 1998. "The Role of Performance Indicators in Public Expenditure Management." IMF Working Paper. Washington, D.C.: International Monetary Fund.

U.S. Department of Justice. National Institute of Justice. "Mapping and Analysis for Public Safety." Washington, D.C.: U.S. Department of Justice. Available at http://www.ojp.usdoj.gov/nij/maps/

U.S. Department of the Treasury, Financial Management Service. 1993. "Performance Measurement Guide." Washington, D.C.: US Department of the Treasury.

Wye, Chris. 2002. "Performance Management: A 'Start Where You Are, Use What You Have' Guide." Arlington, Va.: IBM Endowment for Business in Government. Managing for Results Series.

Chapter 5

Wye, Chris. 2002. "Performance Management: A 'Start Where You Are, Use What You Have' Guide." Arlington, Va.: IBM Endowment for Business in Government. Managing for Results Series.

Chapter 6

Mayne, John and Eduardo Zapico-Goni, eds. 1999. *Monitoring Performance in the Public Sector: Future Directions from International Experience.* New Brunswick, N.J.: Transaction Publishers.

United National Development Programme (UNDP). 2002. *Handbook on Monitoring and Evaluating for Results.* New York: UNDP Evaluation Office.

Chapter 7

Creswell, John W. 1994. *Research Design: Qualitative and Quantitative Approaches.* Thousand Oaks, Calif.: Sage Publications.

Furubo, J. E., R. C. Rist, and R. Sandahl, eds. 2002. *International Atlas of Evaluation.* New Brunswick, N.J.: Transaction Press.

French Council for Evaluation. 1999. *A Practical Guide to Program and Policy Evaluation.* Paris, France: Scientific and National Councils for Evaluation.

Patton, Michael Q. 2002. *Qualitative Research and Evaluation Methods,* 3rd ed. Thousand Oaks, Calif.: Sage Publications.

Rist, Ray C., ed. 1999. *Program Evaluation and the Management of Government.* New Brunswick, N.J.: Transaction Publishers.

Vedung, Evert. 1997. *Public Policy and Program Evaluation.* New Brunswick, N.J.: Transaction Publishers.

Wholey, J. S., H. P. Hatry, and K. E. Newcomer, eds. 1994. *Handbook of Practical Program Evaluation.* San Francisco, Calif.: Jossey-Bass Publishers.

Worthen, B. R., J. R. Sanders, and J. L. Fitzpatrick. 1997. *Program Evaluation: Alternative Approaches and Practical Guidelines,* 2nd ed. New York, N.Y.: Addison, Wesley, and Longman.

Chapter 8

Creswell, John W. 1994. *Research Design: Qualitative and Quantitative Approaches.* Thousand Oaks, Calif.: Sage Publications.

Kumar, Krishna, ed. 1993. *Rapid Appraisal Methods.* World Bank. Washington, D.C.

Rist, Ray C. 1994. "Influencing the Policy Process with Qualitative Research," in Norman K. Denzin and Yvonna S. Lincoln, eds. *Handbook of Qualitative Research.* Thousand Oaks, Calif.: Sage Publications.

World Bank. 2003. International Program for Development Evaluation Training. Available at http://www.worldbank.org/oed/ipdet/ and http://www.carleton.ca/ipdet/

Chapter 9

Leeuw, Frans L., Ray C. Rist, and Richard C. Sonnichsen. 1994. *Can Governments Learn? Comparative Perspectives on Evaluation and Organizational Learning.* New Brunswick, N.J.: Transaction Publishers.

Rist, Ray C. 1997. "Evaluation and organizational learning." *Evaluation Journal of Australasia.* 9(1&2).

Chapter 10

Boyle, Richard and Donald Lemaire, eds. 1999. *Building Effective Evaluation Capacity: Lessons from Practice.* New Brunswick, N.J.: Transaction Publishers.

Georghiou, Luke. 1995. "Assessing the Framework Programmes." *Evaluation.* 1(2): 171–188.

Ittner, Christopher D., and David F. Larcker. 2003. "Coming Up Short on Nonfinancial Performance Measurement." *Harvard Business Review.* 81(11): 88–95.

Mayne, John and Eduardo Zapico-Goni, eds. 1999. *Monitoring Performance in the Public Sector: Future Directions from International Experience.* New Brunswick, N.J.: Transaction Publishers.

Pollitt, Christopher. 1995. "Justification by Works or by Faith?" *Evaluation.* I(2): 133–154.

———. 1997. "Evaluation and the New Public Management: An International Perspective." *Evaluation Journal of Australasia.* 9(1&2): 7–15.

Index

A-311
KIM
Sp'09